Interestingly, Steven Isserlis was born knowing the cures to all known diseases, and the answers to all the major scientific problems that have perplexed mankind for the past few thousand years. Unfortunately, however, he forgot all of this vital information just before he learnt to speak, so it was rather wasted. Instead, at the age of six he decided to learn to play the cello; and has spent the years since trying to do so.

These days, he spends most of his time travelling around the world playing concerts, and eating large meals. He has made many recordings – including music by four of the composers featured in this book – and, as well as playing concertos with orchestras, enjoys equally giving recitals with piano, playing chamber-music with friends and giving concerts for children. He is also Artistic Director of a course for young professional musicians in Cornwall, and has fun pointing out all the mistakes they're making.

Steven lives in London with Pauline (who's been putting up with him for about 25 years now) and their son Gabriel (who's only been putting up with him for sixteen years, but is already showing the strain) – as well as their hamster Speedy, who sleeps most of the day anyway, and is therefore quite tolerant. In 1998, he (Steven, not Speedy) was awarded a CBE, since when he's been trying to convince everyone around him how important he is.

by the same author
Why Beethoven Threw the Stew

Why Handel Waggled his Wig

And Lots More Stories about the Lives of
Great Composers

Steven Isserlis

Illustrations by Susan Hellard

ff

faber and faber

First published in 2006
by Faber and Faber Limited
74-77 Great Russell Street
London WC1B 3DA

Typeset by Faber and Faber Limited
Printed and bound by CPI Group (UK) Ltd, Croydon, CR0 4YY

A CIP record for this book
is available from the British Library

ISBN 978–0–571–22478–4
ISBN 0–571–22478–4

To Gabriel (as usual) and my two favourite (and, for that matter, only) nieces, Isabel and Natasha; and also for my lovely Godson Leonardo Tognetti; and to Oliver and Adam Weber (who are the only people who have ever praised my football skills); but really for all of my young friends, whose company make THE WHOLE THING WORTHWHILE.

A Note for Parents

Each chapter is in three parts: a portrait of the composer, which children can read (or have read to them); a short biography of each composer, with more stories relating to their lives, which may be dipped into, or read in one go; and a brief description of the music, with a guide to some pieces that the children (and you!) may particularly enjoy.

Contents

Contents

Introduction

In 2001, a little book I'd written called 'Why Beethoven Threw the Stew', about the lives and personalities of six composers, was published. That was very nice (for me, anyway). Originally I'd started off writing it just for my son Gabriel; but then the idea rather took off. It was extremely gratifying when other children read the book, and seemed to enjoy it; and even more gratifying when those children turned up at concerts, and enjoyed *them*.

So I was very pleased; and I went back to my normal life – well, as normal as a cellist's life ever gets. Over the next few months, though, a question started to surface with rather disturbing regularity: "Who's going to be in your next book?" I'd explain politely that I wasn't *going* to write a new book; I'd written one, and that was that. But as time went on, my friends started to give me advice on who should be in my new book. "There isn't a new book!" I'd say, a bit more firmly by now. My friends, however, being the rude people they are, decided to ignore me; sometimes they'd start to argue with each other about which composers should be in the new book, while I just sat silently, only intervening if they seemed to be getting into an actual fight. Eventually, however, I had to get tough, and spell it out for them. "Look,' I said. "I'm really frantic, what with playing my cello, and organising concerts, and so on. I don't

1

have time for anything else in my life. To write a second book would be madness."

So here's the second book, in which you'll meet six more fascinating characters who happened to be musical giants. For the past two years or so, they've taken over my life. I've read about them, I've listened to their music, I've asked endless questions about them; and I hope that I've come to know them a bit. The wonderful thing is – that I really like them! They were all unique, amazing people; and as for the music they wrote – well, you'll see (hear).

I do hope that you'll make at least six new friends over the course of the next however-long-it-takes-you-to-read-this-book. As for me - I'm a busy man now. I'm going to switch off my phones, disconnect the doorbell, unplug the computers – anything to ensure that none of my friends can ever contact me again; and I'm going to plunge myself into a new range of activities, which will occupy me from here on. I'd better get on with it; there are so many windows to be looked out of, such a variety of comfortable chairs to be sat in, and at least two thumbs to be twiddled ...

George Frideric Handel

1685–1759

mm . . . I think that something funny must have been going on in 1685: something in the stars, or storks behaving strangely, or whatever. Because in that year – and there's never been another year like it – no fewer than three great composers were born. One of them, the German genius Johann Sebastian Bach, is often described today as the greatest composer who ever lived. Another, the Italian Domenico Scarlatti, is famous mostly for his six hundred or so weird and wonderful sonatas for the harpsichord (the keyboard instrument that ruled before the piano took over). Scarlatti invented all sorts of exciting effects, such as crossing his hands and playing at the low end of the keyboard with his right hand and at the high end with his left – until (the story goes) he got so fat that he couldn't get his hands over his stomach any more, and had to abandon that particular thrill.

And then there's Handel. George Frideric Handel was born in

a town called Halle (the "hall" pronounced a bit like the first syllable of "hallo", and the "e" like the "e" in "butter"), in Prussia, Germany, on February 23rd, 1685.

Actually, it's not *quite* that simple.

He was christened Georg Friederich Händel (the two dots above the "a" in German make it sound like an "e", for some reason). And through the course of his life, he was known as Hendel, Endel, Haendel, Händeler, Hendler (don't know how they got to that one) or Handell; the poor man must have had a bit of an identity crisis! But once he settled in England, where he spent almost fifty years, he decided that he'd call himself George Frideric Handel; so we'll settle with that.

So much for the name; then there's the date.

We know that he was born on February 23rd; the register at his local church tells us that he was baptised on ♂ February 24th (♂ being the astronomical sign for Tuesday; strange!). But February 23rd in 1685 wasn't the same as the February 23rd we know and love these days. In 1685, British calendars were ten days behind German ones; in 1700, in a moment of shocking carelessness, they fell yet another day behind. Not that that would have mattered much to the young Handel as he blew out the candles on his cake, because at that point he'd probably hardly even heard of Britain; but later, he was to make his home in London, and would spend more birthdays there than anywhere else – so then it must have been a tad confusing. Fancy spending your birthday wondering whether it really *was* your birthday – wouldn't that slightly dampen the celebrations? (Actually, it can happen. I have a friend who was born on February 29th; when he was sixty, he celebrated his fifteenth birthday!) Not until 1752 did the British draw level with the continent. That year, the people of Britain went to sleep on September 2nd, and then woke up the next day to find that it was now September 14th – talk about over-

4

sleeping! But at least they'd caught up at last. (Britain does tend to be a bit slow on the uptake sometimes. As I write, we're still driving on the left, when everywhere else in Europe, they're driving on the right; and the reason we drive on the left is that in the old days, people on horses needed to be able to swipe with their swords at people riding the other way – perhaps not *entirely* necessary today; and anyway, rather tough if you were left-handed.)

So that's Handel's birth-date dealt with. Well, at least we're sure that he was born in Halle, Germany; but even here there's a snag. Although Halle was officially in Prussia, Handel considered himself a Saxon – i.e. from Saxony, another part of Germany. And by the way, he preferred writing in French to writing in German.

So that's all clear, then – glad we got it settled.

Anyway, to the story: Handel's father – who was called Georg too, just in case things weren't confusing enough – was sixty-three years old when Handel was born. He was a barber and a surgeon; the two often went together in those days – strange thought. I can't quite imagine it today: "Hello, barber – could I have a short back and sides, please? Oh – and while you're about it, could you take out my appendix? Thanks." Well, that's the way it was in those days – perhaps because the barber had to have such a sharp knife to shave people that he thought he might as well cut them up with it as well.

We don't really know much about the early lives of most composers who lived such a long time ago; but fortunately, in Handel's case we know quite a bit. In the year after his death, a book called 'Memoirs of the Life of the Late George Frederic Handel' was published, written by a man called Mainwaring; it was the first proper biography of a composer ever written.

The book tells us a fair amount about Handel's childhood and youth. We know from it, for instance, that Handel senior thoroughly disapproved of music – which was a pity, because Handel junior even more thoroughly approved of it. Handel senior found out about this, and was furious; he forbade Handel junior to have any musical instruments in the house, or even to go to any other house where instruments were kept. But our Handel had other ideas. Somehow he managed to get a clavichord (the softest of all keyboard instruments) smuggled into the attic of his home; and when his family was asleep, he used to go and practise up there. Seems strange that no one heard him – but his father was probably deaf by then, and perhaps he snored loudly; and maybe Mrs Handel secretly approved, and turned a blind ear.

Handel junior was a product of his father's second marriage, so young George Frideric had several half-brothers and sisters. (By the time Handel senior died, he had twenty-eight grandchildren, as well as two great-grandchildren – not bad going.) One day, the old gentleman announced that he was going to a nearby court to visit his son Karl, who was nearly thirty years older than his little half-brother. Our Handel begged to be allowed to accompany his father; but the old man was having none of it. George Frideric was far too young for such a journey, and besides, it would look silly for a dignified gentleman to arrive with a little boy as his companion at the important court where Karl was employed. (George Frideric was probably around eleven by then.)

Our Handel – obstinate little fellow – wasn't going to be put off so easily. He waited until his father set off in the horse-drawn coach, and then started running after it. The horses

can't have been quite the fastest in the world, because soon after the coach had left the town, little Handel overtook it. This time he begged so hard, and generally made such a nuisance of himself, that his poor father was forced to give in; and George Frideric was off on his first trip – what a thrill! Once at the court, the boy seems to have taken every opportunity to show off (as little boys do – just occasionally . . .). On one occasion, he was allowed to play the organ in the chapel after the service; the Duke, Karl Handel's employer, happened still to be in the church, and noticed something unusual about the organist. He asked Karl who was playing; and was amazed when Karl told him that it was his little brother.

The Duke demanded to see the prodigy, and told Handel senior that it would be "a crime against the public and posterity" if this young genius were not allowed to study music. Handel senior was shocked, and argued that music as a profession was undignified. (Humph.) However, he couldn't really quarrel with such an important Duke; so he agreed, reluctantly, to find a music teacher for his son when they returned to Halle – so long as his son kept up his other studies as well. The Duke was pleased; Handel junior was very pleased (especially since the Duke gave him lots of money as a reward for his beautiful playing); and old Handel was probably in an *appalling* sulk as they rode home. Well, it's good for us that Handel didn't bow to his father's wishes and become a lawyer – this would have been such a boring chapter!

When they got back to Halle, a teacher was found for young George Frideric; this was the organist at one of the local churches, and conductor of the choir there, a man called Zachow. Zachow seems to have been very pleased to have had such a brilliant pupil – partly because Handel must have been exciting to teach, and partly because it meant that Zachow could go off and enjoy eating and drinking with his friends, leaving Handel to do his jobs for him. Good for both of them, really.

Handel's life then continued quietly for a few years; but meanwhile, his father's discontinued quietly, just before Handel's thirteenth birthday. Handel contributed a sad poem to the funeral, signing himself "George Friedrich Händel – dedicated to the Liberal Arts"; rather grand for a twelve-year-old! A few years later, perhaps to honour his father's memory, Handel actually enrolled as a student at the University at Halle; he may even have studied law there for a year. But music was the life for him; and he was making remarkable progress. At some stage, he went to Berlin and was offered financial support by the King of Prussia; but he turned it down, because he and his friends were worried that if he accepted it, he'd be stuck there. Handel didn't want to spend his life entertaining some prince – he wanted to conquer the world! He did take a job as an organist in Halle, but not for long; he needed to stretch his wings, to travel, to learn, to become a great composer. Mainwaring tells us that at this point it was decided that the best place for Handel would be the north German city of Hamburg, because the operas were so good there; and therefore Handel was sent there (the book tells us) "on his own bottom". (An interesting turn of phrase; I wonder on whose bottom he *could* have gone, if not his own? Presumably it means that he paid for the journey himself – but it does sound a touch strange.)

He reached Hamburg in 1703, at the age of eighteen – a young man ready for anything. For three years, Handel became a Hamburger; during that time he became very famous as an opera composer. Next, having got the opera bug, Handel decided that he wanted to travel to the land where opera had been invented, and where it was (and still is) most popular – Italy. So he resolved that as soon as he could afford it, he would go there ("on his own bottom" again, Mainwaring tells us – good to know).

Handel spent around three and a half years in Italy, and seems to have had a great time – well, he seems to have received lots of attention, anyway, which for most musicians is the same thing. He wrote beautiful music for the Catholic Church (even though he himself remained a Lutheran Protestant for his whole life); and also successful operas – in Italian, of course, as all operas were at that time. It was quite an amazing achievement for a German to go to Italy and to be taken seriously as an opera composer by the Italians, who felt that they owned opera. Handel was taken extremely seriously; in fact, he was adored – and not just by the audiences. This is the only time in his life when we know fairly definitely that Handel had a love affair: the object of his affections was a soprano called Vittoria. It seems that she transferred her affections from a local prince to Handel; dangerous behaviour – princes tended then to have short tempers, and to cut off heads off when they were *really* annoyed. But the lovers survived; perhaps music was more important for the prince than love! (The same seems to have been true for Handel; we really don't know anything about his love life after that. But perhaps he just kept it very well hidden – and we're unlikely to find out any more now.)

Despite his triumphs in Italy, in 1710 Handel decided to return to Germany and look for a job. (We have no idea what Vittoria thought about that; maybe he was running away from her by that time?) He was offered a job as court musician to George, Elector of Hanover. (Rulers of parts of Germany were known as Electors, because they were allowed to vote in the election of the Emperor of the Holy Roman Empire of the German nation – that must have made them feel important.) Handel worried that this job would stop him travelling. No problem, said the Elector, travel as much as you like – just remember to tell people that you're an employee of mine. A perfect job offer! So Handel accepted the generous salary, and left immediately. First he went to Halle to see his ailing mother, to whom he had always sent a fair proportion of any money he had earned – a good boy. And then he was off, for the first, but by no means last time, to England. In fact, from his second trip there in 1712 until his death, England was his home. Not that he ever seemed very like an Englishman; he never seems to have lost his strong German accent, for a start. But it was the place where he chose to make the main part of his career, where he became a household name – and where he made lots of money, to which he didn't object at all.

It is in England that we get to know him best – well, sort of. The good thing is that there were more newspapers, journals and pamphlets published in England at that time than anywhere else in the world; the bad thing (for us) is that Handel seems to have been a very private man, who rarely confided his inner feelings to anyone, at least in letters – or rather, in any letters that survive today (the only exception being a sad letter, in German, that he wrote to his brother-in-law on the death of his mother in 1730). So we know lots about Handel's public activities – the concerts and operas he put on, and how they were received; we even have his bank statements! But we know less about what he was really like as a person, and about how he felt about everything that happened in his life.

Still, there are enough descriptions of him, and stories about him, to allow us to build up quite a strong picture. What we do know is that everything about Handel seems to have been on a huge scale. He was hugely successful in his musical life – but also had huge problems to contend with, and huge failures. He had a ferocious temper – but could also be very kind and generous, and funny too. He had a vast appetite for food and drink – and, it seems, a pretty vast stomach to match. And he wore an *enormous* white curly wig.

To deal with his professional triumphs and trials first: he was probably the most famous composer in Europe in his day; there was even a statue of him in Vauxhall Gardens, London's most popular park. (I wonder how he felt when he walked past it?) He was often called upon to compose for important royal occasions; in fact, his music is still performed at British royal ceremonies today. For thirty years or so, his operas (still in Italian) were perhaps the most talked-about events in London; and then for the last years of his life, he turned to "oratorios" – which were musical settings of stories, like operas, but without any acting or scenery, and so could be done anywhere, not just in theatres. These oratorios, usually based on biblical tales, were also very successful on the whole. He never exactly starved, as we can tell from his bank accounts (and the size of his stomach); but both operas and oratorios brought a bucketload of worries onto his head (right through his wig).

For a start, there were the singers. The opera stars were the worst. At one point he had two Italian "prima donnas" (leading ladies) in his company at the same time, Mesdames Faustina and Cuzzoni. Since they were in the same operas, they should have been happy to sing together and be friends; not a bit of it – they were deadly rivals. Not only that, but each had a band of followers who hated the other faction. Fights broke out, both inside and outside the theatre. One prima donna would start singing, and the supporters of the other would start hissing and whistling; then the same would happen in reverse – and so on. Eventually, there was such an outbreak of "indecencies" between the members of the two fan clubs (in the presence of royalty, too – shocking!) that a performance had to be brought to an abrupt halt. Not exactly helpful for people who wanted to listen to the opera properly; Handel must have been furious.

We don't know what he thought of Faustina, who was apparently very nice; but Cuzzoni – short and squat, with a cross little face – seems to have driven him crazy. Once, she complained about an aria he'd written for her first appearance in London; the aria wasn't flashy enough – she wanted to knock the audience's socks off! Handel wasn't impressed; in fact, he lost his temper – just a *little* bit. "Madam!" he shouted, "I know

that you are a true she-devil; but I'll have you know that I am Beelzebub, *Chief* of the Devils!" And, with that, he picked her up by the waist and swore that if she made any more trouble, he'd throw her out of the window! That's one way to deal with singers . . .

Then there was the royal family: it was difficult to sell opera tickets unless the public (or at least the rich snobs among them who bought the expensive tickets) knew that the royal family was going to be present. It often happened that the various members of the royal family hated each other, so that if one went to an opera of Handel's, another would ostentatiously *not* go – and wouldn't allow any of his or her friends to go, either.

There were lots of other things that could prove difficult, as well. Sometimes the weather in London would be awful (unbelievable though that may sound . . .). The theatre management would announce that fires were to be lit in the theatre (sounds dangerous); and the doors would be closed whenever possible to keep the warmth in. People wouldn't be convinced, though; they preferred to stay at home, by their own fires. Or there would be the threat of war; again, people would stay in their houses, or else retreat hastily to out-of-the-way places in the country.

And when the audience *did* come, on normal nights, they'd often be badly behaved, talking during bits they found boring (which tended to be the bits called "recitatives", speech-like passages of sung conversation – as opposed to the "arias", which were the bits where the singers would sing their beautiful melodies). Particularly rude people might shout at the singers, or start walking around (even onto the stage – a bit confusing if one was trying to follow the story!). Then there would be exciting stage effects (put in more to create a sensation than to help the story) that might go wrong – live sparrows, for instance, that were liable to deposit something unwanted on the heads of performers or audience. Or there was the time when the Queen came to the opera, carried in a royal chair, and the chair came to grief – a tad embarrassing: queens aren't *supposed* to fall out of chairs.

And even if the singers and audience weren't causing difficulties for Handel, there were the rich sponsors who supported the opera, with all their commands and demands; and then there were the greedy managers of the companies. One of these was called Owen Swiney, and lived up to his name by running off with all the money; another, although a good manager, was described by everybody as the ugliest man ever invented. There were also some musicians who thought they were better than Handel; they started making trouble even before Handel first arrived in London. "Let him come," said one of them. "We'll handle him!" What a wit *he* must have been . . .

No wonder Handel's wig was white.

The oratorios generally caused Handel fewer problems than the operas; but they weren't all plain sailing, either. Many of the stories of the oratorios were taken from the Bible, two of them directly quoting text from the Holy Book. Some people were shocked by this – to them, it was sacrilege to set sacred text to music intended for performance in theatres. And then, when the stories *weren't* from the Bible, the same people would complain that it was wrong to present *non*-religious stories during Lent – which was when the oratorios were generally performed. Nothing was easy. At one stage, there was a series of earthquakes in London, around the time of Handel's oratorio performances; people were too frightened to come to the theatre, especially since manic preachers kept telling them that the quakes were God's punishment for their many terrible sins – which of course included going to the theatre!

There were also difficulties with the people who wrote the words – or the 'libretto', as the script for an opera or oratorio was called. The most troublesome 'librettist' was a man called Jennens, who selected the text from the Bible for Handel's most famous work, 'Messiah' (often called 'The Messiah' today, but it should really be just 'Messiah'). Jennens was a good writer – but he could also be a major pain. He criticised Handel's music quite nastily at times; he complained that Handel had "maggots on his brain" – charming. (Actually, in those days it was a fairly common expression expression that meant "a fanciful obsession"; but still, it doesn't sound very nice.) And he once wrote Handel such a horrible letter that it made him ill – much to Jennens' delight. Not impressive. Still, he and Handel produced great works together; and it has to be admitted that Handel probably wasn't an easy collaborator, either. There was a story told (probably not true, but it's a good story anyway) that another writer, Morell, sleeping peacefully in his country house, was rudely woken at 5 a.m. by Handel yelling at him from a carriage outside his window. "Vat de devil means de vord 'billow'?" Handel shouted (in his unique accent) at the sleepy author. Morell explained that it meant a wave of the sea. "O, de vave," said Handel – and was off on the long journey back to his house, without another word.

Some oratorios were more successful than others. 'Messiah' became a huge hit, once people had got used to the choice of subject-matter; but others – for instance, one called 'Theodora' – didn't do so well. Some eminent professors once applied to the great man himself for tickets to hear 'Messiah'; instead of thanking them politely, Handel lost his temper. "You are tamnaple tainty!" he raged. "You vould not come to 'Teodora' – der was room enough to tance dere, when dat was perform!" (Translation – I think: "You're damnably dainty! You would not come to 'Theodora' – there was room enough to dance there, when that was performed.") Not the best way to ensure a full house, perhaps. At other times, though, he could survey an empty house and be quite philosophical – "de moosic vill sound de petter."

When his difficulties got too much for him, at least there was the comfort of food and drink – preferably lots of it. He would order twelve gallons of port at a time – he took his enjoyment seriously! Mind you, that could lead to embarrassment as well. Once he gave a dinner party at his house for some of the principal performers of one of his oratorios. Sitting among them, Handel would suddenly get a far-away look in his eyes. "Oh – I have de taught," he would exclaim. Much bowing and scraping – the Master had a thought! Of course he must go and write it down – the moment must not be lost. This did seem to happen rather often, though; and eventually the musicians became a little suspicious. One particularly doubtful man followed Handel to the private room to which he had retired with his "taught", looked through the keyhole – and saw that Handel was just sitting there drinking from a particularly fine bottle of Burgundy wine that he didn't want to share with anybody else!

Ahem.

Oh well – so Handel had his fair share of problems and embarrassments; but great men always do. And since his greatness still matters and his problems don't, let's spend some time with him on one of his *good* days. We'll start by watching him in bed in the house in London which he leased for £35 a year from 1723 until his death. (Before that, he'd lived at the grand abodes of his rich English patrons.) It's a lovely house (which has today been beautifully restored as the Handel House museum, joined with one devoted to a rather different musician who lived next door a few hundred years later – the rock guitarist Jimi Hendrix!). There are

15

beautiful paintings all over the walls, because Handel collected them (one slightly less-than-beautiful drawing that's hanging up now probably wasn't there in those days – a caricature that appeared in the newspapers of his time, in which Handel is depicted as a pig playing the organ!) In the master bedroom, the great man is starting to wake up in his grand red four-poster bed. (It's rather short; but that doesn't matter, because Handel sleeps propped up on pillows – he thinks it's healthier not to lie flat.) If he's not wearing a nightcap, we can see that he's bald; and presumably the first thing that he'll do is to baldly go to the loo, which is a little ceramic pot kept inside a long wooden bucket at the end of his bed. We'll leave the room for a few moments while he does that, and the servant carries it away.

Thank you. When it's safe to go in again (and hopefully Handel has been washed by his servant – not *always* the case in the eighteenth century, by any means; he'll have been shaved, anyway), we can follow him to his dressing room next door. A servant will fetch some posh clothes from the large walk-in closet, and dress his master; and then it will be time to fetch the imposing wig from its wig-block and fix it onto the great man's head. (All we know about Handel's politics, incidentally, is that he once voted for the party known as the Whigs – not surprisingly.)

Perhaps he will feel ready to compose now, and will descend the stairs to his composition room, sit at a table (with a harpsichord nearby, in case he wants to try anything out), and start scribbling away. If he's in a really inspired mood, he'll move himself deeply with the beauty of his own ideas; and the servant who brings him his morning hot chocolate might find his master in floods of tears. (It was said that sometimes Handel even forgot to eat when he was carried away with composing; those must have been *very* strong bursts of inspiration!)

He may need a visitor to bring him back to normal. It's worth waiting for Handel's happy moods; although he frowned a lot, it was said that when a smile eventually arrived on his face, it was like the sun bursting through clouds. There'll certainly be a lot of sunshine if the visitor is a distinguished gentleman who comes to the house to place an order for a copy of one of the master's latest published works. And if it's an especially good day for Handel, he'll hire a sedan chair (a sort of chair-taxi), and two *extremely* strong men will hoist him up on poles and carry him off to the Bank of England, to deposit some money in his account. Positively midsummer on Handel's features!

Coming back, he'll probably have a nice big lunch, and a rest; or perhaps he'll go to the room next to his composition room, the rehearsal room (which doubles as his dining room) to conduct a rehearsal. Sometimes up to forty musicians are crammed into this small space; they'll be sweating madly – especially after Handel, lording it at his harpsichord, has finished barking at them for not singing or playing his music exactly as he wants it. Maybe some rich lords or ladies will come swaggering in to listen to the rehearsal; but woe betide them if they're late – they won't be swaggering then, because Handel will be rude to *anybody* who interrupts his rehearsals, be they royalty or chimney-sweep.

Once he's playing the harpsichord, Handel will be completely carried away, often making up all sorts of wonderful passages as he goes along. Sometimes this can be distracting for the singers; he's supposed to be accompanying their singing, after all, rather than them accompanying his playing. There was a famous incident (which may have occurred in this room) when a tenor, finding himself completely put off by Handel's flights of fancy, threatened to jump into the harpsichord to shut him up. The master was not impressed. "Let me know ven you vill do that," he requested, "and I vill advertise it; for I am sure that more people vill come to see you jump, than to hear you sing."

Or perhaps there won't be a rehearsal, and instead Handel will work with his secretary and copyist, John Christopher Smith. (Many years earlier Handel had persuaded an old friend from university, Johann Christoph Schmidt, to come from Germany to England; Mr Schmidt arrived, renamed himself John Christopher Smith – Christopher Smith for short – and took up a position as Handel's right-hand man. Later, John Christopher Smith was joined in Handel's employment by his son, who was called – er – John Christopher Smith.) But perhaps Handel *should* have a rest this afternoon, because tonight he has a performance of one of his oratorios. On another night, he might have gone to the house of some rich music-loving lady, or even to the Crown and Anchor Inn (a pub/restaurant), and played the harpsichord for hours on end, much to the delight of the assembled company; but not tonight – there's work to be done.

So later, when he's rested and dressed in his evening finery, we can follow him out of the house, observing him walking – or perhaps waddling – along, with his roly-poly gait, through the streets of London on his way to the theatre in nearby Covent Garden (where operas are still performed today, although in a newer building). If he's worried about being on time, we may see him consulting his beautiful silver watch, with pictures of musicians on the cover. If he's worried about something else, perhaps we might hear him muttering to himself in his own special brand of English. When he gets to the theatre, though, we'll leave him at the stage door and go inside the theatre to join the audience.

The place is full. The rich gentlemen and their wives – or, more likely, girlfriends – sit in boxes close to the stage; the more gallant gentlemen hold candles for the ladies throughout the evening, so that the ladies can follow the words in the pro-gramme-book. At 6.30 sharp, the excited chatter stops as the great man enters, with two wax lights being carried in front of him. There is a loud burst of applause as he takes his place at the small portable organ, on which the lights have been placed; he faces the players, his back to the audience. A movement from his hands – and the performance starts, all the players and singers (sometimes more than a hundred of them) with their eyes fixed firmly on Handel. The music is dramatic; the kettle-drums, borrowed from the Royal Artillery, sound like guns. It is also incredibly beautiful, and people are deeply stirred. Handel doesn't want just to entertain people with his oratorios; he wants (as he says) to "make them better". And indeed, everybody there is caught up in the ecstasy of this amazing music. There may be the odd annoying know-it-all who beats time to the music or, worse, counts aloud or discusses the performance as it goes on; but we hope that the real music-lovers will shut them up.

Between the acts of the piece, Handel plays an organ concerto he's written, and amazes everybody with his incredible skill; how does he manage to be so precise with hands so large that his fingers look like toes? Well, somehow he manages it; and it is, all in all, a great occasion. It's hard for the audience to tell what Handel thinks about it all, because they can't

see his face; but actually, there's a sure sign that all is well – his wig is wag-gling! Not a huge waggle – but there's some sort of movement. That's a relief; it would be a bad sign if it were completely still. No, all is well – something's definitely happening there; it's nodding up and down, vibrating a bit. Mr Handel is enjoying himself.

Facts of Life

·1·

It's difficult to see where Handel got his musical talents; there certainly don't seem to have been any accomplished musicians in his immediate family. Mind you, his grandfather on his father's side had been a deeply important man: he was appointed official bread-weigher to the town of Halle. I hope you're impressed . . .

A multi-talented father . . .

Handel's father, apart from his main job as a barber-surgeon, had another business for a time, selling wine. That must have meant that he could offer his customers a full service: first he could make them healthy by operating on them, then make them look tidy by cutting their hair, and finally make them feel good by plying them with wine. His greatest claim to fame, though (apart from having been Handel's father, of course) was the operation he performed on a young boy who had rather foolishly swallowed a knife. Handel senior managed to remove the knife; the boy recovered, was nicknamed (not very imaginatively) "the Halle Sword-Swallower", and later became a successful surgeon himself.

·2·

Handel was just seventeen when he was appointed to his first job, as organist to the Cathedral in Halle. His contract required "an upright organist" (a good thing – it's hard to play the organ lying down) who would be "always in church in good time and before the pealing of the bells ceases", and "for the rest, to lead a Christian and edifying life". In fact, it would seem as if

Handel did just that: he was a deeply religious man. The appointment must have been quite a relief to him; it was only a month earlier that he'd signed up at the university. This job must have given him the perfect excuse not to go to many of the classes. Handel was too busy to go to university, anyway; when he wasn't at the Cathedral, he spent his time in Halle (as he remembered later) "composing like the devil"!

Composers Handel met – and didn't ...

One nice friendship that Handel made at this time was with a young man who was also to become a famous composer, Georg Philipp Telemann. Famous for the quantity as well as the quality of his music, Telemann is supposed to have written more music than any other composer before or since. Telemann was studying in Leipzig, about twenty miles from Halle. Leipzig had a small opera house, run by a gentleman lucky enough to be called Mr Strungk; and it may have been thanks to Telemann that Handel saw an opera for the first time. Almost fifty years later, Handel sent Telemann a crate of rare and exotic plants, to show that he hadn't forgotten his old friend after half a century. Unfortunately, the person charged with delivering the plants returned with the sad news that Telemann had died: a slight problem. Some time afterwards, however, someone else brought the happier news that Telemann really wasn't that dead after all. A few years later, Handel tried again; and this time, another crate of plants found their way to the still very much alive – and sniffing – Telemann.

Unfortunately, Handel never met Bach; just once, in 1719, Bach may (we don't know for certain) have journeyed from Leipzig to visit his fellow genius, when he heard that Handel was visiting his old mother in Halle. By the time he got there, however (the story goes), Handel had just left – rather a long way for Bach to go just to practise his U-turns!

· 3 ·

Once in Hamburg, Handel joined the opera company, first as a violinist (at which he pretended to be very bad – presumably he didn't want to be stuck in the violin section), then as a harpsichordist (at which he astonished everybody by being brilliant); and then as a composer. He wrote his first operas there (including one, unfortunately lost today, called 'Love Obtained by Blood and Murder, or: Nero'. Sounds great!) Another opera, however, does survive – 'Almira', Handel's first. It was a big success; and Handel used bits of it in later pieces – a very definite habit of his throughout his life. He was very much in favour of recycling; if he liked a tune he'd written, he'd tend to use it again (and again). And if he liked a tune that *another* composer had written, he'd use that too – not always to the other composer's delight! Hmm . . .

An irritating friend . . .

Perhaps the first friend Handel made in Hamburg was a musician called Mattheson – composer, harpsichordist, singer and pain in the neck. He and Handel seem to have had a love/hate relationship. The worst moment came when the company was performing an opera by Mattheson, who was also singing the main male part. His character committed suicide about half an hour before the end of the opera, which gave Mattheson half an hour to loiter around without getting any attention. So he used to go and shove Handel – who up to that point had been playing the harpsichord – off the instrument, and play it himself for that last half-hour. One night, Handel (probably in a bad mood, or just fed up with pain-in-the-neck Mattheson) refused to budge; and the two got into a fight. Much to the excitement of the crowd around the opera house, the two men went outside and drew their swords! Mattheson thrust his sword towards Handel's chest – but, very luckily for Handel (and for us), he

was wearing a coat with large metal buttons, and the sword
shattered. (Can't have been much of a sword.) After which,
Handel and Mattheson decided that, since they were obviously
not destined to kill each other, they might as well be friends
again; so they went off and had dinner together, before going on
to a rehearsal of Handel's new opera. An odd little story.

Handel and Mattheson shared another strange experience, as
well. Both of them were invited to apply for the post of organist
at nearby Lübeck, a well-paid and important job. Both, it
seems, might have been tempted to take it – but there was one
slight problem: whoever was appointed to the post would have
to marry the daughter of the retiring organist, Buxtehude.
Neither Handel nor Mattheson – nor Bach a couple of years
later – could face that prospect; and so they all refused the job.
Not exactly flattering for the poor woman!

In later life, incidentally, Mattheson kept writing to Handel,
asking him to write the story of his own life for a book about
musicians that Mattheson was compiling. Handel kept refus-
ing, and Mattheson grew sulkier and sulkier – thus ended the
great (or grating) friendship.

· **4** ·

In Italy Handel was a star. He was employed by rich princes
and cardinals to write operas, cantatas (shorter works for
singers and orchestra, without acting) and his first oratorios.
His rich patrons catered to his every need; in one palace,
where he stayed for several months, he was provided with
forty-five pounds of ice, presumably just to keep his drinks
cool – luxury! After the first performance of one of his operas
in Venice, the crowd went mad, exploding at almost every
pause in the music, and shouting out "Viva il cara sassone!"–
"Long live the dear Saxon!" (They weren't to know that Handel
was officially Prussian, not Saxon – especially since Handel

doesn't seem to have known it himself.) A cardinal who was a patron of Handel's wrote long verses in praise of "the dear Saxon" – which Handel then set to music. Oh well – geniuses don't have to be modest, I suppose.

He also met his fellow 1685-er, Scarlatti, who adored him. There was a fancy-dress party in Venice, to which Handel went in disguise; as usual, he started playing the harpsichord. Scarlatti happened to be at the same party: "Either that is the famous Saxon," said he, "or the devil." It was said that in later life, every time Scarlatti heard the name "Handel", he would cross himself reverently – a wonderful compliment.

A cruel practice ...

In Rome, Handel had to switch from operas to oratorios; the reason was that the Pope had forbidden opera there – too frivolous and theatrical. Still, oratorio performances there weren't exactly shabby: in one case, a special theatre was constructed in a prince's palace, with an amazingly ornate stage, room for a huge orchestra, and seats for a large and distinguished audience. The only problem was that the day after the first performance, the prince was told off by the Pope for having had one of the roles sung by a woman singer!

One way of getting around that problem and still having high singing parts was to have them sung by "castrati". The castrati were a breed of singers (now vanished, I'm glad to say) who were born as normal boys; but, unfortunate enough to possess beautiful singing voices, they were given an operation that prevented them growing up into normal men. That way, their voices would always stay high; and the best of them apparently sang with an unearthly beauty (or, as someone rather rudely put it, in a "celestial whine".) Perhaps the really successful ones thought it was worth it; but what about the ones who didn't make it? Their lives ruined for nothing – an awful thought.

The ones who did *make it became superstars, though. The castrato who was most closely associated with Handel was called Senesino. He kept quarrelling with Handel, and looked just like a pig – but it was said that he had the voice of an angel. The audiences at operas must have been a bit confused; female characters were sung either by women or by castrati – and male characters could be sung by either men or women. Opera is a really strange business.*

·5·

The Elector of Hanover, Handel's employer, must have been extremely keen to have Handel on his staff – or at least to be able to boast about having him on his staff; he put up with Handel's absence from Hanover for a very long time. Meanwhile, the Queen of England, Anne, who was a fan of Handel's, paid him an extra salary on top of his one from Hanover – Handel was clever about money! Handel did go back to the Elector's court in 1711 after his first visit to England, which had lasted about nine months; but the next year he returned to England, and this time he "forgot" to go back to Hanover. Ahem. Not surprisingly, the Elector seems to have become a bit tetchy. Things could have become quite dicey for Handel, especially because, thanks to complicated family relationships, the Elector was next in line to the throne of England (despite not speaking a word of English). Handel could have been in trouble in two countries; but he managed to wriggle out of the difficulty by acting as a SPY – shocking!

Before the Elector could become George 1 of England, Queen Anne would have to vacate the throne. In 1714, she became very ill and seemed to be dying; but she was being very indecisive – she kept getting a bit better, and then a bit worse, and confusing everybody. Very selfish, really, but it worked in Handel's favour. It so happened that Handel was a great friend of the Queen's doctor, who would give him all the latest news; Handel would in turn pass this on to his Hanover contacts. These powerful people were very anxious to put George onto the throne the moment Anne snuffed it, before anyone else could get the idea that they'd look better with a crown on their head than George would; so every snippet of information that Handel could provide was useful. Handel also passed on gossip from Hanover (carefully tailored by his Hanoverian friends) to people in England who wanted to know what was going on over there. So: "George Frideric Handel – Composer and Spy". It sounds quite good, really.

Friends in high places ...

The British royal family was very important to Handel – and he was quite important to them, too. Some of his most famous works were written for royal occasions – beginning with a 'Te Deum' (not to be confused with tedium!) performed at the first important service to be held at Sir Christopher Wren's newly built St Paul's Cathedral, in 1713. In the following years, Handel produced a series of masterpieces for ceremonial occasions. There was, for instance, his 'Water Music', written for an amazing sailing party that the king held one evening in 1717. The musicians floated in a barge up the River Thames, playing as they fol-lowed the King's barge. This went on for about three hours, until the King

got off the barge at Chelsea and spent another three hours hav-
ing his dinner there – while the musicians went on playing.
And then, at two o'clock in the morning, the King went back up
the river, with the musicians following, still playing. I hope they
got paid overtime! (And didn't suffer from seasickness.) Many
years later, Handel was to compose music for the Royal Fire-
works, too – of which a little bit more a little bit later . . .

He also wrote music for the coronation of George II in 1727,
for the funeral of George's wife, for some victories in battle, and
for various other ceremonial events. In addition, he taught
music to several members of the royal family. The royal family in
turn did him several favours (apart from paying him for his
services). King George I, for instance, granted Handel exclusive
rights to publish his own music, "strictly forbidding all our
loving subjects" to put out editions without paying Handel
anything. And one of the same king's very last acts was to grant
Handel British citizenship in 1727, sending his command to
the House of Commons via an exceedingly important person-
age – the Deputy Gentleman Usher of the Black Rod, no less
(though, it must be admitted, no more either).

· 6 ·

From 1712, when he came to live in England, until 1719,
Handel supported himself with occasional operas and
commissions from rich patrons (as well as his salary from
Hanover, and the British royals). In 1719, however, some of
his aristocratic friends banded together to create an opera
company to be called "The Royal Academy of Music", with
Handel as musical director. (Many of the patrons were
members of something called the Kit-Cat Club; and tickets
were sold principally at Mrs White's Chocolate House. It all
sounds quite delicious!) Subscribers could buy "silver tickets"
(really made of metal), which would be good for admission to

the opera every night of the season for, it was hoped, twenty-one years. In the end the company lasted only nine years; but there were some glorious operas composed and performed during that time.

It doesn't seem as if the collapse of the company in 1728 made too much difference to Handel. He continued to buy and sell shares on the stock market; and immediately after the Royal Academy of Music closed, he entered into an agreement with the theatre manager Heidegger ("the ugliest man in existence") to go on with his opera seasons. As Handel's biographer Mainwaring tells us, at this point Handel "embarked on a new bottom"! (Clever of him.)

Handel was really the king of opera in London for many years. But he made enemies: in 1733, another company was formed, called the Opera of the Nobility, basically with the thoroughly noble intention of ruining Handel. The problem was partly that the King and Queen, along with their eldest daughter, the Princess Royal, supported all Handel's productions; but their eldest son, the Prince of Wales, hated his family, and wanted to ruin Handel as a way of getting at them. So the Prince got all his cronies together to form the new company; rehearsals for the operas were held at his palace. It became a huge fight, with the Opera of the Nobility often getting the upper hand; there were reports of the King sitting almost by himself at Handel's opera performances. In the end, both companies collapsed. The Opera of the Nobility ended in 1737; Handel carried on for a little longer, but wrote his last opera in 1740 (Incidentally, the Prince of Wales later decided that he liked Handel after all, and was very good to him. So he's forgiven.)

Singing superstars . . .

One of Handel's tasks as musical director of the Royal Academy of Music, and as chief of the later opera seasons, was to go abroad and find singers with wonderful voices, and persuade them to come to London and sing there (for vast fees). In this way, he found the fighting "prima donnas", Cuzzoni and Faustina, the castrato Senesino, and various other odd-sounding stars: one poor soprano who apparently sang beautifully, but was nicknamed "the elephant"; one castrato who was said to have a square mouth and sometimes to sound like a distressed calf bleating (I wonder what he got paid for that?); a soprano who had a good voice, but was very small and crooked; another who was called "the Pig" and made "frightful mouths" – and so on. At least "the Pig" was loyal to Handel – perhaps pigs are loyal? But no – Senesino looked just like a pig, too, and at the first opportunity he defected to the Opera of the Nobility. (Just before he did that, though, Handel got a small revenge in advance: in a performance of Handel's opera 'Julius Caesar', just as Senesino had proudly sung the words "Caesar does not know what fear is", a piece of scenery fell down on the stage. Senesino fell down on the floor trembling and whimpering, and everybody laughed at him. Served him right.)

It wasn't really Senesino's treachery that threatened to ruin Handel, though – it was that the Opera of the Nobility managed to engage Farinelli, the most famous castrato who ever lived. He created a sensation in London, until he was lured to Spain, where he was paid a fortune to sing privately for the Spanish king, who suffered from depression. Only music could make this king feel better – and only a few pieces of music, at that. Farinelli had to sing the same songs every night for nine years!

· 7 ·

Handel's last opera performance was in 1741; that was really it for his operas – it seems that not one of them was revived after Handel's death until 1920! (Several of them are popular again now, I'm glad to say.) But he knew that he was on to a safer bet with his oratorios, which he'd been producing steadily since the 1730s. For a start, he didn't need costumes, scenery and so on, so it was much cheaper; then he was spared some of the off-stage dramas that always go hand in hand with operas. The singers seem to have been generally less temperamental; oratorios, frequently religious in character, just didn't produce stars in the same way that operas did, and that was basically a good thing. There was a problem in the early days of the oratorios, when Handel employed some Italians who either sang in an English so bad that it annoyed (or perhaps worse, amused) the audiences, or else sang their parts in Italian, which was a bit unsettling; but by the 1740s, he was only employing suitable singers.

Instead of opera seasons, Handel now put on oratorio seasons. It was less risky altogether; but there was still uncertainty involved. Sometimes the oratorios were all the rage – packed, and the talk of the town; but sometimes they were a disaster, empty and deserted. This would be either because of the usual natural causes – the weather, a threat-ened earthquake, or somesuch; or because of certain very unnatural causes – horrible high-society ladies and gentlemen who, for whatever reason, had it in for Handel. One of the worst of these was a certain Lady Brown, who made sure to hold her fashionable balls and card-parties on the same nights as poor Handel was performing his oratorios, and to invite everybody she could think of who might otherwise have gone to the performances – sweet of her. There was also a group of louts – presumably paid by one of Handel's rich enemies – who went around pulling down the posters advertising his performances!

So in 1745, a very sad letter from Handel appeared in a London paper, announcing that, since no one loved him or his music any more, he was cancelling the rest of the season of concerts he had planned, and was going to roll himself up into a little ball and hide in a corner. (Well – words to that effect, anyway.) Luckily, a very nice letter appeared in the same paper the next day, saying that his fans *did* love him really, and encouraging all his subscribers (who'd bought their tickets for the whole season in advance) not to ask for their money back. Handel seems to have cheered up immediately, and resumed his performances. Within a year or so, his concerts were full to bursting again. As one lady of the time put it, "Those oratorios of Handel's are certainly (next to the hooting of owls) the most solemnly striking music one can hear." Quite so. Even today, Handel is probably most celebrated for his oratorios, which are the most beloved works of their kind ever written.

Nights to remember – for one reason or another . . .

Perhaps the most famous concert that Handel ever gave was the first performance of 'Messiah', in 1742. This took place, not in London, but in Dublin – then the second-largest city in the British Isles. It was Handel's first and only visit there – and they made a huge fuss of him. Handel built up the excitement carefully; he started off by giving several concerts consisting of other works of his. The first concert took place just before Christmas 1741 – 'Messiah' wasn't to be unveiled until April 1742. In the months between, Handel's local celebrity grew, both as a composer of genius and as a major character. At one performance, a solo violinist called Dubourg took off on a flight of fancy, and got rather lost; eventually he found his way back to the place where he'd left off. To the delight of the audience, Handel's voice resounded loudly through the hall: "You are velcome home, Mr Dubourg!"

The forthcoming new work was the talk of the town. Eventually a rehearsal was held, attended, according to the 'Dublin Journal', by a "grand, polite and crowded audience"; the same paper informed its readers that 'Messiah' was the "finest Composition of Musick that ever was heard" – not a bad review! Then came

31

the first performance, given in aid of some worthy charities;
it was a triumph. Even though the concert hall was full to
bursting (there were a hundred more people in the hall than
were officially allowed – no fire regulations then), it had to be
repeated a few weeks later, when, because of the crowded
audience and the hot weather, several panes of glass had to be
removed from the windows. These performances were historic
events; 'Messiah' has taken its place ever since as the most
famous oratorio of all time.

A slightly less glorious occasion was the first performance, in
London in 1749, of another well-known work by Handel, 'Music
for the Royal Fireworks'. This was written as part of the celebra-
tions for the end of a long war, in which Britain had claimed
victory. One man, a certain Mr Servandoni, had designed a huge
wooden structure for the occasion, which was being erected in
Green Park; another man, called Charles Frederick, had been
given the title of "Controller of his Majesty's Fireworks as well as
for War as for Triumph" – grand, as titles go; and Handel had been
asked to compose music for the opening ceremony. The rehearsal
of the new piece went well; it was attended by a vast crowd of
people – one newspaper with a lively imagination claimed that
there were twelve thousand of them! Anyway, there were enough
of them to cause a three-hour traffic jam on London Bridge. But
the great occasion itself – oh dear. A lot of the fireworks wouldn't
light at all – and one of those that did set the wooden structure
on fire. It burnt to the ground, Mr Servandoni attacked Charles
Frederick with a sword, and everybody got furious with everyone
else. Not exactly a successful night out . . .

· 8 ·

Basically, Handel had the constitution of an ox who does
press-ups on a regular basis. All the guzzling can't have been
good for him (especially since he may have developed lead-

poisoning from the wine he loved so much – something to do with the way it was made at that time). His exercise can't have been that vigorous, either – people with bow-legs and roly-poly walks tend to move rather slowly. But on the whole he was surprisingly healthy, except for a couple of worrying attacks (strokes, perhaps?). The first occurred when he was fifty-two; his right hand was paralysed, and he seemed to be affected mentally. Fortunately, it didn't last long: he went off for a rather fierce cure of vapour-baths, took three times the recommended dose, and, to everybody's amazement, bounced back to robust health – this was a strong man!

But in February 1751, real disaster struck: Handel realised that he was going blind. In the middle of composing a chorus to the ominous words "How dark, O Lord, are thy decrees", he had to break off, writing a note in the manuscript saying that he'd had to stop because his left eye was "so relaxt" (that's one way of putting it!) A couple of weeks later, there was some improvement, and he went on composing; but it didn't last. That summer, he completely lost the sight in his left eye; and his right eye was failing too. Various operations were tried, but none of them really helped. The last was by the famous (or infamous) eye surgeon (or, as he described himself, "opthalmiater" – extraordinary word!) John Taylor, who had operated (unsuccessfully) on Bach, as well as on camels and dromedaries (probably unsuccessfully too, but since they never talked about their experiences, we don't really know). Not *very* surprisingly, he didn't do Handel any good.

The first few months of blindness must have been truly awful for Handel; there is a sad report of him sitting unhappily at an oratorio performance, unable to play and ignored by the audience. Later, he found it particularly painful to hear his own setting of the words "Total eclipse – no sun, no moon, All dark amid the blaze of noon," (from his oratorio 'Samson'). It was a dark time for Handel, in every sense. Wonderfully, though, he rallied; although he had to be led to the organ, and to be led back towards the audience when it was time to bow, he resumed playing and directing. Rehearsals were held at his house, and he still managed to play organ concertos between the acts of his oratorios – either playing old ones from memory, or giving the orchestra simple accompaniments to play and making up the solo part as he went along. His last perform-ance, of 'Messiah', took place just eight days before he died.

Handel's favourite charities . . .

Although Handel continued to put on his oratorio seasons for the general public (and his own bank account), an increasing amount of his energy in his last years went towards helping good causes. His charity performances became celebrated occa-sions. One organisation which he helped a lot (and to which he left £1000 in his will) was "The Fund for the Support of Decayed Musicians and their Families"; this had been set up after the children of an oboist who had died in poverty had been seen driving donkeys outside the opera house where their father had formerly played. The fund still exists – although it's now known, less colourfully but more cheerfully, as "The Royal Society of Musicians". Another charity for which Handel raised money was one that helped "fallen ladies".

But the organisation with which Handel was most closely associated in his final years was the Foundling Hospital, which took in poor orphans. Handel presented the hospital with an organ for its chapel, became a governor, and gave annual performances of 'Messiah' for its benefit (as well as leaving a manuscript score and set of orchestral parts of it to the hospital in his will). The performances became major events, attended by the cream (both fresh and sour, probably) of society, as well as by the unfortunate (actually, comparatively fortunate) orphans themselves. The concerts were packed: for the perform-ance given in 1750 to celebrate the installation of the organ

*which Handel had presented, so many people were expected
that ladies were asked to come "without hoops" (not the toys –
large dresses, that would take up too much room) and the
gentlemen "without swords". (Funny – I wouldn't have thought
that swords would have taken up too much room; but I suppose that if they'd tried to remove them from their sheaths in a
really crowded space, a nasty accident might have occurred –
and it's true that that would have significantly detracted from
the gentlemen's enjoyment . . .)*

·9·

Handel's end, when it came, was very peaceful. Shortly after
his last performance of 'Messiah', he went to bed – and stayed
there. He had hoped to die on Good Friday (wanting, it was
said, to meet "his sweet Lord and Saviour on the day of His
Resurrection"). But despite newspapers having eagerly reported his death on the Thursday, he actually died at 8 a.m. on
Saturday April 14th, 1759. He was visited on his deathbed
by various old friends, including some with whom he had
previously quarrelled; he made peace with them all. He had
made his will in 1750, but as he'd outlived several of the
people to whom he had originally left money, he'd had to alter
it four times since – the last time just three days before his
death. The document contains a (slightly immodest) request
to be buried with a private funeral in Westminster Abbey
(where only kings and queens and *very* important people are
buried); he also left "up to £600" for a memorial to himself
there – he really wanted to be remembered!

His request to be buried in the Abbey was granted – but not
the request for privacy; around three thousand people attended the funeral on April 20th. The monument was built: it was
to be the last work of Roubiliac, the same sculptor whose first
commission had been Handel's statue in Vauxhall Gardens –

so he'd had practise. Handel was laid to rest nearby – to be joined in a neighbouring grave 111 years later by the great writer Charles Dickens; I wonder if their skeletons talk to each other at night? Handel left lots of money, so his favourite charities were well taken care of, as were his assistants, his favourite niece in Germany, some other relatives, and his servants, one of whom bought his house and its contents – fixed wig block, lead cistern, and all. Many years later, a cheeky upstart

GEORGE FREDERICK HANDEL

whose name happened to be Handel, and who decided that he should therefore have some of the estate, tried to get his hands on it; but I am glad to say that his scheme was foiled. The nerve of it!

Handel's music was carefully disposed of, too; most of his manuscripts have survived, which is good. His will also gives a list of several interesting-sounding friends to whom he left money: they include a perfumer, two lawyers, a rich merchant and others. It's a little glimpse into Handel's private world; but only a little one. It would be good to know him a bit more intimately, perhaps; but what's most important is that his music and reputation have survived . . .

. . . and survive they most certainly have

For the British, who'd adopted him, or rather, been adopted by him, Handel was a national treasure, to be celebrated and boasted about (a touch annoying for the Germans, who'd produced him!) Three years after Handel's death, Roubiliac's memorial was unveiled – very grand it was (and is), too: a bronze Handel in a swirling cloak, holding one of the most famous arias from 'Messiah' ("I know that my Redeemer liveth"), with the title page of 'Messiah' (missing one "s", for some reason) behind it, an organ behind that, and an angel, sitting very comfortably on a cloud and playing a harp, over Handel's head. The only slight problem is that the date of birth is wrong: it says that Handel was born in 1684. Oh well.

Performances of Handel's music (not the operas, but the oratorios, ceremonial music and instrumental works) kept his name alive; but what really cemented his fame was the celebration of his centenary in – ahem – 1784. (Handel fans were evidently deeply muddled people.) It was a huge event, finishing with a performance of 'Messiah' in Westminster Abbey, with over five hundred performers. From then on, Handel festivals were held regularly in London and, increasingly, elsewhere. Probably the largest performance of all came in London in 1883, when an orchestra of five hundred and a choir of four thousand took part in a Handel festival which drew in an audience of more than 87,000 – phew! I wonder what Handel would have thought of it? He'd probably have been shocked by the loudness and heaviness of it all – utterly different from his own performances; but then, perhaps, once he'd got over that, I suspect he might have been rather pleased at all the attention and fame (and at the money flowing into the box office). And who knows? Perhaps his wig would have waggled – just a little . . .

The Music

I'm not sure there has ever been a composer whose music is as *thrilling* as Handel's. Somehow he manages to tell you, right from the first notes, that something special and important is about to happen – or is already happening. It's not surprising that he was commissioned to compose works for so many great occasions; they couldn't fail to be memorable events, with that music going on! He likes drums and trumpets, and generally lots of noise; but he doesn't need them to create excitement. It's his pounding, zippy rhythms, the extraordinary combinations of voices and instruments, the spicy harmonies that do the trick; nobody has had a finer sense of drama than Handel.

It's not *just* excitement and drama that set Handel's music apart, though; there's also tenderness, wit, and lots of gorgeous and easily remembered tunes. And he manages to make us feel totally involved, even though the gods and goddesses, kings and queens and so on in his operas and oratorios aren't exactly like the people that one generally knows. (How many kings and queens do you meet on a daily basis?) We end up caring about them, because the music draws us into their world. Even if they're heroes and heroines and we're not (well, you may be, but I'm certainly not), their emotions are universal, and so they speak directly to us.

We don't get to know Handel himself through his music – at least, not about his love-life and such; he's not that sort of composer. His works are dressed up, as it were, in formal clothes and a wig; but what magnificent clothes, and what a glorious wig! His music can be dark and tragic, as often as it's joyous and celebratory; but it always leaves us with the feeling that life is better and more interesting than we thought, that the world is a great and exciting place after all. And for that, may we be truly thankful to Mr Handel.

What to listen to

The trouble with recommending any particular Handel piece is that he wrote so much – over six hundred works, including more than sixty huge operas and oratorios. So – where does one begin? Well, perhaps you should start with some of the ceremonial music. If you can get a recording of it, listen to 'Zadok the Priest', with the volume fairly high (not *too* high, or you'll get a fright – and annoy the neighbours). It starts softly, not much seeming to happen – but there's a feeling that something momentous is about to take place; and it is. Suddenly the choir enters, singing for all they're worth at the very tops of their voices; it's one of the great moments in music. 'Music for the Royal Fireworks' is fun, too; lots of pomp and ceremony there. Another piece to keep you dancing around the room is 'The Arrival of the Queen of Sheba'. (Actually, Handel never appears to have called it that, and anyway, nobody seems to know where Sheba was; but that's what the piece is usually called today.)

When you want to start getting to know the bigger, more important pieces, 'Messiah' is a must, of course. Again, it's probably worth getting hold of a recording, and listening to it several times before you go to a live performance; it's almost two and a half hours long, so it's good to be looking forward to your favourite bits – and there'll be lots of those! (There's a famous chorus known as the 'Hallelujah Chorus'; that by itself is worth the price of admission.) All the big oratorios are worth getting to know – 'Theodora', 'Israel in Egypt', and many others. Make sure that you have a copy of the words in front of you as you listen, because that makes it all far more enjoyable. The same goes for the operas: it's important to know what's going on! If you can get videos of them, it might be best to start with those – although of course, they're never going to have the same effect as live theatre. Try 'Julius Caesar' (sometimes known by its Italian title, 'Giulio Cesare'), or 'Alcina' (a magic opera about a sorceress with a rather nasty habit of turning people into rocks, streams, trees or wild beasts) – both masterpieces. And maybe the funniest is 'Xerxes', which is about a complicated set of love-pairings that all go wrong (and then right again, naturally).

Another thrill is a choral work he wrote in Italy at the age of twenty-two, called 'Dixit Dominus'. Then there's lots of breathtaking orchestral music – the 'Concerto Grosso', Op. 6, No. 5, for instance. It's really hard to choose just a few of his works though; the trouble is that they're all so good! So – just start exploring: there are endless treats in store ...

Franz Joseph Haydn

1732-1809

now – I hope that you've dressed neatly today, because we're off to a little house just outside Vienna, in Austria, to visit an old gentleman who sets great store by cleanliness and tidiness. He himself, although very old for his time (well into his seventies, at a time when the average life expectancy is under forty) has spent at least an hour and a half getting dressed – or rather being dressed by his servants, as he is too weak to dress himself. We will be met by a smiling housekeeper; she'll make us wait while she announces us, before returning to usher us into a small room. Here is the old gentleman sitting in an armchair, wearing a powdered wig with curls shaped like éclairs covering his ears. (In fact, we've heard little panic-struck noises from inside the room while we've been waiting outside: he has to get the wig on before he can see any visitors.) Round his neck is a white band with a gold buckle; his waistcoat is also white, and made of heavy silk, with an impressive frill on it; over that is a coffee-coloured suit with embroidered cuffs over the wrists; on one of his fingers is a diamond ring (a present from a Very Important Person); and on his coat a red ribbon, also a sign of Importance. On the upper part of his legs he is wearing half-trousers made of black silk, on the lower part white silk stockings; his feet are in posh shoes, with large silver buckles; and on the little table next to him is a pair of white kid gloves. He's all dressed up, in fact – but with nowhere to go, because as his visiting card (which he will no doubt hand us at some stage) puts it, rather gloomily: "Gone is all my strength; old and weak am I" (a quote from one of his own songs). He's stuck in this little house, which is deeply frustrating for him, and sometimes he gets very depressed. Not today, though. We're lucky – this is a good day; perhaps our visit is even cheering him up. He welcomes us with a toothless – well, almost toothless – smile; such a charming smile, despite the lack of molars, that it brings a rush of warmth to our hearts. (We mustn't get carried away, however, as a famous French violinist did; he gave the old man such a fierce hug that he almost knocked out the two remaining teeth!)

But where are my manners? I do apologise. Time for introductions: the elderly gentleman whom I should like you to meet is the famous Austrian composer Franz Joseph Haydn (Hide-'n); and Doctor Haydn, I'd like you to meet my reader. (What was your name? My memory is getting worse and worse – shocking, it is.) Joseph Haydn (forget the Franz bit) isn't exactly a beauty – he never has been. He is rather small, with short legs, and a pockmarked face; his nose is a bit too big for its own good, and inside it he has an unfortunate growth (a "nasal polyp" to its friends) that distorts the shape of one of his nostrils and often makes breathing uncomfortable for him. (He was going to have it operated on once, by a famous surgeon in London; this was well before the day of anaesthetics, so several strong men were employed to hold Haydn down in a chair while the surgeon did his stuff. Haydn was so terrified that he started screaming and struggling, and wouldn't stop; eventually the surgeon gave up in disgust. Personally, I don't blame Haydn one little bit.) But for all the seeming faults in his appearance, Haydn looks lovely – because he has such a kind, good-humoured expression. No wonder that everybody (well, *almost* everybody) adores him.

Haydn likes children; in fact, his housekeeper often brings local children into the house to play in front of the old man, because it gives him pleasure to watch them. So it probably won't be long before he tells you to call him "Papa Haydn"; most people, adults or children, call him that. It also won't be long, probably, before he shows us the contents of a rather splendid box that he keeps near him; inside it are the many gold medals he has been sent regularly, especially in recent years, by musical societies and music-loving aristocrats from various parts of Europe. They are a great comfort to Haydn, reassuring him that his name will be remembered by posterity, so that, as he puts it, "I shall not wholly die."

He certainly won't! His music sounds to our modern ears as fresh, as lively – and as funny too, at times – as it must have sounded to the audiences of his day. And at whatever stage in his life it was composed, it sounds like the music of a young, vigorous man, who loves his life and lives it to the full. Of course he *was* young once; believe it or not, all of us "grown-ups" were, at one time! And he certainly wasn't born wearing those grand clothes. (A good thing too: it might have been a bit uncomfortable – as well as a bit surprising – for his mother.) In fact, he was born into rather a poor family, in a quiet village called Rohrau (pronounced Roe-row – "row" rhyming with "wow", that is). His father, Mathias, was employed by the local bigwigs to repair wagons, to make wheels, and to paint houses; he was also a local magistrate for twenty years, making sure that the locals went to church every week, and didn't get up to any funny business. Before her marriage, Haydn's mother Maria had been employed by the same bigwigs, as a cook (preparing, among other delicacies, tortoise. Horrible thought – I wonder how she served it? Tortoise on toast? Tortoise omelette?) Mathias and Maria had twelve children, seven of whom survived infancy; Franz Joseph, the second-born, was the oldest son. After Maria died, Mathias, evidently an energetic type, married his nineteen-year-old servant and had five more children (although sadly, none of them lived).

Both of Haydn's parents were musical: Mathias played the harp and sang, and Maria sang along with him. Little Joseph used to join in from an early age, perfectly in tune and with a beautiful voice; then, having seen the local schoolmaster playing, he would take two sticks and pretend to play the violin, keeping time to his parents' songs with surprising accuracy. One evening, the Haydn family was visited by their nearest and dearest, Mr Franck – well, perhaps not quite *nearest*: he was the husband of Haydn's father's stepsister, which made him Haydn's step-uncle-in-law. But besides holding this impressive position, Mr Franck was also principal and choir director of a church school in Hainburg, a town not far from Rohrau; and maybe that made him the Haydns' dearest. He offered to take little Sepperl (as Joseph was called) away with him, and to take care of his general and musical education – both essential if the boy was to grow up to be a priest, which was his parents' dream.

So five-year-old Sepperl was taken off to school, and would never live with his parents again. Perhaps that was more normal in those days than it is now; but it can't have been easy, for them or for him. And life at the school in Hainburg was certainly far from easy. Apart from having to work ridiculously hard for a boy his age, Haydn had to live with the Francks, who neglected him. His mother had always made sure that he was clean and tidy; but the Francks couldn't have cared less about that – and Haydn, to his horror, found himself becoming a "ragamuffin". His hair became so dirty that he started wearing a wig – and he continued to wear one for the rest of his life.

From a musical point of view, however, it was a success. Haydn made so much progress that when a man called Reutter (pronouced "Royter") came to Hainburg, looking for young boys to sing in the choir at the famous Cathedral of St Stephen in Vienna, the future composer was taken to sing to him. Reutter was impressed, and invited Haydn to join the choir. He was surprised, though, that Haydn didn't know how to do a trill (two notes next to each other, alternating rapidly). Haydn was so quick to learn, though, that as a reward Reutter took a plate of delicious-looking cherries, and poured them into Haydn's pocket. Every time Haydn heard a trill after that, he thought of cherries!

Vienna was – is – a great city, the capital of Austria; arriving there must have been a bewildering experience for the eight-year-old boy. I'm sure he was excited; but life at the cathedral school turned out to be even harder than at Hainburg. Haydn – who was always extremely fond of good food – had been hungry at Hainburg; in Vienna he practically starved! The only way he could get to eat a really good meal was by being engaged to sing at private concerts given by posh people; so Haydn made sure that he sang well enough to be engaged for lots of them. As for Reutter, he turned out to be a snake-in-the-grass, not at all interested in the boys, and *extremely* interested in earning as much money as possible. (He'd even steal from the boys, given half a chance.)

Haydn had to endure this for nine years, staying in the choir even after his voice had started to break and he could no longer sing like a little angel; in fact the Empress of Austria eventually complained that his solos sounded like the "crowing of a cock". Finally, after his voice had broken fully, his solos were taken over by his younger brother Michael, who had arrived at the school five years after Joseph. From that point onwards, our Haydn was fairly useless to St Stephen's – and that meant that sooner or later snake-in-the-grass Reutter was going to get rid of him. The excuse came one day when Joseph had come into possession of a new pair of scissors. Being a practical young man, he wanted to try them out – so he snipped off the pigtail of a fellow chorister; fair enough – how else could he have found out whether they were sharp enough? We don't know what the young boy whose scalp had just become a pigtail-free zone felt about this, but we do know that Reutter was furious, and threatened to cane Haydn on the hand. Joseph, now seventeen and above such treatment, resisted: "I would rather leave the school!" Reutter compromised: first, he caned Joseph – and then he kicked him out anyway.

And so Haydn was out on the street, alone and penniless. He had a lot of practical experience now as a musician, but he'd never really had any composition lessons and, although he was a good all-rounder, he wasn't brilliant at any particular instrument. What was he to do? All he knew was that he wanted to be a musician, and not a priest, even though that was what his parents wanted – and even though Haydn himself was a deeply committed Catholic, who in later life ended all his manuscripts with the words "Praise be to God".

His prospects looked bleak; but for once, he was lucky. Wandering around Vienna, not knowing where to spend the night, he happened to meet a singer whom he knew slightly, a Mr Spangler. In old English, a "spangler" was something that glittered like a star; and in old Vienna, it seems to have meant the same thing – at least in this case. Mr Spangler was a real star: he took pity on the poor friendless youth, and invited him to come back to his tiny apartment, which he shared with Mrs Spangler and Baby Spangler. Of course, Haydn took this offer up with relief and gratitude. Now that he had somewhere to live – if only very temporarily, particularly since Baby Spangler Mark 2 was on its way – he could set about earning enough to eat. He managed to scrape by, giving some lessons, making occasional musical arrangements, playing at dances and, above all, busking. (The Viennese loved their music, indoors or out-doors.) It wasn't glamorous, but at least he didn't starve to death.

Musical geniuses (genii? No, I prefer geniuses) suffer when they can't express themselves in music, as writers suffer if they can't express themselves in words; and Haydn couldn't express himself in composition, because no one had taught him how to compose. He tried writing very complicated-looking pieces, because he thought that if he covered whole sheets of paper with notes, the music would be good; but it wasn't. It took him years to get to a level where he could be proud of his work. During several of these years he lived – having de-Spangled himself – in a miserable attic, under a leaking roof; in winter his breath froze in front of him, and when he fetched water for his morning wash, it would turn to ice before he got it upstairs to his room. He was busy earning a meagre living from daybreak until dusk; and then – when he wasn't out busking, which at least gave him a chance to try out his new compositions – he would spend most of the night sitting with his new best friend, a worm-eaten old harpsichord, teaching himself how to compose.

Gradually, as signs of Haydn's genius started to appear in his works, his reputation began to spread; and finally, in his mid-twenties, he was hired for his first proper job, as Music Director for someone called Count Morzin. The Count, like many rich men of the time, had a small orchestra of his own; he also had a beautiful wife, who put Haydn into a complete spin by wearing a low-cut dress and leaning over him while he was trying to play. Ahem.

Haydn was always partial to attractive ladies – which makes us wonder why, of all the approximately 400 million women in the world at that time, he chose to marry his wife, Maria Anna. The way they got together was a bit peculiar to start with: a few years before he got his first job, Haydn had fallen in love with a pupil of his, the daughter of a wig-maker (perhaps Haydn occasionally traded lessons for a new wig). Sadly for Haydn, rather than become the wife of poor (as he certainly was then) Joseph, his pupil decided to enter the Convent of the Order of Poor Clares. He was (we can presume) heartbroken. The earliest music of his that survives was written for her ceremony of initiation – perhaps he preserved it because of its sad associations. However, four years later, he accepted a consolation prize: the wig-maker's rather unappealing older daughter, Maria Anna. She, according to one of Haydn's first biographers, had "a wooden head" – not the most attractive of features, unless perhaps you happen to be a carpenter short of materials. From what we know of her character, she must have had a touch of dry rot, too.

The marriage was not what you might call a raging success, judging by Haydn's later remarks. In one of his letters to another lady, he describes his wife as "that infernal beast" – not the *most* loving remark; and he claimed that she couldn't have cared less whether he'd been an artist or a cobbler. His biographers are almost all horrible about her, telling us that she regularly used Haydn's manuscripts as curling-paper for her hair – inexcusable, no matter how nice the curls may have looked. We are told that she spent a fortune, which Haydn certainly couldn't afford, entertaining her religious friends (she was almost as devout a Catholic as her sister, the nun); and then complained that if Haydn were to die suddenly, there wouldn't be enough money in the house to bury him (which doesn't sound like a very loving remark, either). The couple lived apart for most of their married life. So little noticed was her death in 1800, that three years later a close associate of Haydn's sent him a handkerchief as a gift for "Mrs Haydn"!

She doesn't seem to have been either sympathetic or intelligent; but perhaps this impression is unfair – she never gets a chance to defend herself. The only document of hers that we have is her will, which shows us (a) that she couldn't write or spell properly and (b) that she left the little she had to her husband, which implies that she didn't hate him, anyway. It was also said that she took around with her a portrait of Haydn and couldn't bear to be parted from it (although his explanation for that was that she'd had a love affair with the artist who'd painted it!) We don't even know what she looked like, since nobody seems to have thought it worthwhile to commission a portrait of her. So perhaps we shouldn't judge her too harshly; but we can say fairly definitely that the Haydns were not a happy couple. Divorce was not an option, however – their Catholic beliefs ruled out that possibility; so they were stuck with each other.

Still, while his personal life may have been a bit of a disaster, Haydn's career was finally taking off. His first job fizzled out in 1761, because his employer lost his money and had to sack his orchestra; but Haydn was almost immediately hired by the famous Esterházy family (with the stress on the "Est", but with a rather long "a", sounding like "ah" – hence that funny-looking accent). He was to be employed by the family for the rest of his professional life, serving under four of the Princes Esterházy – Paul Anton, Nicolaus I, Anton, and Nicolaus II. From 1761 until 1790 Haydn spent most of his time either at the Esterházy family's castle in a place called Eisenstadt, not far from Vienna, or at the amazingly grand palace in Hungary known as the castle of Eszterháza, which Nicolaus I (also known as Nicolaus the Magnificent) built over a period of twenty years or so.

Both castles were equipped with theatres and halls large enough to house concerts and operas, and there was a permanent company of Esterházy musicians.

The wonderful thing about this was that Haydn therefore had at his disposal a whole orchestra and cast of singers, and was able, in the relative isolation of Eisenstadt and Eszterháza, to make musical experiments to his heart's content (so long as his employers enjoyed the pieces he wrote). It was during these years that Haydn became a truly great composer; as he put it himself, "I was cut off from the world . . . and so I *had* to become original."

The bad thing was that he was essentially a servant, and treated as such; he had to fight for his right to sit among the more important officials at the employees' table, and was frequently answerable to "base souls", as he called them. His responsibilities were huge: apart from having to compose whatever the Prince felt like hearing – whether it be a symphony, an opera, a piece of chamber music or whatever – and having to conduct almost all the rehearsals, performances and church services, he was responsible for the good behaviour and welfare of all the musicians. He often had to defend them when they were threatened with the sack for such lapses as missing performances, or getting married without the Prince's permission; or for other rather more unusual misdeeds, such as the time a flautist was out shooting at birds, but actually hit the roof of a house instead, setting it on fire, and then – far worse, of course – forgot to take off his hat in the presence of the official who was doling out his punishment. Or the ghastly occasion when an oboist and a cellist had a fight in the local tavern, and the cellist, who was wearing a ring, punched the oboist in the face and knocked out his right eye! Yuk. (Moral of the story: never trust cellists.)

Haydn usually managed to smooth things over, to the immense gratitude of his musicians; it was from them that he acquired the nickname "Papa Haydn". He was badly paid for it all, though – to the extent that when he was given a pair of horses by an aristocratic admirer, he had to apply to the Prince for extra money to buy horse-fodder. Moreover, for several years, under his initial contract, all his compositions belonged legally to the Prince, so that Haydn couldn't even make any extra money by having them published. (This changed gradually, on an unofficial basis, but not officially until 1779.) He did eventually manage to buy a house in Eisenstadt, with the help of a loan from Nicolaus the Magnificent; it had a rather bad habit of burning down from time to time, however, which meant that Haydn had to apply for more help from his Prince to rebuild it. So he was almost constantly in debt, which for Haydn, who was extremely careful with money, must have been very upsetting.

At least Eisenstadt was near the great city of Vienna, so Haydn could get there occasionally – when the Prince allowed him to leave the estate. Eszterháza, on the other hand, was miles from anywhere, in the middle of a huge swamp. Furthermore, in Eszterháza all the musicians and music copyists, as well as some actors, painters and even some of the other servants, had to live in one none-too-large house. You'd have thought that in such a grand and spacious castle, with its amazing grounds, they wouldn't have had to be squished together like musical sardines – but that was the way it was. So cramped were the living quarters, in fact, that in 1772 Prince Nicolaus gave strict orders that no musicians (except for the four most important ones, including Haydn – who was probably happier by himself anyway) were allowed to bring their wives or children to Eszterháza; and they were expected to stay in the Prince's beloved castle until he took it into his head that he wanted to go back to Eisenstadt. As usual, the lonely musicians appealed to Papa Haydn for help. Luckily, Papa H. managed to come up with a brilliant idea: he composed a new symphony for the Prince, known as the 'Farewell' Symphony. It went on normally – and beautifully – for the first three movements; but then in the last movement, one by one, the musicians' parts came to an end. They blew out their candles, tucked their instruments under their arms, and left the stage. By the end, only the first violinist and Haydn himself were left on the platform.

At least Nicolaus the Magnificent could take a hint; the very next day, orders were given to pack up and leave Eszterháza.

Haydn appreciated the musical freedom he had working for Nicolaus I, and was loyal to the Prince personally, appreciating his genuine love of music and basically generous nature. Also, he was glad of the musical freedom he was given at Eisenstadt and Eszterháza. As the years went by, however, he became increasingly frustrated by his life at the court. On all his all-too-rare visits to Vienna, he had a wonderful time: he was gradually becoming a celebrity among the artistic circles there, and was treated as such, going to musical parties, enjoying the fine food and drink and – no doubt – flirting with lots of lovely ladies. He also enjoyed the company of a young friend he'd made, a composer called Wolfgang Amadeus Mozart: the two geniuses adored each other and spent a lot of time together, listening to each other's new works, and playing chamber music together. (That must have been quite something!) And then, after all that stimulation, it was back to one or other of the Esterházy palaces, where Haydn was still treated like a servant. One of his most touching letters is the one he wrote to his favourite Viennese musical hostess when he arrived back in Esterházy in February 1790: "Well, here I sit in my wilderness; forsaken, like some poor orphan, almost without human society, melancholy, dwelling on the memory of past glorious days . . . I found everything at home in confusion . . . I slept little, and even my dreams persecuted me, for when I fell asleep and was under the pleasant illusion that I was listening to 'The Marriage of Figaro' [one of Mozart's greatest operas], the blustering north wind woke me and almost blew my nightcap off my head; I lost twenty pounds in weight in three days . . . Alas and alack, thought I to myself, would that I now had many a titbit that I despised in Vienna! Here in Eszterháza no one asks me 'Would you like [hot] chocolate with or without milk? Will you take coffee with or without cream? What can I offer you, my good Haydn? Will you have vanilla ice or strawberry?' If only I had a piece of good Parmesan cheese . . ."

And so on – poor Haydn! He sounds like a schoolboy sent back to a horrible boarding school after the holidays. And things were to get worse before they got better. Shortly after that letter was written, Prince Nicolaus I's wife died, and Haydn and his musicians were expected to lift the Prince out of his depression with their music. They had to be very careful to play the right pieces, because anything too emotional might plunge the Prince into even deeper gloom. Then, later that same year, Nicolaus the Magnificent himself died.

Sad though that was – because he does seem to have been a great man, in his way – in retrospect it was the best thing that could have happened to Haydn. Prince Nicolaus's son, Anton, didn't care about music and dismissed all but a very few of the Esterházy musicians. Haydn's job was spared, but he no longer felt the loyalty and attachment he had felt to Nicolaus. He rushed off to Vienna as soon as he could; and very shortly afterwards, he received an interesting proposal.

According to Haydn, it happened like this: he was sitting in his room in Vienna one day, trying to decide which of a few offers he should take, when a stranger walked in and announced himself. "I am Salomon from London, and I have come to fetch you," said the stranger strangely. "Tomorrow we will conclude an agreement." With that, according to Haydn, he vanished – no doubt leaving the great composer all of a-twitter. Anyway, the long and the short (principally the long) of it was that Haydn did go to England, twice, both trips lasting well over a year. And what a time he had! It was in London that Haydn became a *true* celebrity, a household name – and where he made his fortune: having been fairly poor before he first went there, he returned from the second trip a rich man, having earned roughly twelve times the amount he'd managed to save in all his previous years. He was also awarded an honorary doctorate by Oxford University – he was now "Doctor Haydn", no less.

Virtually everybody he met in England seems to have adored Haydn: the musicians he conducted – he used to call them "my treasure", "my angel", and so forth, which helped; the public – once they'd forgiven him for being a foreigner; and all sorts of grand and influential people, including the King and Queen – although they were a bit offended when he eventually refused their offer to settle in England, and returned to live in Vienna. The only people who seem to have had mixed feelings about him were Salomon's rival promoters, who brought over a former pupil of Haydn's, Pleyel, and tried to convince everyone that Pleyel was Haydn's most dangerous competitor – in fact, much better than Haydn because he wasn't so old. However, Haydn got on so well with his old student, and wrote music so much finer than Pleyel's, that he completely defused the situation.

Haydn wrote some of his very best music in London, including his last twelve symphonies, all of which are amazing. One of them, No. 94, is known as the 'Surprise'. This came about because members of the audience often came to the concerts after having scoffed a large dinner with plenty of wine, and would fall asleep, snoring loudly for good measure. Haydn was annoyed by this, so he wrote a very soft opening to the slow second movement – followed by a sudden CRASH from the orchestra (including loud kettle-drums), which sent the audience shooting out of their seats! It still works today.

Before his first trip to London, Haydn had never taken a journey longer than a few hours in a horse-drawn carriage: although he spoke good Italian and some French, he'd never even been to Italy or France. But he was now in a huge city (far larger and busier than Vienna), over 750 miles away from home – two weeks' journey over land and sea. Furthermore, English people spoke a strange language (with which Haydn struggled, eventually with some success – although his spelling remained startlingly original), and had some even stranger customs. But Haydn, now officially an old man, was far from daunted – he was fascinated. So excited was he by all that he saw and heard, in fact, that he kept a "London journal", which ran to four volumes and gives us some fascinating glimpses into his experiences – and into his preoccupations. There are an awful lot of entries about money, for instance, but there are also jokes, little stories, recipes, bits of gossip, complaints about the weather and so on.

He wrote and received a lot of letters in London, too, and from some of those that survive we find out that – well, that Papa Haydn was rather a naughty Papa at times. Hmm . . . The letters to and from his wife are lost – but we know that she would write to him once a month. Her letters were so horrible, though (according to him), that he stopped opening them, and threatened never to come home again unless she became "much more sensible". We don't know exactly what was in those letters, (apart from a nasty bit of gossip, telling him that Mozart was "speaking very ill" of Haydn. Haydn was obviously bothered by this, but decided (a) that he didn't believe it, and (b) that he forgave Mozart anyway.) We can surmise, though, that Mrs Haydn's letters were probably full of jealous rages – and who can blame her? Her husband's other letters show that he was in the middle of at least three romances with other women, and was thoroughly enjoying all of them.

First, there were letters to and from the lovely lady to whom Haydn had written his lament on arriving back in Eszterháza a couple of years earlier. She was a rich, married society hostess and talented amateur musician called Maria von Genzinger (although Haydn, never the greatest of spellers, could never quite decide what her name was, calling her in various letters Gennsinger, Gennzinger or Gennziger). Haydn obviously adored this lady; but she was married – happily, as far as we know. That didn't stop Haydn, though, from making flirtatious remarks such as: "I kiss your Grace 1000 times – on the hands." (Where else, I'd like to know?) Also, he had to reassure her when her letters to him, or his to her, went astray; after that he put his letters in an extra envelope to keep them from "the eyes of curious people, male or female". Slightly suspicious . . . Their relationship was probably fairly pure, however – if only from necessity; as Haydn said in a letter to Maria: "I have my thoughts." I bet he did!

However – gosh, gossip is fun, even if it's over two hundred years old; in fact, *especially* if it's that old, because it can't hurt anyone's feelings now! – we're pretty certain that he had more than "thoughts" about an Italian singer called Luigia Polzelli, who had been one of the Esterházy singers. She was married, too, with two sons; it was rumoured that Haydn was father to the younger one! (True or not, Haydn was lovely to the boys, treating them both like sons – but that wasn't so unusual for Papa Haydn. More surprising, perhaps, is that Mrs Haydn seems to have been very nice to the older boy when he came to stay with them in Vienna; a point in her favour.) There are some really quite shocking letters from Haydn to Luigia written from London, in one of which he writes, after her husband has died but Haydn's wife is still alive and (no doubt) kicking: "Perhaps, perhaps, the time will come, of which we both dreamt so often, when four eyes are closed. Two are closed, but the other two – enough of all this, it shall be as God wills." That's pretty awful – longing for his wife's eyes to close for ever. And one wonders whether Luigia was really worth it: she was always getting money out of Haydn, and she seems to have been quite a drama queen as well. On one of his letters to her from London, there's a note in her hand: "He will die – an enemy has followed Haydn to overthrow him." Scary! Still, she was presumably attractive; even her passport describes her as having a graceful figure. Of course, poor Mrs Haydn did eventually die; but it seems as if by that point Haydn had gone off Luigia. He didn't marry her after all; so she made him sign a most peculiar agreement instead, promising not to marry anyone else, and to leave her a regular income after his death. (In fact *she* married again; but Haydn still left her something in his will.)

What makes Haydn's letters to Luigia yet more shocking is that he also had a devoted girlfriend in London. In fact, just three days before he'd written to Luigia – "I hope, as God is my witness, to be the same to you as I have been. I love you" – he'd received a gushing letter from his London friend telling him that "I FEEL for YOU the FONDEST and TENDEREST AFFECTION the HUMAN HEART is capable of." (Perhaps she thought he wouldn't believe her unless she used capitals.) This London lady was a comely widow called Rebecca Schroeter, to whom Haydn had given lessons. She was obviously dotty about him, constantly worrying about how his health was, how he'd slept, when he would next visit her, and so on. And the reason that we know about her is that Haydn – rather unsubtly – copied out her letters to him into his London notebooks, for all to see. I wonder whether she knew? And what she'd have felt about her private love letters being read by posterity?

So – Papa Haydn was no saint, at least in the lady department. His rather lame excuse was that because "my wife was unable to bear children . . . I was less indifferent towards the attractions of other women". And he admitted quite freely (indeed, proudly) that in his life he had been loved "by many a pretty woman" (adding modestly that "they can't have been led to it by my beauty.") Also, while we're on the topic of his faults, it has to be admitted that he was also far from saintly towards his publishers. To a Viennese firm he wrote, with a touching display of loyalty, that he'd had a visit from an English publisher, who'd "wanted to purchase various pieces from me; but on your account he did not receive a single note". Funny, that, since

Franz Joseph Haydn

the English publisher returned home and published two major works of Haydn's, that he just *happened* to have in manuscript. I wonder where he could have got them from? Ahem . . .

Ah – but that's about the end of the catalogue of Haydn's less-than-lovable aspects; apart from those flaws, he was pretty saintly. He was so noble to so many people, and so good-humoured and charming and kind: no wonder he was so beloved. And no wonder that the English begged him to stay in London for the rest of his life, as Handel had done. But Haydn wouldn't; he wanted to spend his last days in Austria, his home. He was quite a patriot, in fact: in Britain he was so impressed by the National Anthem, 'God Save the King', that he decided to write one of his own for Austria. The result, 'God Save the Emperor Franz', is still in use today – though in Germany rather than Austria. And the words are different, of course, since God couldn't really save the Emperor Franz for *that* long. Haydn's anthem is gorgeous! (You might know the tune, actually, without necessarily knowing what it is – it gets everywhere.)

So in August 1795, Haydn left England for the second and last time, and headed home for good. Officially, he still had his job with the Esterházys. He'd been worried that Prince Anton would sack him for taking three years' leave of absence (with a six-month return to service in the middle, between the two London trips); but Anton, though annoyed, had kept him on the payroll. Now Anton had snuffed it, and a new Prince, Nicolaus II, was Haydn's boss. This Nicolaus was very keen on music, which was good; but he thought he knew more about it than Haydn did, which was bad. He had an annoying habit of wandering into rehearsals and criticising. On one such occasion, Haydn snapped: "Your Highness, it is *my* job to decide this." Exit one Prince, much offended; cue for several musicians to suffer panic attacks. Papa Haydn had just insulted their all-powerful employer! But no harm seems to have come from the incident – apart from a slight bruise to the Prince's over-large ego, perhaps

Anyway, from now on, Haydn was really focused on Vienna; in fact, his greatest triumphs there were still to come. Now in his mid-sixties, he composed the work generally considered his masterpiece: 'The Creation', a religious work for solo singers, chorus and orchestra. (The text is in German, but it is a translation of an English original that may originally have been prepared for Handel.) 'The Creation' was first performed at two grand concerts in April 1798 – and the people of Vienna went mad. These were actually private performances, for rich types and their rich friends only. However, so many people crowded outside the palace where the performances were held that twelve policemen and eighteen guards on horseback had to be called in to keep order. Haydn himself was carried away by the thrill of the wonderful music he'd written: "One moment I was cold as ice, the next I seemed to be on fire." 'The Creation' was an instant hit, and over the next few years, Haydn raised a huge sum of money for charity by directing various performances of it. It was also heard in every major city in Europe, and beyond. It was played in small places, too – including a little town in Bohemia where the church authorities for some reason forbade the performance in the local church, on the grounds that it wasn't religious enough (rubbish). When the performance went ahead anyway, the local people were forced to kidnap their priest and lock him up, so that he wouldn't get into trouble with his bosses!

Three years later, Haydn followed the success of 'The Creation' with another choral masterpiece, 'The Seasons'. It certainly shows no sign of flagging inspiration – but Haydn always claimed that the strain of writing it finished him off. He wrote a few more works after that, but not many; in fact, his last string quartet, written in 1802, lacks a last movement. In its place, Haydn has written on the manuscript the words that we saw on his visiting card: "Gone is all my strength; old and weak am I." The quartet is a bit short, but it's beautiful nevertheless; as Haydn put it, "It's my last child, but it still looks like me." He was still teaching a bit, overseeing the Esterházy musical activities, and making quite a bit of extra cash by supplying a publisher in Edinburgh with his settings of British – mostly Scottish – folksongs, which were very popular (even though Haydn may actually have got his students to do some of them for him, whilst passing them off as his own works – more naughtiness). But in time even these gentler activities tailed off and Haydn, now in his seventies, became the frail old man whom we met at the beginning of this chapter.

At least he had his lovely cottage – actually found by his wife, who had wanted him to buy it for her. Haydn had bought it for himself instead, and had a second storey added. He had enough money now to settle into a peaceful retirement (even though he was always convinced that he was broke); but he found it hard. The main frustration was not being able to compose any more. He felt, he said, like a piano that somebody was trying to play – ideas came into his head, but wouldn't stay there long enough for him to get them onto paper.

So his last years weren't easy: he felt useless. "It is high time that the Lord called me to him," he moaned. (In fact, in 1805 a rumour spread around Europe that he *was* dead and two composers wrote works in his memory! Haydn was rather amused, saying that he wished he'd been able to conduct his own memorial concerts.) But there were still some pleasures left: the stream of gold medals and passionate fan-letters arriving from all over Europe, which landed up in his box; the love and devotion of his servants (a pity he didn't have an Indian servant with a turban: he could have been called the Haydn Sikh – sorry); the company of the local children; news and gossip from Vienna, which always interested him. And then there were visits like ours, during which he could remember past glories.

We'd have to leave fairly soon, though, so as not to tire him out; and he'll be wanting to say his prayers, something he does many times each day. So, with much bowing and kissing of hands, we had better leave this wonderful old man, to whom, in his own words, "God has granted talent and a good heart." Out we go into his little garden, shown out by his servant – but he has one more thing to say to us. "Give my love to all the pretty ladies!" he calls out after us. He may be old, but Papa Haydn is still Papa Haydn . . .

Facts of Life

·1·

Franz Joseph Haydn was born on March 31st, 1732, at 4 p.m. – or so he believed. But of course, it's a tradition for composers' birth-dates to be questionable, and now we're not sure whether he was born on March 31st or April 1st. It doesn't really matter *that* much, though, does it? Incidentally, the name of his village, Rohrau, means "Reedy Meadow" – rather poetic.

Local boy made good . . .

Haydn rarely went back to his birthplace, but in his old age, he was thrilled to discover – a couple of years after it had been put up – that a member of the rich family who had employed his parents had erected a monument to him in Rohrau. (The only slight drawback for him was that the monument had the birth-date of April 1st carved on it – but perhaps that was right.) In his will, Haydn left some money for the upkeep of this monument, and of a religious statue that his father had placed in the local church. He also left funds for the education of the two poorest orphans in Rohrau.

· 2 ·

Mr Franck, who'd hauled Haydn off to his first school in Hainburg, was not the kindest of men. Apart from neglecting his
step-nephew-in-law's personal cleanliness, and not giving
him enough to eat, he punished the little boy severely for any
musical mistakes that he made. Having received instructions
from his employers not to pull out his pupils' hair, Franck
caned them instead. But Haydn accepted the beatings as part
of life, and in fact remained grateful to Franck for his teaching:
he always kept a portrait of the music-master hanging on his
wall. Apart from improving his singing, little Haydn learned to
play almost every keyboard, wind and string instrument, and
even the drums. Unfortunately, though, he decided to practise
drumming on a little basket that he found perched on a chair,
not realising that it was a baker's basket, full of flour – which
spilled out as he drummed, and ruined the chair.

Snake-in-the-Grass Reutter in Vienna was far worse than
Franck had been. Not only did he starve the boys under his care
(despite being given an allowance for their food), but he also
couldn't be bothered to teach them; he was too busy accepting
lots of different jobs, both at St Stephen's Cathedral and at the
royal court, in order to earn as much money as possible. This
meant that he was required to provide music for lots of different
events; so he would use the boy choristers for these – cheap
labour! At least Haydn got to know some wonderful choral
music; this was practically the only musical education he
received from Reutter, who gave him perhaps two composition
lessons in the nine years that Haydn was at his school. What a
slithery snake Reutter the Rotter must have been. There was
even a story told that when Haydn's voice started to break,
Reutter tried to persuade him to keep it high by having the
operation to become a castrato. Shocking – but very possibly
not true, so perhaps we'd better not waste indignation on it.

A schoolboy prank . . .

Despite the fact that Haydn was semi-starved at both his schools, he kept up his high spirits; sometimes, in fact, they were too high. Once in Vienna, the choristers from St Stephen's were taken to the palace of the Empress of Austria to sing for her. This wasn't unusual – but what was unusual, and tempting, was that there was scaffolding around the palace, left by builders who'd been working there. Boys being boys, the choristers quickly swarmed up to the top. Unfortunately for them, the Empress happened to look out of a window and saw them. The boys were ordered to get down in double-quick time, with the threat of a thrashing if they did it again. The next day, they were back at the palace for another event. This time, just one boy couldn't resist monkeying his way up the scaffolding – guess who! And this time he received the promised walloping.

· 3 ·

One wonders how Haydn survived his eight years of poverty in Vienna after he'd been dumped out onto the street – but survive them he did, despite all the hardships. Strangely, in later life Haydn would occasionally tell people that he'd been happier during these years of struggle than he was afterwards, when he was famous. I doubt whether that was true, though – people often get nostalgic about their youth, even when it's been horrible. His attic must have been depressing, to put it mildly; and not knowing how he would get the money for the next day's meals must have been dreadful. Eventually, however, things started to look up – a little. The arrival of the old harpsichord was a great event in Haydn's life; he also acquired some music by C. P. E. Bach (son of *the* Bach, J. S., and a major composer in his own right). From this, and from some Teach-Yourself-Composition manuals, he started along the long road to greatness.

In the same house as Haydn, but in much nicer apartments on the lower floors, lived a famous Italian poet called Metastasio (some of whose words Haydn would set to music in later years). Metastasio – great name! – shared his apartments with a well-to-do Spanish friend of his, who had two daughters. Through the recommendation of the poet (perhaps he'd heard the harpsichord-playing in the middle of the night), Haydn was engaged to teach the elder girl the piano, receiving proper meals as payment; he also played the piano for her singing lessons with a distinguished old Italian composer, Porpora. Through this contact, Haydn was engaged to accompany some of Porpora's other lessons; as a result, Porpora invited the young and hopeful musician to travel with him to a fashionable summer resort. Haydn's official job was to play the piano for the singing lessons that Porpora gave there; but he had also to act as coat-beater, shoe-cleaner, wig-arranger and general dogsbody to the crotchety old composer. During the course of the summer Haydn was on the receiving end of an interesting array of Italian insults, as well as several unwelcome pokes in the ribs – but he didn't mind. Porpora actually gave him some composition lessons, practically the first he had ever had; Haydn was thrilled! Finally, finally, he was getting somewhere as a composer . . .

A bold young man . . .

Around this time – now in his very early twenties – Haydn wrote his first little opera (now lost, unfortunately), called 'The Limping Devil'. It was written at the request of a famous clown, whom Haydn met under what could have been uneasy circumstances. He had composed a serenade, which he and some friends were performing under the window of the clown's beautiful wife. Presumably they thought that her husband was away; but he wasn't – and he was mighty interested to know who was serenading his wife . . . Luckily, he was so intrigued by

*the music that, instead of punching Haydn on his already
rather mis-shapen nose, he decided to give him a test. He asked
the young composer to improvise some music depicting a man
swimming in the sea – but Haydn had never seen the sea! So the
clown lay face-down over several chairs, made paddling movements, and ordered his servants to push the chairs around the
room. This gave Haydn the inspiration he needed: he produced
some music that the clown loved, and was rewarded by a near-
smothering with clowny kisses, and a commission to write the
music for a libretto written by his new friend. 'The Limping
Devil' was quite successful; but it didn't get many performances,
because some pompous nobleman decided that he was the
model for the title role, and had the opera banned. Spoilsport!*

*So Haydn certainly had nerve – in fact, his nerve often helped
him get on in life. Another time his cheekiness brought a
reward was when he joined a pilgrimage to a shrine at a little
village: once there, he introduced himself to the local
choirmaster, and asked to be allowed to sing in the choir. The
choirmaster took one look at the shabbily dressed young man,
and told him to get lost. So Haydn waited until there was a
church service, hid behind the males in the choir and, just
as a solo was coming up, snatched the music out of some
unfortunate singer's hand and sang the solo himself. Hmm . . .
he sang it so beautifully, though, and everybody was so impressed,
that he was invited to stay for a week. He accepted with pleasure,
and seems to have spent the whole time (when he wasn't
singing) eating to his heart's – and stomach's – content.*

· 4 ·

Gradually, Haydn was becoming busy – if still poor. He had
lots of musical odd jobs in Vienna, at churches and in private
homes. At daybreak he'd play first violin at a church service,
then he'd go to another church to play the organ, then on to

another to sing tenor. The afternoons were presumably given over to teaching his various students; and then there were the all-night composing sessions – he must have been tired! At least he managed to escape from his attic to a new lodging. Mini-disaster struck when his new room was burgled, and all his possessions stolen, but kind friends helped him out. Haydn could always make friends.

From our point of view (and probably his too), one of the most important events in Haydn's life around this time was an invitation to the country home of a rich man who loved chamber music. The other musicians there were the manager of the estate and a priest, who both played the violin, and a cellist. Haydn could play the viola, so he wrote quartets for the four of them to play together for the rich man's pleasure. In this way, he (almost) invented the string quartet, a piece of music written for two violins, a viola and a cello – from his time onwards, the most popular combination in chamber music. Haydn duly became known as the "Father of the String Quartet", creating eighty-three of the little blighters. (Actually, they're amazingly wonderful . . . and not all that little . . . and definitely not blighters.)

Then, around 1758, came his first proper job, for Count Morzin, for whose small orchestra Haydn wrote his Symphony No. 1 – the first of 104! Haydn was also to be known as the "Father of the Symphony". Obviously the fatherly type – well, he *was* Papa Haydn . . .

Mad about dogs . . .

Haydn and Maria Anna Aloysia Apollonia Keller (to give her her full title) got married – shackled – on November 26th, 1760; it can't have been a day Haydn celebrated in later years with great enthusiasm. But, despite all the negatives, there must *have been some positive aspects. And even if he was miserable with Maria Anna, he certainly didn't take it out on her family;*

in fact, for one of the family members, he was a real godsend. A brother of Maria Anna's owned lots of dogs – as many as ten. For this reason, everybody around him decided that he must be mad, and sent him off to a mental asylum. Haydn petitioned the Ministry of Justice to get him out, and succeeded – but only for a year. The second time the poor man was sent to the asylum, Haydn went himself and got him out, lending him lots of money for good measure. I wonder how grateful Mrs Haydn was for this kindness to her brother? Probably not as grateful as the dogs.

Haydn seems to have been particularly fond of dogs, actually. Many years later, he composed a canon in praise of an English bow-wow called Turk, who had died and been buried in his master's garden. The text was taken from the headstone of the dog's grave: "Turk was a faithful dog and not a man" – rather an odd epitaph, really, but Haydn set it anyway. He wrote another piece of canine music, as well: one day, he received a strange letter from a young lady whom he'd never met. She told Haydn that she was in love with an officer, and enclosed a poem telling a story about her beloved and his dog. The officer owned a poodle, and had trained it to find coins and to bring them to him. The officer bet a friend that he could bury a coin under a bush, and that the poodle would find it and bring it back. All would have gone smoothly, except that a passing traveller, a tailor, found the coin first and put it into his trouser pocket. A problem – but the clever poodle smelt the coin and attached himself to the tailor, following him to the inn where he was staying. The poodle stayed all night; but in the morning, when the door was open for a moment, he grabbed the trousers and ran back to his master with the trousers hanging out of his mouth. The poem described this moving tale (about the moving tail) in a rather flowery fashion; the young lady told Haydn that, if he were to set the poem to music, she could sing it to her officer, and that then she was sure he'd marry her. Of course

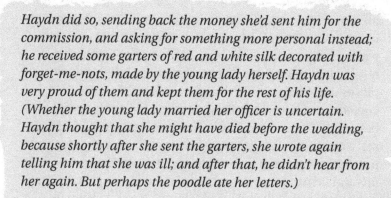

Haydn did so, sending back the money she'd sent him for the commission, and asking for something more personal instead; he received some garters of red and white silk decorated with forget-me-nots, made by the young lady herself. Haydn was very proud of them and kept them for the rest of his life. (Whether the young lady married her officer is uncertain. Haydn thought that she might have died before the wedding, because shortly after she sent the garters, she wrote again telling him that she was ill; and after that, he didn't hear from her again. But perhaps the poodle ate her letters.)

·5·

Haydn's first contract with the Esterházys, dated May 1st, 1761, makes interesting reading. He was actually second-in-command for the first five years, to an old composer called Werner, who was considered too infirm to do all the work himself, but resented having the young upstart ("Heyden", as he called him) thrust upon him – especially since "Heyden" was soon being paid considerably more than Werner. (The good-natured Haydn bore no grudge for Werner's grouchiness, though; many years later, long after Werner's death in 1766, Haydn arranged for some of his works to be published in Vienna.) The Esterházy contract lists the many duties that Haydn (calling him "Hayden" this time – odd that even an official document would get it wrong) was expected to perform: one important one was to make sure that all the musicians turned up for all their services in "white stockings, white linen, powdered, and either pigtails or hair bag, all, however, of identical appearance". (This was before Nicolaus the Magnificent, who was fond of bright colours – he himself had a famous coat studded with valuable diamonds – started introducing new and glamorous costumes for the musicians. The orchestra's first set was blue and silver, while Haydn's, made out of swanky Dutch material, was blue and gold. I bet he preened a bit.) Haydn was also told not to eat and drink with the other musicians, because then they wouldn't respect him enough; to be prepared to compose whatever pieces the Prince required, and not to let the music be copied, in case anyone else were to get hold of it; to appear before his Prince every day both before and after midday, to ask whether the Prince wanted a concert or an opera to be put on that evening; to look after all the music and the musical instruments; to instruct the female singers (he may not have minded that clause too much!); and to keep in practice himself on the various instruments that he played. And at the end of all that, it was noted that whereas, should he want to leave, Haydn would have to give the Prince six months' notice, the Prince could dismiss Haydn without any warning "should he see fit to do so". No wonder Haydn felt like a slave!

His position gradually improved over the years, however. Nicolaus the Magnificent was a strict but appreciative employer who really cared about music. He was even a prac-tising musician himself, working seriously at the baryton, a funny-looking string instrument that is almost forgotten today, despite the many works that Haydn composed for it. These were mostly fairly straightforward pieces, written to show off his employer's rather limited skills. Nicolaus was none too pleased when Haydn, having secretly learnt the instrument himself, surprised his patron with a performance on it one night. "It is no credit to you to play better than I do," snorted the jealous Prince. "It is your duty." Touchy people, these Magnificent types . . .

Still, Haydn and Nicolaus I had a good relationship on the whole – and it's great for us that the Prince was so demanding, and ordered Haydn to write so much music! Haydn's fame was gradually spreading, and the Prince realised that it was actually good for his own reputation if his Director of Music became a celebrity. He soon allowed Haydn to have his works copied (often by a team of different copyists working on the same piece, so that one copyist couldn't sell pirate copies to unscrupulous publishers or to rival princes) and printed. He even allowed Haydn to accept commissions from other music-lovers, such as the priest in Spain who commissioned a series of movements to be called 'The Seven Last Words of our Saviour on the Cross'. These movements, depicting in music the seven last exclamations of Jesus as reported in the Bible, were to be played – interspersed with sermons on the mean-ing of the words – in a darkened cathedral draped in black; all very dramatic – and very long. The door had to be kept locked to keep the congregation in! Legend has it that as payment, Haydn received . . . a chocolate cake. He was furious, until he cut into it (perhaps fury had made him hungry), and found that it was full of gold pieces – that was more like it.

In 1779, Haydn signed a new contract with Nicolaus; this agreement, while still rather unnecessarily requiring that Haydn "conduct himself in a manner which is edifying, Christian and God-fearing", and demanding that Haydn perform whatever music the Prince chose, whenever and wherever he was commanded to do so, was much more reasonable than the first one. Haydn would be allowed to cancel the arrangement should he wish to (unlikely though this was – he'd recently told someone that he wished "to live and die" in the Prince's service). In addition to his salary he was to receive such extras as wine, beef, cabbage and beets, lard (yuk), candles, fodder for his two horses, twelve cords of firewood, and a whole pig (presumably a pig that had already gone to the great sty in the sky, not a pet. Haydn might have pointed out that he didn't need a live pig anyway – he had his wife. But maybe he wouldn't have been so mean – I wonder . . .)

How to party, eighteenth-century style ...

Eszterháza Castle must have been incredible. Talk about luxury: grand rooms full of astonishing furnishings (such as an arm-chair that played a flute solo when you sat on it – a bit alarming perhaps, but better than a whoopee cushion); an opera theatre that could easily seat an audience of four hundred; a marionette (puppet) theatre; a huge park with impressive statues, temples and fountains; two vast state rooms, decorated in stunning white, for concerts, large-scale parties and balls; and so on. In 1773, Haydn's old friend the Empress of Austria came for a simple little three-day visit, along with her friends, followers and servants. As soon as they arrived, the Empress and her gang were driven in fifteen magnificent carriages around the grounds, no doubt ooh-ing and aah-ing at the splendour of it all. Then a Haydn opera was performed, and the Empress was deeply impressed: "If I want to enjoy a good opera, I go to Eszterháza," she announced – no thrashing for Haydn this time! Next came a masked ball in the dazzlingly lit Chinese Pavilion, accompanied by musicians dressed in their smart costumes (deep-red and gold, at that point – Nicolaus kept ordering new designs); and then the Empress was taken to a concert of Haydn's orchestral works conducted by the composer. That was the first day – at least, that was it for the Empress; most of her crowd stayed up dancing until dawn. The next day started with a great banquet, with accompanying music from the orchestra. (It was probably at this meal that Haydn, a keen hunter and fisherman in the little spare time he had, presented three grouse to the Empress; he claimed to have bagged them with one shot! Sounds a touch unlikely; anyway, the Empress graciously consented to stuff her royal face with them.) In the afternoon the great lady attended an opera that Haydn had written for the Esterházy marionettes (I hope they appreciated it!); then it was time for supper, after which there was a breathtaking fire-

work display. Finally, Prince Esterházy led the Empress to a huge, brilliantly lit open space where, as if from nowhere, a thousand colourfully dressed Croatian and Hungarian dancers and musicians suddenly appeared and performed their national dances. The next morning, the Empress distributed expensive presents, including a gold snuffbox filled with money for Haydn. And then, off she went with her retinue – now that's what I call a party!

· 6 ·

There are a lot of official letters from Haydn written during these years spent in Eisenstadt and Eszterháza, many of them addressed to the Prince himself. These aren't the most intimate of documents, though: it's never exactly "Dear Nicolaus – hope you're well. How's the wife?" None of that; they all had to start: "Most Serene and Noble Prince of the Holy Roman Empire, Gracious and dread Lord!" – just a *touch* less chummy. There are also many letters to publishers, often involving understandable tantrums when Haydn's music had been printed with annoying mistakes (one copyist, he ranted, "ought to have his paw chopped off" for all his misprints). Although some of these are fun to read, again they don't tell us much about Haydn's personal life. We get to know him much better from his letters to Maria von Gennsinger/Gennzinger/ Gennziger/Genzinger, written from 1787 onwards. Haydn really opened his heart to Maria about his life at the court and its difficulties. Whenever he was away from Vienna, he clearly suffered from loneliness; he told Maria that he was "often deeply hurt" – presumably a reference either to those on the estate who treated him badly, or to his unfortunate marriage.

On the positive side, however, Haydn at least managed to

surround himself with friends and family (despite complaining to Maria that he had no true friends – he was probably exaggerating to win her sympathy). For instance, he brought the good Spangler's daughter – the former Baby Spangler Mark 2, for whom he'd had to make way in the Spangler household so many years earlier – and her husband, a good friend of his, to join the Esterházy singers; and he also engaged his younger brother Johann, and looked after him for the next twenty-five years. (Michael Haydn was by this point quite a famous composer, living in Salzburg – where he was friendly with the Mozart family – so he didn't need Joseph's help.)

Anyone to whom Haydn was even distantly related could count on as much financial support as he could possibly afford to give; many of his relatives came to live near him, in order to enjoy his protection. Only very occasionally did he rebel, as in the case of a good-for-nothing who had married a rather-less-than-favourite niece of Haydn's; the good-for-nothing constantly got into debt, and then expected his uncle-in-law to pay. Eventually Haydn put his elegantly clad foot down. Fair enough. He also had lots of godchildren, because the musicians at the Esterházy court would ask Papa Haydn to be godpapa to their offspring. There's a charming letter from Haydn to one of these lucky youngsters, who had become a successful composer: "Dearest Godson! When I took you in my arms after your birth, and had the pleasure of becoming your Godfather, I implored Omnipotent Providence to endow you with the highest degree of musical talent. My request has been heard." The godson in question must have been thrilled by that; what a wonderful godfather to have! Then there were all the people with whom Haydn worked on a daily basis; and Luigia Polzelli, of course. Surely he could never have been *that* lonely – he was loved by too many people.

A friendship between geniuses . . .

Of course, one extremely special friend was Mozart. Mozart was almost twenty-five years Haydn's junior, but that didn't prevent the two men from becoming close. They probably met for the first time in 1784, and from that point onwards were very important to each other. In 1785, Mozart wrote a set of six string quartets and dedicated them to his "dearest friend" Haydn, hoping that Papa H. would "be indulgent to their mistakes". (As if Mozart ever made any mistakes in music!) Haydn went to a musical party in Vienna to hear the quartets; at the end, he exclaimed to Mozart's father: "I tell you before God, as an honest man, that your son is the greatest composer known to me either in person or by reputation." Quite a compliment! There was no jealousy in Haydn – just the opposite; when he was asked to compose an opera for a theatre in Prague, Haydn generously replied that it would be a better idea to ask "the unparalleled Mozart" instead. Mozart and Haydn used to play string quartets together, with two other well-known composers. I wish they'd had tape-recorders in those days! (Incidentally, both Mozart and Haydn begged to be allowed to play the viola part, so they'd be right in the middle; it's surprising how many great composers have played the viola.)

When Haydn was planning his first trip to London, the only person who seems to have been gloomy about his prospects was Mozart; Mozart thought that Haydn was too old to undertake such a journey, and would feel isolated, since he spoke no English. As they parted the day before Haydn set off, Mozart had tears in his eyes. "We shall meet no more in this world, Papa," he said sadly. Haydn was worried; it was true that he was old – and travelling was dangerous in those times. Perhaps Mozart was right, and he would never come back. It probably never occurred to him that Mozart himself might be dead before

Haydn returned to Vienna; but that's what happened, Mozart dying tragically at the age of thirty-five. Haydn was devastated when he heard the news; for the rest of his life he would weep whenever Mozart's name was mentioned. He was always wonderfully kind to Mozart's widow and children, too, helping them in any way he could.

·7·

Haydn arrived for the first time in "Dower" (as he called Dover) on New Year's Day 1791, very proud that he had survived the channel crossing "without vomiting" (lovely). The next day, he arrived in "the endlessly huge city of London"; and a few days later he made his first public appearance, attending a concert where he was led up the centre of the hall to the front of the orchestra and given an amazing ovation. After the concert, he was invited to sit at the head of the table at a dinner for two hundred people. Overwhelmed, he refused – but he couldn't get away without joining the company in drinking a toast. This set the pattern for both his visits to London: he was a megastar – and people drank a lot. It's fun reading the journals he kept, sketchy though they are; the few entries in English are especially characterful. In those days, English money used to be more complicated than it is now: a pound consisted of twenty shillings, while many prices were in guineas, a guinea being one pound plus one shilling. So the first English entry in the journals tells us that "6 schirts" cost "8 guinees'; and a "watch from gold" thirty guineas, with the "chen" – presumably the chain – costing an extra guinea. His English evidently got much better – pretty impressive for a man in his sixties – but he still insisted on his own spelling of names. Bristol was always Pristol, Bedford Pedfort, and so on. Money is a source of endless fascination for him: we are told, for instance, that in January 1792 a roasting chicken cost seven shillings, a turkey nine shillings, a dozen larks one crown (i.e. five shillings); and "NB: a duck, if it is plucked, costs 5 shillings". Good to know. He also records, rather indignantly, that "I had to pay $1^1/_2$ guineas for having the bells rung at Oxforth" (he means Oxford) "in connection with my doctor's degree, and $^1/_2$ a guinea for the robe. The trip cost 6 guineas." He also complained about having to walk around "Oxforth" for three days wearing the robes. (Grumbling aside, he later told his biographer that he owed his introduction to English high society, which helped him a lot, to his Oxford doctorate.) The journal also contains nuggets of deeply useful practical advice: on how to keep milk fresh for many months, for example. (No fridges in those days, of course – though even with a fridge, the thought of many-months-old milk is rather more appalling than appealing . . .)

There are also lots of stories – some just short anecdotes that he'd heard, such as one that is rather frustratingly cut off: "The little story of an errand boy who ate cow dung". (I wonder what the rest of the story was? Perhaps it's just as well it's missing.) Most, though, are about Haydn's own experiences. There's his dinner at a Mr Shaw's, where he notices that Mrs Shaw ("the most beautiful woman I ever saw") and all the other ladies present were wearing headbands with the name "Haydn" embroidered in gold, Mr Shaw also sporting the name sewn onto his collar in shiny steel beads. Haydn had a good time that night! Then, in a more dramatic vein, he claims almost to have been eaten by a tiger at the Tower of London. Mind you, Haydn was somewhat prone to exaggeration. There's another entry about a visit to the house of a rich banker, Mr Brassey (or, according to Haydn, "Brassy"). Haydn writes: "NB: Mr Brassy once cursed because he had too easy a time in this world." By the time Haydn got around to telling his biographer this story, several years later, he had changed the story a bit: now Haydn remembered that, while he had been telling his host about his own deprived childhood, Mr Brassey suddenly jumped up, swore frightfully and shouted: "Bring the pistols! I'm going to shoot myself." Haydn (who'd initially thought that the banker was going to shoot *him*) and the other members of the household tried to calm Mr Brassey down; they begged him to tell them what was wrong. It turned out that the problem was that Mr Brassey had never known any misfortune; he'd been happy and prosperous his whole life, and was sick of it – so he'd decided to kill himself! A very strange tale – and funny that Haydn didn't mention all those elaborate details at the time . . .

There is also a lot of talk about musical events, of course – including the sad story of a clergyman who, upon listening to the slow movement of one of Haydn's symphonies at a concert, went home immediately, convinced that he had heard the music the night before in a dream, and that it was a premonition of his death; within a month, the poor man was dead. On a more cheerful note, there are comments about Haydn's own concerts, and about other people's performances. A famous violinist, we learn, "played like a pig"; but of four thousand poor children singing, he says that "no music ever moved me so deeply in my whole life".

We have also lots of written reports from other people of Haydn's visits to England, and of his concerts there. One of the major British newspapers reported of the "extacy of admiration" with which his works were received; and the London correspondent of a German journal reported that Haydn "is indeed a grateful, candid, honest man, esteemed and loved by all". Of course. There were several poems written in praise of Haydn as well, one of which he set to music; it does seem an odd thing for such a modest man to do – but maybe it was expected of him, and he didn't want to be rude. Or perhaps he wasn't *that* modest!

Talking of composers who set their own praises to music –

Haydn felt that, although he learned a lot from many experiences he had in London, he learned most from his encounters with the music of Handel. Hearing 'Messiah' performed by about a thousand performers in Westminster Abbey, he burst into tears as the 'Hallelujah Chorus' rang out. "He is the master of us all!" Haydn exclaimed. I wonder if, from a nearby grave, a ghostly wig appeared for a moment and waggled . . .

A troublesome pupil . . .

Since the trips to and from London took around two weeks, Haydn had to break the journeys occasionally along the way (with stops of a few days – not just loo-stops!). He often found that in the German cities where he alighted he was more famous than he'd thought. In Bonn, for instance, during his first trip to London, he went to church and heard his own music being played at Mass; he was pleased, but thought it must be a coincidence. Towards the end of the service, however, someone approached him and invited him into a small private chapel – where to his astonishment he saw the local Mr Important, the Elector Maximilian, ready to greet him. The Elector took Haydn by the hand, and presented him to the musicians who'd been playing with the words: "Thus I make you acquainted with your much-cherished Haydn." A nice ego-boost.

Among the musicians there was a twenty-year-old violist (a violist again!) called Ludwig van Beethoven – the Beethoven, in fact, later to become perhaps the most famous composer of all time. On his way back from London, Haydn stopped in Bonn again; this time, he saw a composition by the young man, and was (not surprisingly) very impressed. It was arranged that Beethoven would travel to Vienna to study with Haydn, with the expenses being paid by the Elector. Alas, the lessons weren't a great success. Beethoven wanted to be trained strictly; Haydn was an inspirational figure, but not a professor who would instruct his pupils in detail. Although

Beethoven continued to go to Haydn for some lessons (and noted in his diary that he'd treated the master to hot chocolate and coffee, which sounds as though they were at least on friendly terms), he was so frustrated by Haydn's relaxed approach that he started going to another teacher at the same time. Fair enough, perhaps; but Beethoven also did something really naughty that put Haydn in an embarrassing position. Despite the fact that Haydn, being the generous man that he was, charged almost nothing, Beethoven complained that Vienna was expensive, and that he couldn't manage on the allowance that the Elector was giving him. So Haydn wrote a begging letter on his behalf, telling the Elector that he had been obliged to lend Beethoven money himself: he asked Maximilian to double the young composer's allowance, and sent along five of Beethoven's compositions as proof of how hard the young man had been working. In reply, the Elector sent a horrible *letter, pointing out that he was in actual fact already giving Beethoven almost twice the sum that Haydn had been led to believe; and that, of the five compositions, at least four had been written and performed in Bonn long before Beethoven had left for Vienna. Furthermore, the Elector wrote, he doubted "whether he [Beethoven] will have made any important progress in composition and taste" in Vienna – not exactly a compliment to Haydn's teaching!*

Poor Haydn, caught between the naughty young man and his haughty employer; it looked as if he had plotted with Beethoven to cheat the Elector. We don't know how Haydn reacted to this whole business – but he can't have been pleased. Still, he and Beethoven remained outwardly on good terms (probably due to Haydn's forgiving nature), occasionally performing in the same concerts in later years. Beethoven dedicated the first works to which he gave an opus number (always a significant event for a young composer), his three piano trios Opus 1, to Haydn.

·8·

It was only during his last years in Vienna, after returning from his second trip to London in 1795, that Haydn finally became a real celebrity in his home city. Once again working for an Esterházy Prince, Nicolaus II, he could have settled back into a certain amount of obscurity – but the success of 'The Creation' changed all that. He was now a public figure, celebrated and cherished – and filled with a new confidence; the works of his last years, including six wonderful masses he wrote for the church-music-obsessed Nicolaus, are possibly the very greatest he ever wrote. At the Esterházy court, he was no longer the servant; he was even invited to dine at table with the Prince and his guests for special feasts – a far cry from the early days!

But of course he was now *really* old for those days – if he'd wanted to be an average sort of man, he'd have made sure to have died several years earlier – and his strength was gradually ebbing away. So eventually, Haydn retired to his little cottage. He conducted public performances of his works in aid of charities (raising a huge sum) until the end of 1803, and still composed and taught a little in 1804. After that, though, he worked on two rather different projects: his will, first drafted in 1801, but subject to constant revisions, especially since old friends and relatives kept dying; and – with the help of Johann Elssler, his devoted copyist, secretary and companion – a catalogue of the works which "he could approximately recall having composed from his 18th to 73rd year". This catalogue, although not complete, has been a great help to Haydn scholars over the years. Apart from that, there wasn't much left for him, except to check the household accounts (which he did very carefully, even though he really loved and trusted his servants), to receive visitors, to talk to two men who were writing books about him, to pray – and to read, and be touched by, proofs of devotion from musicians all over

Europe. To a society in Paris who had sent him a gold medal and an enthusiastic letter, he wrote that the package had "strewn flowers on the path of life that yet remains for me to traverse". Just a few months earlier, Haydn had written to the Esterházy musicians, thanking them for a tribute which had moved him to tears; he was, he said, "attached to them with a truly fatherly love".

Nicolaus II turned up trumps in these final years; he was no doubt influenced in this by his wife Princess Maria (funny how many women in Haydn's life were called Maria). She adored Haydn, and occasionally turned up at the cottage to visit her old friend, giving him much pleasure; he described her as his "good angel". (Haydn still worried about money constantly; he could never feel secure about it. (I wonder whether he ever cast his mind back to a miserable ceremony at which he'd almost certainly have sung as a choirboy: the funeral of the famous composer Vivaldi, who'd died in terrible poverty in Vienna. That must have shocked Haydn, showing him how neglected musicians could be, no matter how famous they had once been.) The last surviving letter in Haydn's own – by now very shaky – hand, dating from late in 1806, thanks Nicolaus for the extra pension that he'd unexpectedly granted to his old employee. The very last – dictated – letter we have is another thank-you letter to Nicolaus from late 1808, this time thanking the Prince for granting Haydn's request to have his medical bills paid for him. "Your serene Highness has freed me from a pressing anxiety, and thus enabled me to await the end of my earthly existence in peace and serenity."

So people cared about Papa Haydn until the very end. There was a golden sunset side to his final years, despite the sadnesses: he had the comfort of knowing that he was much loved, and would be remembered through his music. He was also happy to have eased the lot of so many suffering people through the money his music had raised for charity; and happy in the thought that the bequests in his will might transform the lives of so many of his friends, servants and relatives. Haydn died a rich man, especially since extra money rolled into the estate after his death from the sale of his possessions (one of the most valuable being a parrot that he'd brought from England, and trained to speak!) Both Michael and Johann having died before him, none of his surviving family were musicians; his money went mostly to relatives who had poorly paid jobs – a blacksmith, a shoemaker, a lacemaker, and so on. They must have been truly grateful. There were also (surprise, surprise) lots of little legacies to ladies not related to Haydn, about whom we know nothing (perhaps just as well!); and there was even a bequest – cancelled in a late amendment – to his first great love, his wife's sister. Good thing his wife wasn't around to see that!

A farewell appearance . . .

Haydn was really stuck in the house for those last years, hardly ever venturing out; but there was a glorious exception. On a mild day in March 1808, just before his seventy-sixth birthday, he was allowed by his doctor to attend a celebratory perform-ance of 'The Creation', given in his honour at the university in Vienna. Haydn was carried out of his house to Nicolaus's carriage, generously laid on by his patron; he was then driven slowly to the university, where a huge crowd had gathered to get a glimpse of the living legend. Carried on an armchair into the hall, where a distinguished gathering of aristocrats and musicians (including Beethoven) awaited him, he was greeted with a flourish of trumpets and drums, along with cries of "Long live Haydn!" He was seated among the poshest people in the hall, next to his beloved Princess Maria Esterházy. (Later, she would present him with a valuable box, with the scene at the concert painted on it.) At one point the Princess noticed

him shivering, and wrapped her
shawl around him; not to be
outdone, many of the other
aristocratic ladies sitting
nearby wrapped their
colourful shawls around
him too – Haydn must have
looked like a Christmas
ornament! All sorts of high
and mighty people came to
bow and scrape before
the frail old man; poems
written in his honour
were handed to him. Then the
amazing music started. At one of the
most famous moments – where Haydn sets the words "Let there
be light" with a touch of spine-tingling musical genius, seeming
to travel from darkness to light with just one vast chord – there
was thunderous applause. Haydn lifted his hands to heaven, as
if to say, "It is from there, not from me."

It was a magical, historic occasion. So overcome was the old
man by the whole event, though, that it was thought best to
take him home in the interval. As he was carried out, people
thronging around his chair, the great composer lifted his hand
in fervent blessing – and then Papa Haydn was gone, never to
be seen in public again.

·9·

The end came in May 1809. It was a difficult time for Vienna:
the Napoleonic wars had been raging for several years, and
at the beginning of May Napoleon's army was approaching
Vienna. On May 12th, they started to bombard the city; a
huge cannon-shot landed near Haydn's cottage, shaking the

whole house as if in an earthquake. Three more shots followed in quick succession. Haydn was terrified, but still he thought of others. "Children, don't be afraid!" he called out to his servants. "Where Haydn is, nothing can happen to you." During the day, he got up and resumed his daily schedule; but he was shaken. At least the French army, once they'd occupied the city, treated him well. Napoleon ordered a special guard of honour to be posted in front of the composer's cottage; and then Haydn was surprised to receive a visit from a French officer, who sang an aria from 'The Creation' so beautifully that Haydn cried. But the shock of it all had weakened the old man. One of the few things he was still able to do in music was to play his own hymn, 'God Save the Emperor Franz', on the piano. One day, summoning all his remaining strength, he called his household to the piano and played the beautiful hymn three times over, with "an expressiveness that surprised even himself", according to the devoted Elssler. On the next day, he took to his bed, and lay there peacefully. "Children be comforted; I am well," he whispered. On May 31st he slipped away, "blissfully and gently".

Ceremonies and grave robbers …

So Papa Haydn was no more. Elssler took his death mask, showing his sunken but still recognisable features. (A bit macabre – but interesting.) The funeral wasn't much of an event, because of the war; it seems to have been attended mostly by French army officials, the Viennese feeling too scared to come out of their houses. At least there was music – the Requiem Mass (Mass for the Dead) by Haydn's brother Michael. The official memorial service on June 15th was a far grander occasion; it was here that the cultural elite of Vienna, alongside several high-ranking French generals, took their leave of Haydn. This time the music was the Requiem Mass by Haydn's beloved friend Mozart – his last work.

And that should have been the end of the story. It wasn't, though – not quite. Haydn was initially buried in the Hundsturm (Dogstorm!) Cemetery in Vienna; but Prince Nicolaus thought it would be more fitting to have his tomb at the Esterházy Estate in Eisenstadt. So the Prince applied for permission to have the body brought there, received official sanction – and then forgot all about it for over ten years. He was reminded in 1820 by a visitor, who congratulated him for having employed the living Haydn, and now housing his remains. The Prince didn't disillusion his guest; but as soon as he'd got rid of him, he gave orders for Haydn's body to be brought to Eisenstadt. And it was – or rather, part of it was: the skull had gone missing! The wig was there – but no head for it to cover. Headless Haydn.

What had happened was that two amateur scientists, anxious to do research on the skull and thus discover what makes a genius, had bribed the gravedigger to let them remove it after the funeral, ostensibly "to protect it from desecration". They had a black wooden box made, with glass windows; the skull was placed inside, on a white silk cushion trimmed with black – grisly! Prince Nicolaus was furious; he sought out the thieves, and set the police onto them. The robbers dutifully handed over a skull – but in fact, it wasn't Haydn's. Prince Esterházy probably didn't know and therefore didn't mind; but I wonder what Haydn's ghost might have felt about it? The thieves left the real skull to a museum in Vienna, where it was displayed after 1895. Not until 1954, 145 years after Haydn's death, were the skull and torso reunited, in Eisenstadt – I bet they were pleased to see each other! Now Papa Haydn is whole again.

The Music

Haydn's music is just what you'd expect from him, really: it's totally unexpected! He was one of the most original composers who has ever lived; it's almost as if he couldn't stop experimenting – and his experiments were *always* successful. Amazing things are always popping up in his works. For instance, in one symphony (No. 60), the violins have to tune their strings down a whole tone; there's a shocking moment in the last movement when they seem to have forgotten to tune them up again – the whole piece grinds to a halt, to give them time to put this right. It's apparently meant to represent a bridegroom who gets a nasty fright when he remembers he's supposed to be getting married that day! In another symphony (No. 67), Haydn surprises us by having the violins play with the wood of their bows instead of the hair (which makes a sound like a skeleton dancing); and in another (No. 97), he makes them play right on the bridge of the violin (which makes a sound like fingernails scratching a blackboard). Then there are the antics in the 'Farewell' and the 'Surprise' Symphonies (Nos. 45 and 94) – and many more.

It's not just in his symphonies that astonishing things happen, though. There's the 'Joke' string quartet (Op. 33, No. 2), for example, which keeps ending, stopping, and then ending again; it's really funny – especially since audiences almost always clap in the wrong place. Then there are other, completely different sorts of surprises – far more subtle ones; for instance, there's a particularly wonderful string quartet (Op. 54, No. 2), where in the slow movement the first violin unexpectedly sings a gypsy-like lament – haunting and unique.

For some of his contemporaries, Haydn's originality was *too* shocking by far. A lot of his religious music, particularly, was too cheerful and dance-like for them; religion was supposed to be a gloomy business! Haydn had an answer for these people: during composing, he said, he had thought of God's mercy. "These thoughts cheered me up. I experienced a sure joy so confident that … I could not suppress my joy, but gave vents to my happy spirits." Good answer – I hope that shut them up! His religious music is glorious: it's so human and spirited, as well as being serene and profound.

All in all, Haydn was one of the most fascinating and lovable composers of all time. Whether he was writing hilarious, crazy music or dark, tragic works (there are many of those, too), his own character shone through – and his character was irresistible!

What to listen to

Well, certainly listen to the works I mentioned above; they're all wonderful. But actually, *most* of the symphonies are gems. If you have to choose just a few, try the ones with nice nicknames, such as the 'Bear' (No. 82), the 'Hen' (No. 83), or the 'Clock' (No. 101). And if you want to hear Haydn in a darker mood, try the 'Trauer' (Grief) Symphony, No. 44 – it's really powerful.

For the string quartets, maybe begin with the two I mentioned above, the 'Joke' (Op. 33, No. 2) and the extraordinary quartet Op. 54, No. 2; but you really can't go wrong with any of the quartets with an opus number of 33 or higher. And if you listen to the slow movement of the 'Kaiser' or 'Emperor' quartet, Op. 76, No. 3, you can hear the Austrian national anthem, with Haydn's variations on his own theme. The later piano trios are very fine, too; the early ones aren't quite as interesting, but listen to No. 25 in G (the 'Gypsy Rondo') or No. 27 in C – great pieces.

There are some beautiful masses – the 'Mass in the Time of War' or the 'Harmonie' Mass, for example. Perhaps the most important works of all, though, are the two huge oratorios, 'The Creation' and 'The Seasons'. Take a deep breath, sit down with the words in front of you, and prepare to be taken on an amazing journey – from the first notes of the Creation, representing chaos, to Adam and Eve's blissful emergence at the end; and from the icy winter music that opens 'The Seasons', to the final, warmly triumphant "Amen".

Franz Peter Schubert

1797–1828

rankly, I'm a bit worried. Of course, I worry about all sorts of things all the time, like most people – but the worry that's worrying me just at the moment is this: if I manage to make it to heaven in the next life, won't conversation be a bit awkward? It's not the humans (or ex-humans) I'm worried about – it's the dinosaurs. Humans have ruled the earth (well, sort-of – our hamster would no doubt disagree with that statement, but since he probably won't read this book, I'll leave it in) for around a million and a half years; whereas dinosaurs were here for about 160 million years (give or take a month or two) before that. So isn't it fair to assume that a lot of them must be up there now? And if so, what do I say if I meet one of them? "Excuse me – do you speak humanoid?" "Terribly sorry about all you chaps being wiped out by that meteorite – must have been frightfully annoying." Or what?

Oh well. Perhaps we'll all just stand around in a trance listening to the heavenly music going on. And if we do, I'm pretty sure I know whose music it will be. I bet it'll be by Franz Schubert ("Shoobert"); that's because, of all composers, he's the one who most often opens a door and shows you – paradise. Of course, all great composers wrote music that could be described as "heavenly"; but the others have to take you there. In Schubert's music you hear the very first notes, and you know that you're there already.

Not all of his music is like that, though – not at all. In some pieces, he can take you just as immediately to something more like hell; his music can be really terrifying, in fact. It's strange – because if you'd seen him, you'd never have thought that such an odd-looking little fellow could have produced music of such colossal power. Small and plump – his nickname was "Schwammerl", which means either "tubby", "mushroom" or "sponge" (busy word!) – with brown curly hair, a large head, a thick neck and small hands and feet, he would often spend whole evenings sitting in a corner without uttering a word. Very short-sighted (he wore glasses all the time, even in his sleep!) with a tendency to screw his eyes up tightly, his teeth tobacco-stained, and often with a faceful of pimples, Schubert would have been a non-starter in any male beauty contest. One acquaintance (hardly a friend) of his summed him up neatly: "a lump of dough". Charming – but it's true that Schubert's appearance wasn't promising. He didn't usually smell great, either; he stank of tobacco, and frequently also of wine, of which he tended to drink a bit too much, a bit too often.

On the other hand, this tubby lump of dough/sponge/mushroom was very popular among those who knew him; and he could be very friendly, if he wasn't feeling too shy. He had a small circle of very close friends (all men – he tended to be awkward with women) who meant the world to him. In fact, since he hardly ever had enough money to afford a place of his own, he spent much of the time living at their houses or apartments; they were fond enough of the genial, rather chaotic composer even to put up with his unusual lifestyle. Schubert's ideal day would consist of getting out of bed late, wherever he happened to be staying; starting to compose immediately (well, I hope that he went to the loo and cleaned his teeth first – but that's not recorded); continuing to compose for at least five hours without a break – clicking his tongue and drumming his fingers, and often smoking a pipe, while he did so; then having some lunch at an inn; going for a walk with friends, or resting; going to a concert or an opera, if he or one of his circle could afford tickets; and then eating dinner with a large group at a restaurant, before finishing the evening at a coffee-house, talking and drinking until all hours.

His circle had a lot to talk about: endless gossip (as there always is, always has been and always will be among groups of friends), lots of serious and idealistic talk about the arts and their purpose in life – and a lot of laughter as well. They used to play games – such as one in which they constructed drawings out of a few dots, or poems out of random words; or sometimes a game now called "charades", in which some of the friends would act out a silent scene and the others would try to guess what on earth was going on. One night, coming back from a late-night drinking session, Schubert and his companions came across a building site, with the beginnings of a new house starting to take shape; the group stood in a line and sang a hymn, praying for the house to grow up sturdy and strong. Well, perhaps it seemed hilarious after a few bottles of potent wine . . .

So who were these unusual friends of Schubert's, you may ask (if you feel like it, that is – don't worry if you don't: I'll tell you anyway). Well, they were all young men of around his own age – all with artistic ambitions and few with any money. Actually, the one of whom Schubert was probably most fond, Franz von Schober, was from a rich family, with whom Schubert lived for several months at a time. But Schober's main talents seem to have been for talking brilliantly, and for losing all his money; so most of the time he tended to be as poor as the rest of the group. Most people saw Schober as an untrustworthy character – charming, but lazy and selfish. It's hard to tell now what he was like; but it's true that he never really did anything much with his life, except for managing to annoy almost everyone who knew him well. And besides, he had a thoroughly suspicious moustache – *far* too carefully groomed for its owner's good. On the other hand, Schubert adored him, and was probably closer to him than to anyone else; the pair liked to combine their names: "Schobert".

Other close friends of Schubert's included a really nice guy called Josef von Spaun (pronounced "Shpawn') – a funny name, but he does seem to have been a lovely person; Schubert went to school with him, and they remained friends for the rest of Schubert's life. Another was Johann Baptist Mayrhofer – an even stranger name, and a strange character, too. He was a poet, with whom Schubert lived for a time. But Mayrhofer was moody and miserable, and managed to quarrel with even the easy-going Schubert; many years later, long after Schubert's death, poor Mayrhofer got so depressed that he killed himself by jumping out of a window. Not exactly a happy ending.

And so on – Schubert's friends were an interesting bunch. Earlier composers were usually supported by the church or by aristocrats; not Schubert. Nor was he a famous celebrity. He was, to outward appearances, just part of a group of art-loving, pleasure-seeking young men. Actually, he belonged to a few different groups, some of whom gave themselves names. One of them was called the "Bildung" – which means roughly "self-improvement" – Circle. Another, more promisingly, was called the "Nonsense Society" – that sounds like more fun. And then there was a literary society, which used to get together for readings from great books; but it had to be closed down when it was taken over by rowdy young men who were more interested in drinking beer and eating sausages than listening to literature.

Outsiders invading the societies could cause all sorts of problems; and it wasn't always just a question of beer and sausages, either. Once, Schubert and some of his friends decided that a newcomer to their circle wasn't to be trusted; they believed that he was actually a police spy, who was watching them in case they were planning a revolution. (There was a lot of political unrest in Vienna at the time.) So they kicked him out – and had their suspicions quickly confirmed. Shortly after they'd got rid of the untrustworthy character, they were visited by some thoroughly unfriendly policemen, who arrested all of them. Schubert and most of the others were let off without charge in the end; but one of them was imprisoned for fourteen months, and then expelled from Vienna for ever – awful. So it wasn't all fun and games for Schubert's groups: Viennese life could be quite dangerous.

But Schubert himself wasn't politically minded, as far as we know – sponge-mushrooms aren't, as a rule. It was the arts that really mattered to him. He liked to be around people with talent; in fact, another nickname for him was "Kanerwas" ("kahnervas"), because if he were introduced to a new person, his first question tended to be: "Kann er was?" (Can he do something?). That sounds a bit intimidating for a first remark – thoroughly unsponge/mushroomlike, in fact; and it's true that his friends were constantly reminded that, underneath his tubby exterior, Schubert was a serious, profound genius. The occasions that brought this home to them most forcibly were the "Schubertiads". These were large gatherings in private houses in which Schubert would unveil his newest compositions. Nobody who went to a Schubertiad ever forgot it. Schubert would sit at the piano and accompany a singer (or perhaps accompany himself singing) in performances of his latest songs; or perhaps he would perform his new piano pieces (if they weren't too difficult for him to play

– he was never a virtuoso pianist); or perhaps some instrumentalists would play through his chamber music. Whichever it was, the audience would be transfixed.

And how much new music there was at every Schubertiad! Music just poured out of Schubert; he could produce a masterly song in a few hours. Sometimes he'd even forget that he'd written it, and not recognise the song if it was played to him a few days later – as if he'd been in a trance when he wrote it; curious. There was a typical pattern before a new song came into being: someone would give Schubert a poem to read; if it appealed to him, a little smile would appear on his face. After that, he couldn't wait to get to some manuscript paper. Once he did, his fingers would positively fly over the page as he wrote out the new song as fast as he could – it must have been amazing to watch! It was as if he *needed* to write music, as other people need to eat and breathe.

He didn't always write that quickly, of course; large symphonies and works for chorus and orchestra took him much longer to write, and sometimes gave him more problems as well. A surprisingly large proportion of his works are unfinished, as if he'd got stuck, shrugged, and gone on to the next piece; or perhaps just put aside the manuscript for a time and then forgotten all about it. But almost everything he wrote, short or long, finished or unfinished, was startlingly original and profound; and each year, the works he wrote became deeper. He had always written very beautiful music; but as he got older, it often went beyond beauty. There was a terrible sadness behind much of it; sometimes it was really disturbing. The pieces of this quiet, shy being could unexpectedly erupt into violent anger. It was scary – what was it that was making him sound so tortured?

Well, perhaps some of the music Schubert wrote was tortured and violent just because that was the way the music was; maybe it had nothing to do with his own day-to-day existence. But on the other hand, perhaps it was a direct reflection of his own state of mind – because there was certainly enough wrong with Schubert's life to make him utterly miserable. For a start, he was always poor, and never really knew how he was going to make a living. Not many of his pieces were published during his lifetime – in fact, there were many works of his that he never even heard. (That's why the Schubertiads were so very important: they provided Schubert, as well as his friends, with the best opportunities to hear his music.) Although he did have some successes during his lifetime, they weren't nearly enough to make him rich or famous; music publishers were terribly snooty to him, as were many musicians and so-called music-lovers.

But there was something worse in Schubert's life than lack of money or success – far worse. He was seriously ill; in fact, he was doomed. In his mid-twenties, he had a love affair, or perhaps just a brief fling, with someone – we have no idea who it was – from whom he contracted a horrible, destructive disease called syphilis; nowadays it's curable, but in those days it wasn't. And so poor Schubert knew that he wasn't going to live for long. He poured out his heart in a letter to a friend: "I feel myself the most unhappy and wretched creature in the world. Imagine a man whose health will never be right again, and who in sheer despair over this makes things worse and worse, instead of better; imagine a man, I say, whose most brilliant hopes have perished, to whom the happiness of love and friendship have nothing to offer but pain, at best . . . I ask you, is he not a miserable, unhappy being?" Poor, poor Schubert – what a terrible state to be in! He was twenty-seven years and two months old when he wrote that – and he had fewer than five years left to live.

In the end, he may not have died directly of his horrible illness, but of another; he himself thought that he had been poisoned by some fish he ate at a restaurant. What is certain is that the last years of his short life were overshadowed by the terrible threat of an early death; I think that one can feel it all too clearly in his later music. And yet: if he hadn't suffered as he did, would his music be so wonderfully, irresistibly powerful – would it show us heaven and hell as it does? I suspect not. So for his sake, I wish he hadn't suffered so much; but for our sake, I'm glad that his music makes our life so much richer. Besides, it will give me something to discuss with those dinosaurs . . .

Facts of Life

·1·

Franz Peter Schubert was born at 1.30 p.m. (or thereabouts – it might have been 1.29 or 1.31 – sorry to be so slapdash) on January 31st, 1797, in a house called, for some reason, "The Red Crayfish". Schubert's poor mother, Elisabeth, gave birth to fourteen children – only five of whom survived infancy, sadly – in sixteen years; she must have been exhausted! Elisabeth died when Schubert was fifteen; and within a year Schubert's father, energetic fellow, had married again, this time to a woman who bore him five more children, four of whom managed to live for a respectable time. Schubert's elder brother Ferdinand was even more impressive – from two marriages he managed to produce twenty-eight children! Again, sadly, only

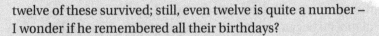

twelve of these survived; still, even twelve is quite a number –
I wonder if he remembered all their birthdays?

A family with a history . . .

*Perhaps in a way it was just as well that little Franz didn't
have too many brothers and sisters living in "The Red Crayfish"
when he was little. The house itself was tiny, with two storeys.
Schubert's father (also called Franz) was a schoolmaster, who
ran his own school; this took up the ground floor of the building – and the entire Schubert family had to live in a one-room
apartment on the floor above! There was a kitchen attached
to the room; and it was in an alcove in this kitchen that all
fourteen children were born. (I wonder if meals were being
cooked at the same time?) So it was a poor family – but
respectable. Franz senior was a serious and dedicated teacher,
and I'm sure that Elisabeth (whose sister, incidentally, was also
her sister-in-law – she married Franz senior's brother Karl) was
really nice. And what makes her just a little more intriguing is
that she had a "skeleton in her cupboard": her father had been
involved in a scandal. He had been imprisoned for financial
fraud, and was forced to leave his native town to try to establish
his family in Vienna. He managed to get there – but unfortunately, died a few hours later. ("Here we are; welcome to this
lovely city. Excuse me for a moment while I snuff it" – plonk.)
Not an easy beginning for poor Elisabeth. She was obviously
quite a free spirit, however – and seems to have married another
one (even though Franz senior was deeply religious). Their first
son, Schubert's eldest brother, Ignaz, was born about seven
weeks after his parents got married. Ahem.*

· 2 ·

Schubert started his general education at his father's school.
Meanwhile, his musical talent showed itself pretty soon; at

the age of nine, having already started on the violin and piano, he began having composition lessons. His teacher was flummoxed: "Whenever I wished to impart something new to him, he always knew it already," he remembered later. How could this be? Well, it just was. When still-rather-little Franz was eleven, he won a scholarship to a classy choir school called the Imperial and Royal City Seminar. This was a great opportunity for a poor boy like Schubert, whose parents certainly wouldn't have been able to afford the fees at such a place. The deal was that Schubert would be allowed to attend the Seminar for free until his voice broke. After that, if his education and his morals proved satisfactory, he would be allowed to stay on; if not – toodle-pip, young Franz. In the event, his studies were consistently described as "good", and his morals alternated between "good" and "very good". His music, of course, was always "very good". Apart from singing, he played violin in the orchestra; every day they would play through some symphony by one of the great masters – Mozart, Haydn or perhaps the still-active Beethoven. Everyone noticed how incredibly musical young Schubert was, and how music seemed somehow to flow through him.

His voice broke quite late, when he was fifteen; a piece of music from the school library has a note on it in Schubert's hand: "Schubert, Franz, crowed for the last time, 26th July, 1812". He was allowed to stay on, though, receiving a scholarship provided from money left by the interestingly named Count Windhag. But then there was another snag: Schubert started to fall behind in maths. The next year he was offered the chance to stay, but only on the condition that he improved. He decided to leave instead – he must have really hated maths!

Schooldays . . .

Music has always been taken really seriously in Vienna – even today, the questions of which singers and conductors should

*be engaged at the Vienna State Opera are the talk of the town.
So perhaps it's not surprising that the choice of choristers at
Schubert's Royal Seminar (which provided the boy singers for
the Emperor of Austria's chapel) had to be personally approved
by the Emperor, even if he was away somewhere fighting a war.
The school orchestra must have been terrific, too; every evening
when it played, a large crowd would gather outside the window
to listen. Schubert, having started in the second violins, was
soon promoted to the position of leader of the orchestra; he also
had the job of looking after the music and instruments, and of
lighting the candles – a little less glamorous. He became a good
pianist, too; and it wasn't long before he started to compose
seriously. His first surviving work dates from 1810, when he was
thirteen; by the time he left the school, he'd already written
piano pieces, quite a bit of chamber music, several songs and
even his First Symphony – which is a lovely piece, by the way.
Not bad going!*

*The main problem with the
school (apart from the maths,
and perhaps a couple of other
academic subjects) seems to
have been the food. Schubert's
first surviving letter is to his
brother, begging him to send some
money so that Schubert can afford to
buy a roll or a few apples to tide
him over the eight and a half
hours between the "middling"
lunch and the "miserable"
evening meal. The uniform
doesn't sound too attractive,
either; it included a three-
cornered flat hat and knickerbockers
with straps. Poor schoolboys.*

·3·

So in late 1813, at the age of sixteen, Schubert left school – or "prison", as he described it). After a few months' study at a teachers' training college (from which he graduated with medium-to-good marks in everything except religion, which was "bad" – he was never a conventional believer), he started on a grand professional career: he was appointed sixth assistant teacher at his father's school! Actually, it was probably pretty hard work: by this time, his father had moved to a slightly (but only slightly) larger house, and had around three hundred boys studying there – in two rooms! Schubert hated teaching, but he stuck it out for a couple of years; later, he used to boast about how strict he'd been with the pupils. One piece of good luck for him around this time was that he didn't have to go into the army, as most young men did – he was too tiny! Schubert was only five feet, one-and-a-half inches – a small package, in fact.

First outpourings of genius ...

Schubert's day job may have been boring – being sixth assistant teacher at his father's school can't have been that *thrilling – but the rest of his time (when he wasn't socialising) was devoted to something he found truly captivating: music! By now, he was turning from a brilliantly gifted child into a great composer. It's astonishing to think that he was almost self-taught. He had had some composition lessons with Salieri (a fictionalised version of whom you may remember from the film or play 'Amadeus', in which he was portrayed as a deadly and bitter rival of Mozart's); the lessons were likely to have been few and far between, however, and Schubert probably didn't learn that much from them anyway. Nothing could stop him composing, though – only the lack of manuscript paper, when he couldn't afford it. If that happened, his old schoolfriends would buy it for him; also, on the rare occasions when he was showing signs of laziness, they'd sometimes lock him into a room and wouldn't let him out until he'd written something! It's nice (and rather rare) when schoolfriends actually encourage each other to work ...*

In 1814, when he was just seventeen, Schubert had a mass performed at his local church, with great success; and in the same year he wrote an amazing song that is still one of his most famous, 'Gretchen am Spinnrade' ('Gretchen at the Spinning-Wheel'), about a young girl sitting and thinking of the man she loves, as she spins her wheel. It's a wonderful song (soppy though it may sound – it isn't, in fact). The next year, he composed another incredible song, 'The Erl-King' – one of the most dramatic songs ever written. A father rides through a storm, clutching his little son, who is ill. The boy keeps crying out that he can see the Erl-King (the King of the Elves), that the Erl-King wants to take him away; the father replies that he can see nothing, that his son mustn't worry. The child hears the Erl-King's voice, pleading with him to fly away to the land of the spirits; we listeners can hear the voice, too – but the father hears nothing. It must be the sad wind, the sound of the mist, he says; he gallops on, clutching the boy to him. But finally, as the journey finishes, the father looks down – and the boy is dead. It's horrible – chilling; but irresistibly powerful.

The words to this song, incidentally, are by Johann Wolfgang von Goethe – pronounced a bit like "Goerter" – the most famous writer and poet of his day. Schubert set many of his poems to music, and twice friends of Schubert's sent Goethe collections of the songs. Charmingly, the great man never deigned to reply; he just sent back the packages. He was a writer of genius, and a major figure in history – but in this instance, he did a remarkably good impression of an idiot.

· 4 ·

1815 was an astonishing year for Schubert: he composed
about 140 songs, four works for the stage, eight or nine works
for the church, and lots of other music – as well as having a
full-time job and a full-time social life, and playing lots of
music at home (including string quartets with his father and
two brothers) and elsewhere. Incredible! He was just a genius
– no other way to explain it. But being a genius didn't help him
in all ways – in money matters, for instance. He applied for a
salaried job as a music teacher, but didn't get it; one laughs
now at the morons who turned him down, but it was probably
no laughing matter for Schubert at the time. At this point,
none of his music had been published, either. It's not until
June 1816, in fact, that he writes proudly in his diary, "Today,
composed for money for the first time!" So all he had to live
on was the miserable income from teaching at his father's
school; and the only encouragement he received was from his
friends – and from his own inner voice, telling him that he *had*
to compose, whatever happened (or didn't happen).

Despite his precarious situation, however, towards the end
of 1816 Schubert took a daring step: bored and frustrated with
the school, he gave up his job there and decided to take his
chances as a professional musician. His prospects weren't
exactly brilliant: he couldn't play any instrument well enough
to make a living as anything but a second-rate performer; he
wasn't a natural teacher; he didn't have any rich aristocratic
patrons who might give him a salary; and he didn't exactly
have a load of publishers begging him to let them be the first
to bring out his works. But his small circle of friends believed
in his talent, and were prepared to help him in any way they
could.

So he left his family home, and moved in to the home of his
friend Schober – him of the suspicious moustache. In fact,

Schober was away when Schubert moved in, but his mother and younger sister were living there. (He'd also had an older sister, but she'd died in rather dodgy circumstances after an unexplained accident with a pistol.) Schubert stayed in the Schober family house as a non-paying lodger for a year.

Since the composer himself was so bad at being pushy, Schubert's friends started to send his songs to publishers; unfortunately, this all too often ended in rejection. Funnily enough, there were two other composers called Franz Schubert around at this time. One of them, the deeply unimportant Franz Schubert of Dresden, received from a publisher a copy of 'The Erl-King', with a letter saying something along the lines of: "Dear Mr Schubert, Thank you for your manuscript. Please have it back. Yours, etc." – the publisher obviously being too stupid even to get the address right. The Dresden Schubert looked at the music – and was furious that anyone could think it was by him! He wrote back indignantly: "I shall retain it in my possession in order to learn, if possible, who sent you that sort of trash in such an impolite manner and also to discover the fellow who has thus misused my name." What a complete, twenty-carat, turnip-peeler!

The princess and the pauper ...

Being a genius doesn't seem to have helped Schubert in matters of the heart, either. Around this time, he fell in love with a girl called Therese, who sang beautifully. She may have been in love with him too; but he just didn't earn enough money for them to get married, so she married a baker instead – a far safer bet. Schubert was apparently very upset. ("Happy he who finds a true man-friend," he wrote in his diary. "Happier still he who finds a true friend in his wife" – although he did add: "To a free man matrimony is a terrifying thought in these days." He really seems to have felt more comfortable with men, and with his bachelor life.) After that, we don't know much about Schubert and love affairs, but it does seem that much later there was a young princess who brought a gleam to Schubert's spectacles. She was called Princess Karoline Esterházy (probably distantly related to Haydn's employers), and Schubert spent two summers with her family at their country estate, giving Karoline and her sister piano lessons. Of course, there could be no question of the humble Schubert – a mere musician – marrying a noble princess; but he was evidently keen on her. She is said to have asked him once why he'd never dedicated any of his compositions to her. "What is the point?" Schubert is supposed to have replied. "Everything is dedicated to you anyway." (In fact, he did end up dedicating one of his greatest works, a Fantasie for piano duet, to her.) Karoline must have been a lovely person – but she must have been a bit odd, too: when she was thirty years old, her mother would send her away to play with her hoop! Just a touch unusual . . .

·5·

Eventually, things started to look up a bit. For a start, in 1817 Schubert finally gained a fan who wasn't just one of his inner circle, but was important and influential in the musical world of Vienna. This was a very tall singer called Johann Michael Vogl, who was a very dramatic performer (although he had a bad habit of fiddling with his glasses when he was about to start singing). Schober and others kept telling this celebrity that he must meet their friend Schubert, an amazing young song composer. Vogl was at first very sniffy; but then he fell in love with Schubert's music – and secured a place for himself in musical history. He was to sing Schubert's songs countless times, making them famous in Vienna and elsewhere. Next, in 1818, an overture that Schubert had written was performed in a public concert and received a good review, the critic writing that Schubert had learned "to touch and convulse all hearts" –

sounds dangerous! Also, one of his songs (he'd written almost 350 of them by now) appeared in print for the first time. That must have been thrilling – a bit like seeing one's baby's first steps, perhaps.

But the same year, short of money and unable to stay with the Schobers, Schubert was back living with his family at their new, somewhat larger house, and probably teaching at the school again; and this time – whether because Schober's laziness had rubbed off on him, or because he was in a bad state of mind, or both – Schubert composed much less. Of all of his years as a composer, 1818 was the one during which he wrote the least.

An idiotic friend . . .

Another friend of Schubert's around this time was called Josef Huttenbrenner. (Don't try saying that name when your mouth's full of sausage!) Josef Huttenbrenner was the brother of a composer called Anselm, whom Schubert already knew quite well. Josef seems to have been quite devoted to Schubert, giving some money towards the cost of publishing 'The Erl-King', and even acting as a sort of secretary to the disorganised composer for a bit; but he also seems to have been something of a pest. In the years after Schubert's death, Josef was busy pumping up his own importance in Schubert's life, and at the same time telling anybody who would listen that his brother Anselm was just as great a composer as Schubert had been. (He even managed to get a Requiem Mass by Anselm performed at Schubert's memorial service, paying the performers with money taken from the fund set up to pay for Schubert's gravestone – very clever!) But far worse than his blithering was the fact that Josef built up a large collection of Schubert manuscripts, and then either kept them to himself, refusing to allow them to be published, or lost them. An early three-act opera of Schubert's met a fate almost as sad as that of its composer: Josef's servants used the manuscript of the second and third acts to light the fires in his house! And since the opera had never been published or even copied, that was it – it's lost for ever. An excuse, perhaps, is that by that stage, Josef had gone completely batty (and so had Anselm, for that matter) – but it's still an appalling story . . .

·6·

So 1818 wasn't the best year for Schubert – and the next few years were pretty mixed, too. One good thing was that in 1819 he completed a short opera called 'The Twin Brothers'; thanks to kind Mr Vogl, this had been commissioned (i.e. paid for) by an opera house. A bad thing, though, was that he had then to wait eighteen months for its first performance. And a mixed thing was that while some of the audience loved it and cheered, others hated it and hissed. Schubert himself sat in the gallery and, either because he was so badly dressed, or because he was so cross about the hissing, or because he was just too bashful, refused to go on stage at the end for a bow. Eventually, Vogl had to go on stage and lie: "Schubert is not present; I thank you in his name." The little party for Schubert and his friends after the performance seems to have been quite fun, anyway, with lots of Hungarian wine (Schubert's favourite); and the opera ran for six nights, which wasn't bad.

Another good thing was that he'd left his family home again, and was living back among his circle; and yet another was that a group of musical friends formed an orchestra which met every week and tried out Schubert's new pieces. That ended, unfortunately (for Schubert, anyway), when the man at whose house they met won a lottery and moved away. A *very* good thing was that a performance by Vogl of 'The Erl-King' (for which Schubert was too shy, or nervous, to play the piano, so he just turned pages instead) was such a hit that the song was published by a major publisher, with financial help from some of Schubert's friends; it appeared as Schubert's Opus 1. Other works soon followed; and performances of Schubert's music started to take place more regularly – put on by such fine institutions as "The Society of Ladies of the Nobility for the Promotion of the Good and Useful". Personally, some good things happened, too: Schubert's favourite group of friends met often, and had a room permanently reserved for them at the "Hungarian Crown" inn. The inn had a clock that played Schubert's tunes; that must have pleased him. And the first "Schubertiads" date from around this time – a very significant development.

So all in all, a lot of good things; but unfortunately, rather too many bad things as well. The influence of the untrustworthy Schober grew on Schubert, and somehow the two of them managed to quarrel with Vogl – not a good idea. Luckily, it was patched up; but Vogl seems never to have liked Schober again. Lots of Schubert's other friends couldn't stand him, either. Perhaps the way Schober decorated his home gives us an idea of his character: the house was full of Turkish curtains or drapes, Arabian carpets, Persian pipes and so on – all *far* too plush and arty for the honest Schubert, who had been born in a kitchen alcove.

It was at this time, too, that Schubert and his friends got arrested; and he got into more money difficulties (although at least the sum he made from the publication of his works helped him to pay the debts he'd built up with his landlord, as well as with the shoemaker, the tailor, and at various inns and coffee-houses). He seems even to have quarrelled with his family; at least, one gets that impression from a most peculiar essay he wrote around then called 'My Dream', in which he talks about being "banished from the sight" of his angry father. Lots of unfortunate developments, in fact – but nothing anywhere near as terrible as what was just about to happen to him . . .

Letters home . . .

One new development for Schubert in 1818 was that, for the first time in his life, he started travelling. He'd hardly ever been outside Vienna before; but that summer, he spent four months with his Princesses Esterházy and their family in Hungary. He was to go back there for another four months in 1824. (Incidentally, it was on this second trip that he fell in love with Karoline – on the first trip she was only twelve years old!) Actually, the stays in Hungary weren't all that much fun for Schubert – but they're great for us! Schubert didn't write many letters as a rule, probably because he used to see his friends every night, unless they left Vienna – or he did. Most of his best letters (there are only about sixty that survive) were written while he was away; and some of the very best date from his Hungarian trips. The first summer started well: "I live and compose here like a God," he wrote – although this particular godlike being was paid far less than the cook, ran out of handkerchiefs, scarves, stockings and trousers, had to live in a house surrounded by forty cackling geese, and wasn't considered respectable enough to sit with the noble family

*at dinner. By the end of the four months, not surprisingly,
he was desperate to get back to Vienna; but still, he sounds
cheerful on the whole. And we can see what an affectionate
friend he must have been ("You who are everything to me!"
he wrote to Schober and other friends); and how lovely he was
to his family. To his brother Ferdinand he was particularly
wonderful, writing a Requiem for Ferdinand to pass off as his
own (in order to impress people who could help him with his
career); and getting very cross with him for offering to pay for
a piano that Schubert wanted to give to him. Schubert was
very fond of his whole family, in fact – and they of him. His
father's letters are interesting, in a gloomy sort of way. There's
one dating from Schubert's second summer in Hungary; it's
full of rather stern good advice, and news about who's died
recently – just the sort of thing to cheer Schubert up.*

*What's really disturbing, though, is to see the difference in the
letters from the two summers, between the basically cheerful
young Schubert of 1818 and the depressed, bitter man that he's
become by the time of his second Hungarian trip. In 1824, he
writes to Schober that he is not surprised that Schober is
unhappy, because that is "the fate of most intelligent people in
this miserable world. And what should we do with happiness,
misery being the only stimulant left to us?" It's heart-rending to
see the good-natured Schubert laid so low by his suffering. But
at least all his personal letters, contented or miserable, give us a
chance to know the real Schubert, through his own, utterly
honest words; it's a different man from the one we read about
in the memoirs of his friends (most of whom just try to tell us
how important they'd been to him!).*

*Anyway, Schubert seems to have been in far better spirits when
he finally got back to Vienna late in 1824; in fact, he was so
overexcited on the way home that he smashed the window of the
coach in which he was riding, and he and his fellow travellers
had to travel home in a freezing draught. Clumsy mushroom . . .*

· 7 ·

Oh dear – now we come to the really awful bit: the beginning of Schubert's illness. We don't know precisely when he became ill, but we know that it was either early in 1823, or late in 1822 (i.e. somewhere – or somewhen – shortly before or after his twenty-sixth birthday). The first we hear of it is in a letter from Schubert written at the end of February 1823; but he had moved back into his family's house in late 1822, so perhaps he was already unwell by then. How he became ill we can only guess; but however and whenever – the point is that he was horribly ill with syphilis. Many people suffered from syphilis in those days: in some cities, perhaps as many as one in five. In most cases, it was a death sentence; not an immediate one – the disease could seem to vanish for a bit before emerging with new symptoms – but a sure one, sometimes bringing madness with it. (At least Schubert was spared that horror.)

The surviving letters of Schubert and his friends don't give us many details; any revealing letters would probably have been destroyed deliberately. Friends of famous people in the nineteenth century tended to portray them after their death as happy, well-behaved angels, and so would try to suppress any materials that showed them in a less than flattering light; very different from these days, when a celebrity dies and with-in minutes there are so-called "friends" queuing up to sell awful stories about them to the newspapers! Anyway, we know that in the summer of 1823 Schubert spent some time in a hospital (which would have been horrible); that all his hair had to be shaved off because of a rash, and that he wore a wig for a time; and that for the rest of his life, his letters would be full either of cries from the heart about the wretched state of his health, or hopeful reports that he was better. It's hard to imagine what he must have gone through. Perhaps his feelings were best summed up in a poem that he wrote in 1823 called 'My Prayer', which contains the following verse:

> See, abased in dust and mire,
> Scorched by agonising fire,
> I in torture go my way,
> Nearing Doom's destructive day.

Poor Schubert . . .

But life goes on . . .

*When he wasn't confined to bed or suffering from too many
obvious symptoms, Schubert's social life went on pretty much
as before. Occasionally, he would even go on holiday. In the
summer of 1825, for instance, he went to Upper Austria with
his tall friend Vogl (they must have looked funny together); the
air and scenery seem to have lifted Schubert's spirits and
health. But all too often Schubert would be fighting new and
nasty symptoms of the deadly disease. Sometimes he would go
on diets for his health; he was a bit fat, so they were probably a
good idea – but they were rather strange. At one point, for
instance, he would have pork cutlets every second day, and a
dish called panada, made of flour, water, breadcrumbs and
milk, on the other days; that can't have done him a lot of good.
At other times, he would forget about trying to get better, and go
on a smoking and drinking binge – with the result that he
would either fall asleep in the middle of a social gathering, or
sit there fuming in a "silent rage", as one friend put it. And he'd
usually suffer for days or weeks afterwards.*

*Schubert knew now that he could never marry. "I renounce it,"
he told his father and stepmother – although actually, it had
renounced him. So he was now more dependent than ever on his
circle of male friends; if any of them went away from Vienna,
Schubert would miss them dreadfully. As long as there were
enough of his favourite people around, however, there could still
be good times. Only with close friends, though; Schubert was no*

good in polite Viennese society. If he were invited to a posh party, he'd either forget to go, or, if he really had to go, would keep himself hidden away as much as he possibly could. Once, at a musical evening, a baron sang some Schubert songs, with the composer accompanying him on the piano. At the end, all the rich guests fluttered around the baron, showering him with praise, and ignoring Schubert. The hostess, embarrassed, apologised; Schubert told her not to worry at all. He was used to being ignored – in fact, he preferred it that way.

Schubert was much too clumsy to dance, of course; but occasionally he would sit at the piano and make up waltzes for the assembled company at a ball. (The Viennese took their dancing pretty seriously; on special holidays, there would be as many as 1,600 balls held in the city, some of them going on until eight in the morning! The guests must have felt wonderful the next day . . .) It's a nice image: the little man sitting at the piano, almost unnoticed as he plays wonderful music that sends the richly dressed dancers spinning around the room in transports of elegant delight.

Once he stopped playing music, though, Schubert could be a liability. There were times when he could open up to friends and talk inspiringly about music and art; but there were also times when he could put his foot in it horribly, even with other musicians. The famous composer Weber ("Vayber") came to Vienna for a performance of his latest opera; he had been very kind to Schubert up till then, and had offered to help arrange a performance of one of Schubert's operas in Germany. Unfortunately, though, Schubert didn't really enjoy Weber's new work – and he went and told him so! Funnily enough, Weber never did put on Schubert's opera . . .

No, the tub of lard really wasn't a practically minded being – apart from one triumph: once, he wanted to smoke a pipe with two friends, using the three pipes he owned – but the bowl of the third pipe was missing. So Schubert found an old

*spectacles-case, somehow managed
to twist it into the right shape, and
was able to puff away to his heart's
content. I bet he was proud of that!*

· 8 ·

As he approached the grand age of
thirty, Schubert was becoming fairly
famous, at least for his songs; but he still wasn't
successful enough to escape from his money difficulties.
(His medical treatments may well have been expensive,
which wouldn't have helped.) His career was by now a
mixture of failure and success; he would quarrel with one
publisher, would be rudely rejected by another, but then
would have something accepted by another. Some nice
articles were written about him in newspapers, in Austria and
even abroad; but his career refused to take off properly – it
was all very frustrating. Of course, he had his ardent fans: a
concert he was giving with Vogl in Upper Austria had to be
stopped, because "after the performance of a few melancholy
songs the female part of the audience began to howl"! (They
had to be plied with coffee and cakes to cheer them up.) The
warmest support Schubert received, though, continued to
come from his circle of friends, and that was what mattered
to him most. He really needed their understanding, as the
dark currents in his soul surfaced increasingly in his music.
In 1827, Schubert wrote a deeply tragic song-cycle called
'Die Winterreise' ('The Winter Journey'). When he played it to
his circle "we were quite dumbfounded by the gloomy mood
of these songs," wrote his old friend Spaun; but Schubert
knew that he'd written a masterpiece. "I like these songs more
than all the others," he told them, "and you will come to like
them too."

An inspirational contemporary . . .

The most famous musician living in Vienna at the same time as Schubert was the great composer Beethoven. Vienna wasn't a huge city; they must have seen each other in the streets, in an inn, at a music shop, or whatever. But did they ever meet? Beethoven was completely deaf by the 1820s, and so it was difficult to talk to him; and Schubert – who worshipped the older composer – was so shy. Beethoven certainly knew about Schubert. Schubert had dedicated a piano duet (which apparently met with Beethoven's approval) to the great man in 1822; and in August 1823, Beethoven's nephew Karl wrote in his uncle's conversation-book (the easiest way to communicate with the deaf composer): "They greatly praise Schubert, but it is said that he hides himself." (Not surprising that he was hiding himself then; that would have been just around the time that he was covered with a horrible rash.) Finally, on his deathbed, Beethoven read through lots of Schubert's songs, and was amazed. "Truly there dwells in Schubert a divine spark," was his reaction.

But scholars disagree to this day about whether the two geniuses actually met. Schubert's brother Ferdinand wrote that they met frequently; Anselm Hüttenbrenner tells us that he was with Schubert at Beethoven's deathbed, and that Beethoven summoned Schubert into his room for a private talk. But by the time Anselm wrote that, he had started blithering; and Ferdinand could have just written his comment in a careless moment, perhaps writing "met" when he meant "saw". Spaun, usually the most reliable of Schubert's friends, wrote that Schubert often regretted never having talked to Beethoven. So scholars keep arguing about whether any meeting took place; and they'll probably keep arguing about it for the next hundred years at least – that's the sort of thing scholars like to do.

Whether they met or not, Beethoven had a great indirect influence on Schubert – perhaps more than ever after his death in March 1827. Schubert was one of the torchbearers at the funeral; later, he went with a few friends to an inn, and spent hours talking about "nothing but Beethoven". After that, Schubert set to music several poems that Beethoven had intended to set himself; wrote a mass for the church in which Beethoven's funeral had been held; quoted from the funeral march in Beethoven's famous 'Eroica' Symphony in two of his own last works; and invited a string quartet to come and play one of Beethoven's last quartets to him as he lay on his deathbed (the last music he heard, outside his own head). He was obsessed, in fact! Perhaps he was responding to a question posed during the oration at Beethoven's funeral: "Who shall stand beside him?" Schubert must have known deep inside himself that he was the only living composer who was on the same level as Beethoven – even if no one else realised it at the time.

· 9 ·

The year 1828 should have started fairly cheerfully for Schubert. At the age of thirty, his health seemed to be better than it had been a few years earlier; he was finally becoming more famous – not nearly as famous as he should have been, but at least it was progress; and some of his best friends who had deserted him earlier, such as Schober and Spaun, were back in Vienna. But at the New Year's Eve party at Schober's (where Schubert was living again), as the first minutes of 1828 ticked away, one of Schubert's friends read out the lines of a poem:

> The magic of speed, the source of songs –
> it too will dry up, divine as it is;
> No longer will songs pour forth in a flood,
> for the singer too will be carried away.

I wonder if Schubert and his friends shivered and exchanged uneasy glances as these words sounded in the middle of their celebrations?

Well, if they did, the moment probably passed; Schubert was a busy man! A couple of weeks later, publication was announced of the first part of 'Die Winterreise'. Then, in February, two publishers wrote to Schubert asking if he had any music that they could publish; in the past, Schubert had had to approach *them*. (Not that anything came of these two enquiries – Schubert and publishers just didn't mix well.)

And then there was the grand occasion of the one and only concert in Schubert's lifetime devoted entirely to his works; it was carefully planned to take place exactly a year after Beethoven's death. The venue was a building known for some reason as "The Red Hedgehog". (Schubert was then living right by another establishment known as "The Blue Hedgehog" – I have no idea why the Viennese were so obsessed with hedgehogs! Nasty prickly creatures with fleas – hedgehogs, I mean, not the Viennese . . .) The concert was a great success. Well, Schubert's friends all yelled and cheered, and the critics wrote fairly warmly about it (although implying that Schubert had a lot to learn from them about music – but music critics have always been like that!) Schubert himself reported that he had "received an extraordinarily enthusiastic reception"; he even made some money from the ticket sales.

But after that, the usual frustrations took over once again: not enough money (he couldn't afford a holiday that summer); too much drinking; and health worries. Still, neither Schubert nor his friends seemed to have thought that the end was looming so close; and his flow of masterpieces continued as unstoppably as ever. On September 1st, he left Schober's apartment, where he'd been lodging for nearly a year, and moved to the house of his brother Ferdinand, outside central Vienna; this move was apparently suggested by Schubert's doctor, who thought that the country air would be beneficial – presumably he didn't realise how damp and unhealthy Ferdinand's house was. Schubert was having dizzy spells, and some other rather nasty episodes; but he was still going on walks – including one to Haydn's grave – and seeing friends, until the end of October.

On the last day of that month, though, he ordered some fish – and is supposed to have pushed it away in disgust, claiming that it was poisoned. From that day on, he seems never to have eaten again. Extraordinarily, however, he did manage to go to a well-known Viennese professor for a lesson in a specialised branch of composition. Schubert had planned to have a series of sessions, but wasn't well enough after that first one. It's rather an amazing thought – the world's greatest composer having composition lessons! Schubert was anything but conceited.

On November 12th, he wrote to Schober: "I am ill. I have had nothing to eat or drink for eleven days now, and can only wander feebly and uncertainly between armchair and bed." He asked Schober to send him books (preferably by Fennimore Cooper – Schubert had enjoyed his book 'The Last of the Mohicans'). There seems to have been no question of Schober actually visiting him; he was probably too worried about his moustache catching a disease. Humph. Others visited, however, and weren't too worried about Schubert: they assumed that he would get better. But instead, he just got weaker and weaker; eventually he became delirious, and started to sing to himself – new songs or old? We shall never know. At one point, he woke up, and asked Ferdinand where he was. Ferdinand assured him that he was at home. "That's not true," Schubert replied. "Beethoven's not here." Beethoven, the man he probably never even met, was such an important part of Schubert's life by now – perhaps he felt that he was finally going to meet him!

All too soon afterwards came his very last words, spoken as he turned his face to the damp wall of Ferdinand's room: "Here – here is my end," he sighed. And indeed, sadly – no, tragically – it was. He died at 3 o'clock on the afternoon of Wednesday, November 19th. We don't know exactly what it was that killed him – probably a combination of things, all made far worse by the disease that had been attacking him for several years. Ultimately, it doesn't really matter what he died of; the fact is that he was dead at the age of thirty-one – this loveable, tubby, awkward genius who loved life, loved his family and friends and loved music. And it's not fair. But he achieved more in his thirty-one years than most people would have achieved in ninety – no, nine hundred – years; and he left it all for us. Thank you, Mr Mushroom.

Schubert's musical legacy . . .

Schubert's friends were in a state of shock. "On Monday I was speaking with him," noted one in his diary. "On Tuesday he was delirious, on Wednesday dead . . . I wish I were lying there, in his place," he continued, a bit strangely, "for he leaves the world with fame." Well, people in shock do say weird things. Most of Schubert's friends wrote glowing tributes, describing Schubert's modesty, friendliness, dedication to music, and denying that he had ever drunk too much (ahem). Only Schober failed to write anything – he whom Schubert had loved best of all, but who had refused to visit him on his deathbed. (Actually, Schober did claim later that he'd tried to write a book about Schubert, but just couldn't manage it.) Schober lived a long time, not snuffing it until 1882 – giving him lots of time to quarrel with lots of people, and to change his hairstyle fairly drastically. One picture of him from 1835 shows that his moustache had acquired a large companion – a thoroughly bushy beard; he looks like a rather bad-tempered Father Christmas. A later picture shows him completely clean-shaven – but still in a bad mood. A strange character; oh well – Schubert liked him, anyway.

Enough about Schober. Ferdinand Schubert had arranged for his brother to be buried next to Beethoven, as Schubert had wished. (Well, almost next to him; unfortunately, the two plots right next to Beethoven were taken, one by a certain Count O'Donnell – hmm . . . Beethoven, O'Donnell, Schubert – spot the odd man out.) Almost sixty years later (by which time they can't have been very recognisable, except perhaps by expert dentists), both Beethoven's and Schubert's bodies were exhumed and taken to lie in grander monuments (next to each other this time) in central Vienna; but their original gravestones remain, in a rather shoddy little space known as "Schubert Park". I wonder whether Schubert would have been proud, or just embarrassed, about the name? He might have thought that "Beethoven Park" would have been more appropriate; but I'm glad it's Schubert Park. It makes up a bit for the slightly condescending inscription on the gravestone there: "The art of music here entombed a rich possession, but even far fairer hopes."

But to be fair, nobody really knew at that point just how much Schubert had written; even his close friends thought of him primarily as a song-composer. It was only in the following fifty years or so that the vast majority of his music came to light. It was a strange phenomenon: compositions by Schubert kept appearing, as if in the years after his death, Schubert had carried on composing (while he was decomposing, as it were). In 1862, a famous Viennese critic wrote: "For thirty years [this

man was a music critic, not a maths professor!] the master
has been dead, and in spite of this it seems as if he goes on
composing invisibly – it is impossible to keep up with him."

   Actually, it does makes sense – somehow, Schubert had
managed to compose over a thousand works (some of them
single songs, but others operas, symphonies, major religious
works, long chamber-music pieces, and so on) in his short life;
but fewer than two hundred of them had been published during
his lifetime. He'd been careless with his manuscripts, too, giving
them away to friends if he thought they'd appreciate them; so
many of his works were thought to be lost, and then turned up
later. It was almost as if, once he'd finished composing a piece (or
very often before he'd finished composing it, in the case of his
many unfinished works), he'd lost interest in it as he moved onto
the next one. So for years and years, as Schubert's name became
more and more famous, manuscripts by him would turn up and
greedy publishers – sometimes the same ones who had treated
Schubert so badly when he was alive – would bring them out as
quickly as they could. Often they had no idea when, where or
why the "new" work had been written. It was ages before anything like a "complete Schubert edition" could be compiled – he
was a cataloguer's nightmare! But at least people came to appreciate his amazing genius; and in fact, it was Schubert, rather
than Beethoven or any of the other great composers who had
lived in Vienna, who was the first composer ever to have a statue
erected there in his honour, in 1872. Ha. What would the modest,
tubby little mushroom/sponge/lump of dough have made of that?

The Music

Now, I know I've gone on about how sad a lot of Schubert's music
is; but have I described enough how incredibly, breathtakingly

beautiful it is? He writes melodies so gorgeous that they stay in your head for days, weeks on end; his music could make rhinoceroses cry. (Well – if you were to make them chop raw onions as they listened, anyway.) The funny thing about Schubert's musical phrases is that they'll often seem to be quite happy; and then suddenly, before you realise what's happened, they'll go around a corner, and be inconsolably tragic. There's nothing quite like it in any other music.

Of course, in the songs, the mood depends entirely on the words he's setting. Some of the songs are endearingly light-hearted and joyous; but it does seem as if, as he got older, Schubert was increasingly attracted to more sombre texts. By the time he gets to 'Die Winterreise' in 1827, he's so far into his own bleak journey that it seems as if he'll never come back. On the other hand, some of the songs he wrote the next year – his last – are charming and full of smiles; so there's no fixed rule.

His instrumental music certainly gets deeper, and usually darker, as he matures. There's still plenty of charm, and glorious melodies and dances; but somehow the charm can be heart-breaking here, because of the contrast with the grief that surrounds it. It is often as if Schubert is looking back to the good things he loved in life, knowing that he is about to leave them for ever. Even his lovely, lilting Viennese dance rhythms can sound tragic in this context.

Hmm ... I hope all this talk of death and tragedy doesn't put you off. Schubert's music isn't morbid or depressing; in the end, it's uplifting, because it's so utterly exquisite. And if you're ever sad, his music will make you feel better; it's as if he understands, and is trying to comfort you (and himself) by showing you a world more beautiful than ours.

What to listen to

I know I've said this before, for our first two composers – but it's true here as well: selecting just a few pieces is difficult, because there's just too much to choose from! But I'll try.

Let's start with the songs. Two of the early masterpieces that I've already mentioned are unmissable: 'Gretchen am Spinnrade' ('Gretchen at the Spinning-wheel'), D118; and the scary 'Erlkönig' ('The Erl-King'), D328. (The D stands for "Deutsch", by the way. Because Schubert's music was published in dribs and drabs, his opus numbers became completely messed up; so a very clever man named Professor Deutsch – which means "German" in German! – catalogued all his works in as near as he could get to chronological order, and gave his name to the catalogue.) Among later songs, there's the charming 'Die Taubenpost' ('The Pigeon-Post') D965A; and the magical 'Auf dem Strom' ('On the Stream'), D943, with horn as well as piano. Those are pretty random choices, though; the complete songs take up thirty-seven CDs, so you've got a lot of exploring to do! At any rate, you should definitely get to know the two big song-cycles, 'Die schöne Müllerin' ('The Fair Maid of the Mill'), and 'Winterreise'. As always with songs, make sure you've got the words in front of you as you listen; that way, you can enjoy the amazing way Schubert illustrates the words he's setting and brings them to life.

From the orchestral music, try the last two symphonies: No. 8, the 'Unfinished' (his most famous incomplete work), and one of Schubert's most serene pieces, the 'Great' C major Symphony, No. 9. As for the solo piano music and the chamber music: what an incredible treasure-trove! For three perfect examples of Schubert's way of opening a door and showing us heaven, listen to the last piano sonata in B flat, D960; the Fantasia in F minor for piano duet, D940; and the slow movement of his string quintet in C with two cellos, D956 – all three works written in his last year, when Schubert was staring death in the face. The two piano trios are magnificent, as well; so are many of the string quartets – maybe start with the A minor quartet, D804, and the 'Death and the Maiden' quartet, D810. And so on – I could go on for pages, but I can't; we've got another composer to attend to.

Pyotr Ilyich Tchaikovsky

1840–1893

Hmm . . . well, that story was horribly tragic; but, believe it or not, this one is even worse. In fact, some of it is so awful – especially the ending – that I wouldn't blame you if you skipped ahead to the next chapter, where a nice cheerful (well, comparatively cheerful) composer awaits you. All right – off you go. See you soon . . .

Still here, eh? Well, OK – but don't say I didn't warn you.

Actually, before we start this chapter, I want to show you some brief film clips. Sitting comfortably? Popcorn at the ready? Then we'll begin:

First of all, we see a totally flat, totally white landscape, stretching as far as the eye can see. It looks as if it's covered with a blanket of sugar; in fact, the whiteness is deep, endless snow. It may not seem very exciting to us – it might as well be a photograph rather than a film, since it's so still; but to a typical nineteenth-century Russian, this was an image that lived deep within his heart, one that he carried inside him wherever he went. It is the silent, profoundly peaceful Russian landscape in winter; an image of "Mother Russia".

Next the film moves to a city street. It's also white, covered with the same endless snow; but there's life here. Horse-drawn carriages roll along the road, while on the pavements, human figures hurry along – not that you'd be sure they were human at first glance: they're so firmly bundled up in fur hats, fur coats and fur boots that they look like furry creatures from another world. (Actually, it *is* another world – the world of nineteenth-century Russia.) There's still no sound; is this a silent movie? No, it's just that the blanket of snow absorbs all the noise.

Now the camera pauses in front of a huge wooden building, with onion-shaped spires of gleaming gold on the top. Entering the doors, we realise that this is certainly *not* a silent movie; the singing of the choir is practically deafening! The basses hold the lowest notes that could possibly emerge from a human throat; the other voices quiver fervently as they sing passionate, almost desperately emotional hymns, imploring God to have mercy on them. In fact, not only does this movie have sound, but I think it must have been filmed in Odorama: the smell of incense is overpowering, the fumes filling the church with a mysterious mist. This is an Easter service at a Russian Orthodox Church, the establishment that represents another

Pyotr Ilyich Tchaikovsky

side of the soul of Mother Russia. Even non-believing Russians (and there aren't too many of those at this point in history) are moved by the passion of these services. The film shows the faces of a few members of the congregation, dramatically lit by the candles they hold: the deeply lined features of an old peasant woman, dressed in grey rags; a fierce Tartar from a distant region of the Russian Empire, with dark, burning eyes; a colourfully dressed aristocratic lady, tears streaming down her cheeks and ruining her elaborate make-up. And then we see the tall figure of the priest, with black hat and black clothes, which go well with his huge black beard. "Christ is risen!" he roars (in Russian) at the congregation. "He is risen indeed!" they roar back in an ecstatic frenzy.

Moving away from that extraordinary scene, we go somewhere quieter: a heavily furnished room where several men sit around a table laden with delicacies such as caviar (eggs from sturgeon, a type of fish – probably the most expensive food in the world, then and now), blini (Russian pancakes), lots of vodka (the very alcoholic Russian national drink), and so on. In the corner, boiling water is bubbling away in a cylindrical brass vessel – known as a samovar – in case anyone wants tea; these men are probably more interested in the vodka, though, downing small glasses of it in one violent gesture. (Wine and champagne are welcome, too.) As soon as any new arrival comes in, the men all stand up – at least while they're still sober enough to find their feet – embrace him, kiss him three times (once on the right cheek, once on the left, and again on the right), sit down again, and start talking, shouting, gesturing, laughing, quarrelling, even crying together; everything at high voltage. It all seems so much more emotional than an English dinner-party; of course, it probably *is* more emotional than a similar English gathering would be – but the sounds of the words help too. The Russian language itself is so full of passion, even the most everyday expressions. Take the commonplace greeting, for instance: in English, we greet someone with the very ordinary word "hello"; or "hallo"; or perhaps, if we have a particularly deep voice, "hullo". In Russian, the word is "zdrastvui" – a sadly expressive sort of word, sliding darkly out of the mouth, implying all sorts of hidden emotions. ("Yes, here I am and here you are – but how we've suffered, what we've been through since we saw each other last, ten minutes ago.")

This dinner-party will probably go on all night, so we'll leave them to it; but before the film stops, the camera has paused in front of one man at the table – the hero of this chapter, Pyotr Ilyich Tchaikovsky (pronounced "Chai" – rhyming with "tie" – "kovski").

Let's look at him at the age of fifty or thereabouts; he might protest, because he's quite sensitive about his appearance, and has been worried about being old since his early thirties. But there are so many photos and written descriptions of him at fifty that it's easy to get a clear picture of him at this age. So – sorry, Pyotr Ilyich (Russians address each other by their first name, followed by the name of their father, so: Pyotr, which is Russian for "Peter", Ilyich, meaning "son of Ilya") but we'll have to meet you at age fifty, even if you'd prefer us to see you in your twenties. Or rather, we'll have to *see* him at age fifty, since meeting him isn't a good idea; he tends to be dreadfully, painfully shy, and the presence of just one stranger in a room full of his friends can cause him to clam up completely. Let's hope that the men around the table are all members of his family, or chosen from his closest friends, because then Tchaikovsky will be relaxed, and we can see him at his best.

Observing him as he sits there, we can see that he looks quite a bit older than fifty. Most of his hair is gone, and the bit that remains is as white as Russian snow. He has a neatly trimmed white beard and moustache; his face is deeply wrinkled, and his teeth are yellow. (In fact, within a year or two, he will lose a tooth or two, meaning that he'll speak with rather a strong lisp; that will make his speech rather hard to understand, even for Russians – much to his distress.) He is impeccably dressed, and his voice is soft and warm; his eyes are soft and warm too – dark brown, with a clear and trusting expression. Everybody in the room seems to adore him; and perhaps for that reason, he seems to be enjoying himself, getting quite giggly as the evening wears on.

Nevertheless, he'd probably prefer us to see him at his own house, just outside a little town called Klin; after years of not really having a home at all, he has settled here all alone, except for his adored – if slightly fierce – servant Alexei, on whom he relies to make his life run smoothly, and Alexei's wife. So let's look at him here. It is in this peaceful place that Tchaikovsky does most of his composing these days. A typical day for him starts at around seven, when Alexei brings him some tea; then Tchaikovsky will read for a bit, or perhaps study English. (He already speaks French perfectly – like most educated Russians – and has also learnt Italian and German. Now he wants to be able to speak English – mostly in order to be able to read the novels of Charles Dickens in their original language.) When he's dressed, he'll take a short stroll through the local countryside that he adores; and after that he'll settle down to compose, in strict privacy – no one is allowed near enough to hear anything, except perhaps Alexei, because he doesn't understand a thing about music and is therefore safe.

Tchaikovsky will work from 9.30 until one o'clock. After that will come lunch, the main meal of the day; and then a walk of exactly two hours. (An hour and fifty-five minutes isn't enough – Tchaikovsky is sure that he needs precisely two hours for the sake of his health.) He has to be alone for this, because he's still composing in his head. The only problem is that the local children know that he's a soft touch, because he loves children, and also because he loves to give his money away; so they will probably ambush him and beg for coins until he gives in and they run off, satisfied.

Afternoon tea is at four o'clock; Tchaikovsky will read the papers as he sips, or talk to guests if he has any. (He prefers to be alone while composing his major works; but if he's just putting the finishing touches to a piece, or composing something small, he may invite some close friends to keep him company.) From five until seven, he'll be busy again, writing down the ideas he's had on his walk. And then, finally, work is over for the day, and he'll relax, maybe going for another stroll, with a friend this time; or playing the piano, either by himself or with the friend. Supper follows, and then letter-writing or reading if he's by himself, or cards if there's company, before he goes to bed, reading some more until it's lights out and sleep.

Sounds fine, you'll say: a lovely life, composing at home or socialising with close friends in the city. What's awful about this story? Well, nothing – yet. The trouble is that when we look behind the calm surface, we can see that Tchaikovsky is a tortured soul – capable of great happiness and even brief moments of inner peace, it's true; but also tormented by painful self-doubt, constant worries and an almost unlimited capacity for suffering. Like many Russians, he is easily moved to tears. Occasionally he cries because he's so happy – when he is moved by a beautiful Russian landscape, for example, and sheds tears of gratitude to the Lord; more often, though, he is liable to sob hysterically – when he parts from someone he loves, or even when he's composing a sad scene in an opera. Tchaikovsky is a deeply emotional man – and life can be hard for people who feel things too deeply.

Nothing in his life is ever really easy or straightforward, but hardest of all are the times when he has to see lots of people. In order to supervise or conduct performances of his works, he has to travel often to the two main cities of Russia, Moscow and St Petersburg; when he's in the city, he's usually in a dreadful state the entire time. "Pyotr Ilyich," people will say, embracing him, "you're here. You *must* come and visit us." And Tchaikovsky, too kind and gentle (and perhaps too weak) to say no, will agree; then he'll go to their homes and sit there miserably, trying desperately to make polite conversation, and longing to get away. Concerts and opera performances are often torture for him, too. By the time we're observing him, he has come a long way as a conductor: when he'd tried to conduct as a young man, he'd been so crippled by nerves that he'd spent the whole performance flailing around distractedly with his right hand (not helping the players one little bit) while using his left hand to hold onto his head – convinced that it was about to fall off! Most peculiar. This particular neurosis has improved with age; but he can still be horribly unsure of himself when he conducts, and often drinks quite a lot before a concert to calm his nerves. If he thinks that the orchestra isn't enjoying a work of his, he's likely to finish rehearsals as soon as he can, no matter how badly the musicians are playing, so that they can stop being bored and go home. Any criticism of his work, or a poor reaction from an audience, can depress him horribly; he has been known to destroy the manuscript of a new piece immediately after the first performance, because he's just decided that it's no good. In fact, he sometimes flees from Russia after the first hearing of a major new work, in order not to be around to hear the comments of the public, or to read the reviews (which, it's true, are often terrible). So he goes abroad as fast as he can; but then suffers from dreadful home-sickness, and can't wait to get back to Russia. (He's not safe from people when he's abroad, anyway; people will always recognise him, and disturb his privacy. Once in Switzerland, a woman approached him: "Pyotr Ilyich!" she cried. "Excuse me Madam, I am not Tchaikovsky," he answered – forgetting that she hadn't actually mentioned the name Tchaikovsky; there were probably thousands of people called Pyotr Ilyich. Whoops.)

It's true that most composers suffer for their music; his was just rather an extreme case. But it wasn't just music, or being bothered by strangers, that made Tchaikovsky's life so hard; any activity, no matter how simple, could cause him pain. Reading, for instance: he read avidly – but if he didn't like a book, he was liable to jump up and tear it into shreds, or throw it out of the window. And if a character in a novel reminded him of a friend, and that character behaved badly, he might sit down and write a furious letter to the unfortunate friend. Cards, too: he loved to play cards – but then he worried that it was an addiction, and that it was bad for his health. Further-more, he'd be depressed if he lost, cursing himself for his stupid mistakes; but would be equally depressed if he won, because he felt that he didn't deserve to, and would feel sorry for his opponents. Oh dear.

Anything could be too much for Tchaikovsky. He was terrified of thunderstorms, and of ghosts – even of telephones. In the early days of long-distance calls, he was put through to a friend in another city; but instantly begged, in a quavering voice, to be allowed to hang up, because the thought of all that distance between him and the caller was making him feel ill. (I don't think he'd have been too keen on video conferencing.) He loved dogs, but agonised about whether he should get one, partly because his servant Alexei didn't like them, and Tchaikovsky didn't want to upset him; and partly because (in his own words) "I worry about them all the time; I continuously imagine that they're hungry, that they want something and can't say so, that they're ill, and so on."

Poor Tchaikovsky. Still, I hear you say (I have fairly good hearing) – not exactly an awful story, is it?

You just wait.

So what made Tchaikovsky into this bundle of neuroses? Well – who can say what makes anyone into what they are? But there are some events that must have contributed, at least; so let's have a brief look at his life.

His early childhood was all right – pretty idyllic, in fact. His father had a good job as an inspector of mines in a fairly remote region, about six hundred miles east of St Petersburg, where the family lived very comfortably. Tchaikovsky adored both his parents, and loved his older brother, Nikolay; so all appeared to be rosy – although even then, according to Tchaikovsky's adored French governess Fanny, he was "a child of glass", because he was so easily hurt and upset. He was a lovable child – a bit messy and disorganised, but deeply affectionate and kind; perhaps his proudest moment came when he rescued a kitten from some cruel children who were threatening to drown it.

Russia, the beloved mother country, was important to him from his earliest years. One day Fanny discovered him holding a map of Europe and trying to spit on all the countries that weren't Russia; rather shocked, she pointed out that this wasn't a very nice thing to do, and that she found it especially insulting, because she herself came from France. It's OK, Tchaikovsky reassured her, I was holding my hand over France, so you shouldn't be cross with me. Hmm . . . a bit strange.

At the age of eight, Tchaikovsky's peaceful world was shattered. His father Ilya heard of a better job in Moscow, and decided to move the whole family there; unfortunately Ilya told a friend of his plans – and that "friend" nipped in first and secured the job for himself. Ilya had already quit his present job, so he was now unemployed; from then on, although they didn't starve, the family's life was never as settled. Fanny had to leave the household, and Tchaikovsky's health and happiness suffered. The family moved briefly to Moscow and then to St Petersburg, before Ilya found a new job in a remote little town, miles from anywhere. There were more children by then: a younger sister, Sasha, had arrived two years after Tchaikovsky, followed by another brother, Ippolit (strange name – say a cheery hello and a fond goodbye to him, because he doesn't appear again in this story). Finally, when Tchaikovsky was ten, twin boys, Anatoly and Modest, were born. Tchaikovsky was to adore these twins more than anyone else on earth; but although he was thrilled by their arrival, it did mean that his mother had less time for him. Besides, it was time for him to go to a good school.

So his mother took him back to St Petersburg – and had to leave him there. Tchaikovsky was totally traumatised by their parting; as his mother rode off in a carriage, the desperate boy clung to the wheels to stop the coach from moving away. It must have been hideous for both of them.

Worse was to come, though. In St Petersburg, he stayed at the house of some kind people, who looked after him well. One day, there was an outbreak of a dangerous disease, scarlet fever, at Tchaikovsky's school; Tchaikovsky didn't get it himself, but unwittingly brought the germs into the house. Within a few weeks the adored eldest son of his hosts had caught the disease and died. How must Tchaikovsky have felt? And then a few years later, when Tchaikovsky was fourteen, his mother died of a dreadful disease called cholera – an illness spread by bacteria that can live in unclean water. (St Petersburg was known then, and is still known today, for its filthy water.) For the rest of his life, Tchaikovsky couldn't speak about her without bursting into tears; every year he would remember her birthday, and would write in his diary about how much he still missed her.

Right – that's enough awfulness for a bit. Life went on – as it does. Tchaikovsky went to a posh school, the Imperial School of Jurisprudence (that's "law" to you and me), where he was very popular. Throughout his life, Tchaikovsky seems to have had a knack of charming people – whether or not he liked them. He graduated in 1859, just after his nineteenth birthday, and almost immediately entered the Civil Service, where he seemed to be settling down to a more or less (probably less) distinguished career in the Ministry of Justice.

The strange thing was that there was really no sign at this point that a great composer was preparing to leap out from inside this civil servant and take everyone by storm. Of course, when they looked back later, people could remember little signs that had shown themselves throughout his life: Fanny, for instance, recalled an occasion when, as a little boy, Tchaikovsky, sobbing, begged her to stop the music going on and on inside his head; his family remembered how fascinated he was by the orchestrion (a huge mechanical musical instrument which looks like an organ) that his father owned – especially when it played tunes by Mozart, who was to be Tchaikovsky's favourite composer throughout his life. Other people thought back and remembered how he used to go to the piano and improvise for hours when he was sad or lonely. But that was in retrospect; at the time nobody, not even his piano teacher, could have predicted a career in music for him – let alone that he would become one of the most famous composers of all time. At this point, all he seemed to want was to be successful at the Ministry, and to lead a fashionable life, going to concerts, theatres and restaurants, taking part in amateur theatricals, dressing as well as he could afford to, knowing lots of people with similar interests, and so on – the merry bachelor existence, in fact.

It wasn't nearly as simple as that, though, even at this stage – because Tchaikovsky had a secret: he was a homosexual, and for the rest of his life he would continue to fall in love with a series of young men. At first it doesn't seem to have bothered him too much: many of his friends were inclined the same way, and several of them were to go off, get married and live "respectable" lives – so perhaps Tchaikovsky thought that he would do the same. Besides, there was a more tolerant approach to such behaviour in Russia at that time than there was, say, in England. However, when Tchaikovsky was in his early twenties, a scandal broke out in St Petersburg, and Tchaikovsky was named as a member of a set of homosexuals. It was a shock to him; for the first time, he felt the weight of society's disapproval.

From that point onwards, he started to keep his private life more private; and he replaced the company of his former friends with that of his twin brothers. Much later, Modest remembered that one evening he and Anatoly were home after school, bored and dejected as on most evenings, when their distant older brother, Pyotr, who was never around because he was always going out and being fashionable, passed them, stopped suddenly and asked, "Would you like to spend the evening with me?" And that was the beginning of a new era for all three of them. Tchaikovsky had always loved the twins, it's true, and, when their mother died, had resolved to show them the love and care that their mother would have given them had she lived; but he'd never had the time to do much about it. Now everything changed: from that evening onwards, he devoted himself to their upbringing, and the three of them formed "a family within a family", bound together by a love that would be a central force in all their lives.

Life with their older brother wasn't easy for the twins, though; Tchaikovsky's relationships were always complicated. Modest in particular had a hard time of it. He worshipped Tchaikovsky, trying to model himself on his beloved Pyotr

(Modest was also homosexual, unlike Anatoly); but he suffered for his adoration. It is true that he became Tchaikovsky's closest confidant, particularly in later years; but he always felt that it was Anatoly whom Tchaikovsky really loved. And what Modest had to put up with! As a schoolboy, he sent a photo of himself to Tchaikovsky; Tchaikovsky thanked him, but added, "Your photograph made me think with sadness that in real life you are not at all so charmingly good-looking as in your portrait." Ouch – no wonder Modest was modest! Later, when Modest wanted to give up his job in the civil service in order to become a writer (i.e., an artist like Tchaikovsky), his elder brother's advice was again full of tact: "You had the misfortune to be born with an artistic soul . . . but as, in spite of your fine artistic nature, you have not been endowed with any talent, for God's sake do not let yourself yield to your desires." Ouch again. In fact, Modest did become a playwright and even wrote the librettos for a couple of Tchaikovsky's later operas; and Tchaikovsky, to do him justice, was eventually very helpful to Modest's career (although there tended to be rather a lot of bullying mixed in with his helpfulness).

Meanwhile, along with the changes in his personal circumstances came a transformation in Tchaikovsky's professional life: he had got the music bug! A Conservatoire of Music was founded in St Petersburg in 1862; and Tchaikovsky, having started to study music seriously the previous year, was one of the first students to enrol. And what a student he was – a fanatic! If necessary, he would work all night, desperate to learn how to compose properly; he also studied the flute and the organ, continued to play the piano and sang quite nicely. But he had such a distance to go; he was writing some music, it was true – but most of it was pretty bad. Would he ever really succeed? It was risky – deeply risky; but in 1863, he gave up his job at the ministry (in which he wasn't progressing as well as he'd hoped, anyway) and became a full-time music student.

His father, older brother and sister were all very worried; but Tchaikovsky held firm. In 1866 he graduated with the Conservatoire's highest honour, the silver medal (despite being too nervous to attend the final ceremony, where a cantata of his was performed); and was immediately offered a job teaching musical theory at the Conservatoire of Music just being started up in Moscow.

So – from a musical nothing to professor at a Conservatoire in four years wasn't bad; and he was pretty successful as a professor, too. He wasn't always particularly kind to the students (especially to the breed of young ladies who, according to him, were only there because music was a "nice" thing for a young society lady to learn); but he was very knowledgeable, and extremely clear in his explanations. In fact, in 1871 he wrote a book about musical theory which, while not exactly a laugh-a-minute, became a standard textbook on the subject for countless future music students. He was also engaged as a music critic by some leading Russian journals – an activity that brought in some much-needed extra income for the next few years.

But of course Tchaikovsky was aiming far higher; he wanted to be a great composer, nothing less. There was some progress – not as much or as fast as Tchaikovsky would have liked, but definitely progress; at least his music was now starting to receive occasional performances, which aroused some interest in his work. Finally, just before his thirtieth birthday, Tchaikovsky produced his first real masterpiece, the "Fantasy Overture" based on Shakespeare's 'Romeo and Juliet' – still one of the most popular of all orchestral pieces; even Tchaikovsky remained proud of it. Now he was really on his way. For the first time, he rented his own apartment in Moscow; he also engaged a young peasant boy, Alexei, as his manservant. That's the same Alexei whom we saw at the house in Klin about twenty years later; he may have been a doubtful character in some ways, but Tchaikovsky became completely dependent on him.

Now that Tchaikovsky is becoming a man of substance – a celebrity, even – let's take another look at him. He's good-looking, with his deeply expressive eyes, his still-luxuriant brown hair, and a fine auburn beard. He is already deeply neurotic and deeply shy; but on the other hand he needs company, and is capable of forming close friendships quite easily. His health is something of a problem. He has a semi-permanent upset stomach, occasional trouble with his eyes, pain in his legs, headaches, small fits, and so on; but it's difficult to tell what's really serious – he's quite a hypochondriac! He has a rather bad habit of telling his relatives, and other people close to him, all about every symptom, and building it up into a huge issue; and then, when he's got everyone into a complete state of panic, he'll suddenly announce that it's all passed, that it had been nothing really, and that he's perfectly well after all. Slightly infuriating . . .

Nothing in Tchaikovsky's life is really simple. In a letter to Anatoly, he describes a typical day: "Yesterday I couldn't wait for lunch to be served. After lunch I waited impatiently to go for a walk. During the walk I was longing for tea. After tea I wanted the moon to rise as soon as possible, then I just couldn't wait for supper, and then – the right to go to sleep . . . to be sorry for the past, to hope for the future, never to be content with the present – that is my life." Sigh.

He is completely unpredictable, too, with a very special talent for saying one thing, and then doing exactly the opposite. Once, a baritone was appearing in one of Tchaikovsky's operas, and was desperate to have a new aria written for him; Tchaikovsky was equally desperate *not* to write the new aria, because he was sure it wouldn't fit into the opera. So that should have been that. But then one day, as Tchaikovsky was sitting in his apartment, he heard the baritone arrive at his door; Alexei informed him that the master was out – but the baritone announced that he was going to come in and wait for the master to come home. Panic stations. Tchaikovsky dived under his sofa, just in time; but the baritone stayed sitting there for three hours! (Must have been one of his busy days.) Eventually, he gave up and left, and a rather squashed Tchaikovsky crawled out; but the perverse thing is that, after all that, he immediately sat down and composed the aria!

Oh well: perhaps geniuses are supposed to be complicated – and weird. Anyway, in this case his weirdness leads us back neatly to our story; because "weird" is probably as good a word as any to describe Tchaikovsky's relationship with a lady called Nadezhda von Meck. In his mid-thirties, Tchaikovsky was still poor, despite his steadily increasing fame. If he ever had any money to spare, he would spend it immediately, or give it away. So he was very grateful when Nadezhda ("Nadiejda" – nice word: it means "hope") came into his life. Nadezhda was rich, but lonely and miserable; nine years older than Tchaikovsky, she was a formidable character whose husband had made a fortune from the railways. He had just died, however, leaving Nadezhda with lots of money, and with eleven children, whom she brought up with a rule of iron.

Actually, the beginning of Tchaikovsky's friendship with Nadezhda was fairly normal. In late 1876, she wrote to him for the first time, about some short pieces she'd commissioned from him, and telling him how much his art meant to her. (It really did have an extraordinary effect on her; once, when

Tchaikovsky sent her a little funeral march he'd written, she wrote him a typically cool, down-to-earth letter describing her reaction to the piece: "I want to sob, I want to die, I long for another life . . . life, death, happiness, pain all merge. I soar above the earth." I think she liked it!) Tchaikovsky was very moved by her enthusiasm, and they became great friends – best friends, in fact. They confided in each other. She told him that she was cut off from the world, sitting at home running her business and arranging for her children to be married off – her rules for their marriages being that the couples mustn't be in love, and that she herself would never have to meet the in-laws' families. Occasionally, she would go to plays and concerts; but she always tried to stay hidden from the rest of the audience. She was, in fact, an unusual woman; Tchaikovsky found that intriguing. In turn, he told her all the secrets of his inner life (except for his homosexuality, which he never mentioned). The two exchanged photos, swore mutual love. Later, he dedicated his first truly great symphony, his Fourth, to her, always referring to it as "our symphony"; the dedication reads simply: "To my best friend". Tchaikovsky would sometimes stay at Nadezhda's various houses; they would take holidays together.

But they never met.

So how did they manage to go on holiday together, how come he stayed at her houses, you may ask – reasonable questions. Well, the answer is that they'd go to all sorts of lengths to be as close as possible, while at the same time making every conceivable effort to avoid an actual meeting; they were worried that a face-to-face encounter would spoil their ideal friendship. With Nadezhda safely out of Moscow, for instance, Tchaikovsky would go round to her house there, inspecting all the rooms (including the bathrooms) and smoking as he prowled around, leaving his smell for her to come home to. That was strange enough; but not nearly as strange as the holidays they took "together". Nadezhda owned a country estate, and in the summer would stay in the main house with her family. One summer, Tchaikovsky went to stay in a smaller house nearby on the estate, was spoilt rotten by her servants and corresponded with her every day – but of course they never exchanged a word in person. It was all very – well, weird. Once, Tchaikovsky hid in the bushes watching a family party that the von Mecks were having; the children knew that he was there, but weren't allowed to mention it – or even to look in his direction. Nadezhda also arranged for Tchaikovsky to be in Florence at the same time as her. There the two of them were sometimes a little too close for Tchaikovsky's comfort; he was worried because he saw Nadezhda at the theatre – and got upset because he noticed her looking into his window as she passed his house every day. (But then, being Tchaikovsky, he was upset when she left and *didn't* look into his window every day.) Only once on these holidays did real disaster strike: Nadezhda and Tchaikovsky came "nose to nose" (as he put it) in a forest, by accident. It was a shock for both of them; but they just bowed slightly to each other, and passed on.

Gradually, Tchaikovsky became more and more dependent on Nadezhda for financial support. Many composers have been supported by private individuals, so that wasn't odd in itself; but of course, between the two of them, it became a peculiar situation. Nadezhda had to beg Tchaikovsky to accept her help, even though he was constantly letting her know how poor he was; he would make her feel terribly guilty about offering him money, giving the impression that he was taking it only in order to make her happy. It was all topsy-turvy; Nadezhda seems to have been more grateful to Tchaikovsky than he was to her (at least on the surface). Eventually, she offered to provide him with a regular income; he responded miserably, telling her that he had been through one of the most dreadful days of his life before deciding to accept it. In 1878, with her encouragement, he finally gave up his professorship at the Moscow Conservatoire; he was a free man! (Of course, while longing to give up the job, he agonised over how to tell the head of the Conservatoire – and then, typically, was hurt when the head said that it was fine for him to leave. Obviously, Tchaikovsky complained, he hadn't been appreciated as a teacher!)

Well, the correspondence-course friendship is a strange story; but at least it's basically a positive one. However, not long after he first encountered Nadezhda, Tchaikovsky got himself involved in another relationship that ended up *far* from positively; in fact, it proved to be a total disaster for everybody involved. Much earlier, in 1868, Tchaikovsky had almost got married to a famous singer – strange, considering that he really wasn't attracted to women; but while he was fretting over whether or not to make a serious proposal, the singer rather settled things by marrying someone else. (Tchaikovsky was probably more relieved than upset – especially when he saw her again years later, and wrote rather ungallantly that she was now "as fat as a bubble".) Now, in 1877, he actually did get married, to a girl called Antonina; it was a hideous mistake.

Antonina had met Tchaikovsky a few years earlier, when she'd been studying the piano at the Moscow Conservatoire.

Tchaikovsky didn't even remember her; but she obviously remembered him, because suddenly she started to write him letters, telling him that she loved and adored him, and that she had to see him. Up to him, of course, she wrote – but she would kill herself if he didn't come to visit her. No pressure, then. Perhaps under normal circumstances (or as normal as Tchaikovsky's circumstances ever were), he would have had the sense to ignore these pleas and threats; or would have dealt with them gently but firmly. But it so happened that around that time Tchaikovsky had become particularly worried about people knowing that he and Modest were homosexuals. The reason was that Modest had just got a full-time job as tutor to a deaf and mute boy (whom Tchaikovsky adored) called Kolya; Modest took his job very seriously, and was a devoted and talented teacher. Tchaikovsky worried about the effect on that relationship if his and Modest's "secret" were to become too public; and so he was keen to get married, if only to confuse the issue.

But there was also another, deeply peculiar reason that propelled him into Antonina's arms. Just around the time that she floated into his life, Tchaikovsky had started to write what would be his most famous opera, called 'Eugene Onegin' (pronounced "On-iay-gin", with a hard "g" – i.e. *not* "one gin" as in "one gin and tonic, please"). The main character in the story, Eugene Onegin himself, is a cold fish who cruelly ignores the love of a young girl: Tchaikovsky got it into his head that if he were to reject Antonina, he would be acting like Eugene Onegin, and that would be unforgivable. So – he proposed to her. It was madness. He wasn't even the tiniest bit in love with her; he told her so, but she didn't seem to mind. She was so madly in love with him (or so she said) and so thrilled to be able to call this famous, kind man hers, that she would have settled for any conditions for the chance to drag him to the altar.

Even before the wedding, Tchaikovsky was horrible about her. To his sister Sasha, whose place in the country had been for many years his favourite retreat, Tchaikovsky wrote that he wouldn't bring his wife there until it no longer seemed to him "impertinent" that Antonina would become an aunt to Sasha's children – as if that were Antonina's fault! He didn't dare tell most people – even Modest – about the forthcoming wedding, because he knew how horrified they would be. Only his father – now almost senile – was happy; in fact, he jumped for joy when he heard the news. Everybody else, as they found out about it, prophesied catastrophe; and how right they were.

But Tchaikovsky, in his twisted way, had decided that "one cannot avoid one's destiny". The wedding took place in Moscow on July 6th, 1877, in an atmosphere more like a funeral than a wedding. Even if he hadn't realised before, he certainly realised that day that he was making a dreadful mistake. Antonina was pretty and probably good-natured; but she was weak-minded, and didn't even begin to understand what made her husband tick. According to Tchaikovsky, all she could talk about was (a) all the men who were in love with her, and (b) how awful her family was. The final straw came when it turned out that, despite protesting undying love for him, she didn't know a note of his music! After the wedding, he spent less than three weeks with her before running away to stay with Sasha for six weeks, officially to give Antonina time to prepare an apartment for them both in Moscow. Eventually, unwillingly, he returned to Moscow and Antonina. It wasn't the happiest of reunions; on his first morning back with her he wrote to Anatoly: "Death is man's greatest blessing, and I long for it with all my soul." Hmm . . . He later claimed that he'd tried to kill himself around this time by standing in a river and freezing himself to death. (If he did, it didn't work; but it must have been awfully cold.) All in all, one could say that the marriage was not exactly going well. It lasted another twelve days – and that was it.

Tchaikovsky had started to hate Antonina with a violent passion; he wanted to strangle her, in fact. So he got Anatoly to send a faked telegram from St Petersburg, signed with the name of a conductor there, inviting Tchaikovsky to come and discuss details for a forthcoming opera performance. Tchaikovsky rushed off immediately, away from the nightmare of Moscow and Antonina. According to Modest, on arriving in St Petersburg Tchaikovsky fell into a coma for two days; even though that was probably an exaggeration, he was certainly suffering some sort of nervous breakdown.

The marriage was over; that was that. Never again would Tchaikovsky even contemplate a romantic relationship with a woman. Occasionally he would dream of putting his head on a woman's knee and kissing her hands, and he was always jealous of happily married couples; but he knew now that marriage could never be right for him. (He did encourage his manservant Alexei to get married "so that there'll be someone to take care of our linen", as Tchaikovsky put it – charming.) Perhaps it was a sensible decision from his point of view to give up fighting against his nature – but poor Antonina! While those closest to Tchaikovsky surrounded him with reassurance and protection (Modest assuring him that he had always been, and continued to be, "the embodiment of all perfections"), Antonina was abandoned.

As soon as Tchaikovsky was fit to travel, Anatoly whisked him off abroad, with Modest taking over as his older brother's minder when Anatoly had to go home; Tchaikovsky didn't return to Russia for eighteen months. Of course, since for Modest and Anatoly Tchaikovsky could do no wrong, in their eyes the whole thing was entirely Antonina's fault. Nadezhda was even worse; deeply jealous of Antonina (although Nadezhda couldn't exactly have married Tchaikovsky herself without at least meeting him once or twice!), she told Tchaikovsky that he had behaved like a saint; and that if Antonina seemed to be suffering, not to worry – her type never really felt anything anyway. Horrible! The only person in Tchaikovsky's circle who seems to have stuck up for Antonina at all was his sister Sasha. Sasha invited the poor woman to stay with her; Tchaikovsky was horrified. "Send her away," he pleaded, " . . . for the sake of all that is holy in this world." And in another, appalling, letter, he added: "I beg you, when you grieve over her sufferings, to recall that forty thousand of her moral sufferings would not compare with all that I have experienced this whole time." Hmm . . . this episode did *not* bring out the best in Tchaikovsky.

Shaken as he was by the marriage disaster, Tchaikovsky felt that it was a "miracle" that he didn't go mad; but then again, he was always being amazed by his continuing sanity, convinced that his sufferings were enough to send most men over the edge. In fact, two of his greatest works were written during this period: 'Eugene Onegin', most of which was written just before and after his wedding, and his Fourth Symphony, the one dedicated to Nadezhda (opening with a trumpet call depicting fate). Eventually, Tchaikovsky was ready to return to Russia, but he was still pretty delicate. There's a rather disturbing account of him at around this time, written by a singer who'd sung many of Tchaikovsky's songs but didn't know him personally. She sent Tchaikovsky an invitation to dinner. The answer came back: yes, he would come – but only if he could sit between his twin brothers, and if the singer would agree not to talk to him directly. Desperate to meet the great man, she agreed to this strange request. Tchaikovsky duly turned up, surrounded by Anatoly and Modest, and sat silently at dinner, with his eyes lowered; sounds like a fun party. After dinner, Tchaikovsky whispered to Anatoly that he'd like to hear the singer singing; she agreed readily, and Tchaikovsky sat at the piano. She prepared to start. No, said the brothers; she was standing too close to Tchaikovsky – could she move a bit further away? Then they sat either side of him as he played, just in case – just in case what? It's hard to know. All most peculiar. Was Tchaikovsky really still close to collapse? Or was he just being

145

melodramatic? Perhaps a bit of both; but then he confused the singer still further by turning up at her house the next morning, all smiles and friendliness, to thank her for the lovely evening! *What* an odd man he was.

Anyway, he recovered in time from his mess of a marriage; and his career as a composer flourished. Tchaikovsky enjoyed his greatest triumph yet when 'Eugene Onegin' was performed in a new production in St Petersburg in 1884, five years after its premiere. (So maybe the opera was worth all the trouble it had caused!) His reputation was spreading abroad as well; performances of his music became more frequent, and despite the nastiness of some critics (a famous critic in Vienna wrote that Tchaikovsky's Violin Concerto "stinks to the ears" – delightful), his works were becoming more popular in several countries. It helped when Tchaikovsky discovered, much to his surprise, that he could conduct rather well; he decided to conduct one of his own operas in Moscow, and was astonished when everybody told him how well he did it. (He reported to Nadezhda on how happy this had made him; even if the pain and terror had taken several years off his life, he wrote, it was worth it.) After that, he was able to accept engagements to conduct concerts of his own music at home and abroad. He probably wasn't *that* good as a conductor, but he wasn't hopeless; and it was exciting for audiences to see the man who'd created this beautiful music re-creating it in front of them.

By 1890, when we first met, or at least saw him, he was one of the most famous men in Russia, a hero to almost everyone who cared about music at all, from the Tsar (the King, or Emperor, of Russia) to the people in some of the most remote Russian cities. He was still very much the old Tchaikovsky though, spending a lot of his time in floods of tears (especially when he was away from the few people he loved), constantly worried about his health, almost always sure that his powers as a composer were dwindling – and so on. One genuinely upsetting thing happened to him in that year: he received a letter out of the blue from Nadezhda, saying that due to financial difficulties she was unable to continue his allowance – and so, sorry and goodbye. By this point, Tchaikovsky really didn't need the money – partly because his music was played so often, and partly because the Tsar was also supporting him by now – so it wasn't the financial blow that mattered; but to be suddenly dropped by this woman who'd been prepared to do anything for him for the past thirteen years, whose love for his music had been, so she had always insisted, at the very centre of her existence, was humiliating (especially when he discovered that her financial difficulties weren't really serious). He, of course, wrote back immediately – and kept writing; but from Nadezhda there was just silence. There was nothing he could do; it was as if she'd moved to another planet. We still don't know why she behaved like that. Perhaps she went a bit mad; or perhaps her family, some of whom were probably very jealous of her love for Tchaikovsky, managed to separate the two friends, first of all by somehow forcing her to write that letter, and then by intercepting his replies to her, so that she would think he had abandoned her, while he thought she'd abandoned him. Whatever the truth, it was a strange – and sad – ending to the strange friendship.

On the other hand, there was another, very positive development in his life: in 1888, after years of living in temporary accommodation in Moscow or St Petersburg, staying with his friends and relatives in the country, or going abroad, Tchaikovsky acquired the house in which we saw him near the beginning of this chapter. In fact, he ended up living in a few different homes in his last years; but they were all in the same area, near Klin, peaceful but also quite conveniently close to Moscow. And, despite his constant complaints and worries, Tchaikovsky did experience contentment and happiness there, fussed over and bullied by the devoted Alexei, and sticking to his strict routine of work, walks and relaxation.

He was coping with his trips to Moscow and to St Petersburg a bit better, too; whenever he could escape from all the people he didn't want to see there, he would surround himself with a group of admiring young men, whose company he enjoyed hugely. This set was headed by Tchaikovsky's beloved nephew, Sasha's son Vladimir, known as "Bob" – a nickname deriving not from the English name Robert, but from a Russian word for baby, "bebinka"; somehow the nickname, which had shrunk to "Bobik" and then to "Bob", had carried over from "Bob's" earliest years. Tchaikovsky had written three orchestral suites (like symphonies, but usually with shorter movements, all based on particular dances); this set of young men was known for some reason as his "Fourth Suite". Bob was really at the centre of his uncle's life now, as much as Modest or as Anatoly, who had moved with his wife and children to far-off Georgia. "Uncle Petya" took enormous pleasure in his nephew's company (although, being Tchaikovsky, he complained that the happiness he felt when together with Bob wasn't as powerful as the misery he suffered when they parted. Always looking on the bright side.) It was to Bob that Tchaikovsky dedicated the work that he felt was his finest of all, his Sixth Symphony. Written in 1893, it was to become known as the 'Pathétique' Symphony; that sounds awfully miserable – but actually the word was probably supposed to mean "passionate", rather than "pathetic". (On the other hand, it's true that whereas most symphonies end with fast, exciting movements, this one ends with a slow, sombre one, which leaves you feeling incredibly sad.) Tchaikovsky admitted that there was a story behind the symphony, but he wouldn't tell anyone what it was. He did say, however, that he suffered "from an anguish that cannot be expressed in words (in my new symphony there is a passage that seems to express it well)". So obviously it was a piece that meant a lot to him.

And now comes the bit I warned you about . . .

On October 10th, 1893, Tchaikovsky arrived in St Petersburg to prepare the orchestra for the first performance of the 'Pathétique' Symphony. As the rehearsals progressed, he was a bit dismayed that the musicians didn't seem to love the piece as he'd hoped they would; so he kept the rehearsals short – too short. Nevertheless, on October 16th, the stage was set for a great event, as the audience crowded into the Hall of the Nobility for the concert. Tchaikovsky came on stage – and the public went mad. Here was their beloved Russian composer, standing in front of them to conduct his important new symphony.

Tchaikovsky made his usual series of rapid, almost violent, bows, repeatedly bending over as far as he could and then straightening up with amazing speed. Finally, when the ovation had subsided into an expectant hush, he turned to the orchestra, put on his little half-spectacles, tapped his conductor's baton on his music stand – and the first performance of Tchaikovsky's greatest work began.

And it failed.

The trouble was that it just wasn't a good performance; at the end, although the audience cheered him loudly, Tchaikovsky could tell that they weren't convinced. It wasn't really a disaster; but it certainly wasn't the triumph for which he'd been hoping. After all he'd poured into this work, it was depressing to feel that it had been rejected. But still, there was a difference from his earlier failures – this time he *knew* that he'd written a great work, and nobody was going to convince him otherwise. So, despite his disappointment, he seemed to be in good spirits over the next few days, as he stayed with Bob in Modest's apartment in St Petersburg, and held meetings, both professional and personal, with various people.

On October 20th, he went to the theatre with Modest and various members of the "Fourth Suite". After the play, Tchaikovsky went to talk to the leading actor. For some reason, the subject of death came up (according to Modest's account). In earlier times, Tchaikovsky had been terrified of "the old woman standing behind his chair", as he described death, and would-n't allow people to use words such as "coffin" or "grave" in his presence; but now he referred to it as "the repulsive snub-nosed monster", and, according to Modest, was no longer so scared of it. In conversation with the actor, he dismissed the subject with optimistic words: "I feel I shall live a long time." Leaving the theatre, Tchaikovsky escorted some of his young men to a restaurant called Leiner's.

It's from this point that the details of the story start to become unclear. It seems to have been a merry enough meal, with Tchaikovsky eating his favourite dish, macaroni, and drinking white wine mixed with soda water; but according to Bob's younger brother Yuri, at one stage Tchaikovsky insisted on drinking an unboiled glass of water, which in disease-ridden St Petersburg, with its filthy water, would have been a foolish thing to do – extremely dangerous, in fact. The trouble is that it doesn't seem as if Yuri was there at the restaurant – so should we trust his account? There are so many different versions of the events of those few days that it's impossible to know which one to believe.

Later that night, Tchaikovsky had stomach trouble: but then he often did, so he doesn't seem to have been too worried. In the morning (according to Modest) he set out to visit a conductor friend; but then, feeling ill, he went back to Modest's apartment instead. He managed to write some letters, one of which was about some concerts he was planning for the next year; and then, although he couldn't eat, he sat with Modest and a guest at lunch. According to Modest, it was now – when he was already ill – that Tchaikovsky insisted on drinking the unboiled glass of water. Modest had suggested calling a doctor that morning (or so he claimed later); but Tchaikovsky, who was scared of doctors and was used to treating his own stomach troubles, refused. Now Modest went out to the theatre to supervise rehearsals of a play he had written; while he was out, Tchaikovsky's condition became more serious. At five, Modest got home; getting alarmed, he sent for a distinguished doctor called Dr Vasili Bertesson. Dr Bertesson was out, unfortunately, so Tchaikovsky's sufferings continued without any relief; but Modest can't have been *that* alarmed, because he went out to the theatre again from five until eight.

By the time he got back, things were getting desperate. Tchaikovsky was losing everything he'd eaten for the past few days – or rather, it seemed, everything he'd eaten in his entire life! Finally Dr Bertesson got Modest's note, and arrived. Tchaikovsky, super-sensitive as ever, apologised for ruining his evening; but Dr Bertesson wasn't worried about missing his planned trip to the opera. He had something more pressing on his mind: it looked to him as if his patient, Russia's most famous composer, had developed one of the most dreadful of all diseases – cholera, the illness that almost forty years earlier had killed Tchaikovsky's mother. Dr Bertesson rushed off to fetch his brother Lev, who was an even better-known doctor; from then on, the two of them took turns looking after their distinguished patient. Meanwhile, Tchaikovsky was in agony, ghastly things happening at both ends. (I'll spare you the grisly details – well, most of them.) His head and extremities started to turn blue; and for a time, nasty black spots appeared on his face. Modest, Bob and whoever else was around massaged him furiously all over, in an attempt to alleviate the pain. At one point, Tchaikovsky turned to his brother: "It's not cholera, is it?" he asked. "No, no," said Modest soothingly, "it can't be." Shortly afterwards, however, Tchaikovsky overheard the doctors giving instructions to Modest about precautionary measures to be taken for avoiding the spread of the disease. "So – it *is* cholera," gasped Tchaikovsky.

By the next morning, though, his condition appeared to have become more stable. Dr Bertesson arrived at eleven, and asked the patient how he felt. "Vastly improved," was the answer. "Thank you – you have snatched me from the jaws of death." If only. It was true that the main stage of the disease had passed; but it had done so much damage to Tchaikovsky's body that complications were bound to follow. At least he was no longer infectious – not that the fear of infection would have kept his desperate relatives away. He apologised to Bob, who had helped to mop up all the horrible substances emerging from his uncle's body. "You'll never respect me again after this," Tchaikovsky said sadly. He kept telling everybody to go to bed, to get some rest; but they wouldn't leave him. There was too much to do, anyway: some close friends and relatives had to be told what was happening; the police had to be notified (since cholera was a disease that had to be officially controlled and monitored); and there was constant work to be done to keep Tchaikovsky in as little discomfort as possible. Word was beginning to spread around St Petersburg that the great man was dangerously ill. People started to arrive at the apartment; few were allowed in, but they stayed outside anyway, hoping for crumbs of information. Eventually, Modest wrote out bulletins about the patient's health, and had them posted outside the building. The news wasn't good.

The main worry was that Tchaikovsky's kidneys weren't functioning; and that always proves fatal. The doctors recommended immersion in a warm bath, as a last resort; all the Tchaikovskys were worried about that, though, because Tchaikovsky's mother had been given that treatment, and had died at the very moment she'd been put into the bath. But by October 24th, when all else had obviously failed, the family gave in, and Tchaikovsky was placed in the bath. At first, he murmured that it was quite pleasant; but then he felt so weak that he asked to be taken out. His condition hadn't improved at all. The doctors had failed; now there was nothing more they could do. Tchaikovsky seemed to give up too; he became delirious, and – again according to Modest's account – uttered curses on the name of Nadezhda von Meck. A priest read prayers for the departing, as Tchaikovsky slipped into unconsciousness. At around three in the morning on October 25th, his eyes opened suddenly; they rested on the faces of Modest and Bob with a look of "infinite love and anguished farewell". Ten minutes later, Tchaikovsky was dead.

It's one of the most horrible stories of any composer – and there are enough terrible ones!

The aftermath was hideous, too. Of course, people from all over Russia were stunned and overwhelmed by the news. Just a few days earlier, the great man had been alive and well, conducting his new symphony (and preparing to go to Moscow to conduct the first performance there). And now – he was gone. Dead. It was widely known that Tchaikovsky had had a secret life that people weren't supposed to talk about; so perhaps it's not surprising that rumours started to fly around St Petersburg from the moment he died, if not before. What *is* rather surprising is that they're still flying around today.

As often happens in such tragic cases, people started looking for someone to blame. First, they rounded on the establishment where Tchaikovsky had supposedly drunk the fatal glass of water; that put Leiner's restaurant into serious financial difficulties – a bit unfair if he hadn't actually drunk the water there in the first place! But it turned out that many of the restaurants in St Petersburg *did* have a bad habit of cooling down the glasses of boiled water they served their patrons by adding tap water – a crazy thing to do in St Petersburg. (So perhaps the one good thing to come out of the whole ghastly business was that

that custom was stamped out.) Then some of the newspapers turned on the doctors who had treated Tchaikovsky: they should have called in other doctors, cholera specialists, said the newspapers; they should have put him in the bath earlier; they should have spent more time at his bedside; and so on. It must have been incredibly painful for the doctors to read that stuff; it was true that they weren't cholera specialists, but they had followed the practices of the time, and had done their best. What *was* true, however, was that if they had been called in just a few hours earlier, they might possibly have been able to save the patient. And for that, Modest probably felt like a murderer; perhaps if he hadn't been out at the theatre . . . but how could he have known? Guilt isn't always built on reason, though; I'm sure he was haunted by remorse for the rest of his life.

In time, even darker rumours started to surface. Some of them were plain silly – such as the one that claimed that Modest had murdered Tchaikovsky over a quarrel about a lover; but some took hold, and people still believe them today. The main one was that Tchaikovsky was so depressed about the failure of his symphony, and about his secret life, that he deliberately drank the glass of unboiled water. "What does it matter, anyway?" he is supposed to have muttered. That would have made his death suicide – or perhaps semi-suicide, since he couldn't have been absolutely sure that the water would kill him. Or was it water at all? Another version insists that Tchaikovsky actually took poison – arsenic, perhaps. But he does seem to have known that people would eventually come to appreciate his symphony; and he'd lived with his secret life for a very long time now. So why else would he have killed himself?

Again, there were various murky theories. These were fuelled by the second performance of the 'Pathétique' Symphony, which took place in St Petersburg shortly after Tchaikovsky's death. A bust of the composer, surrounded by palm trees, overlooked the orchestra; at the end, as the music trailed away into the tragic silence that ends the symphony, the only sound was of sobbing – the whole audience was united in desperate grief. And now they thought they understood that last movement: Tchaikovsky, knowing that he was going to kill himself, had written his own Requiem. The fact that he'd composed a few pieces after the symphony didn't matter; this was his last will and testament. All sorts of new explanations were given for his suicide: there was a story of him being screamed at in the street the day before he "fell ill", by a woman who claimed that he had ruined the life of her son; another story had it that he'd been having a love affair with a member of the royal family; and so on.

Perhaps the strangest rumour of all didn't surface until the 1960s. According to this story, Tchaikovsky had been having a love affair with the nephew of an aristocrat; the aristocrat found out, and threatened to expose the shocking secret. This could have meant total disgrace and exile to Siberia for Tchaikovsky; it would also, according to the old boys of his former school, the Imperial School of Jurisprudence, have brought disgrace upon the school and on all the boys who had ever been there. It sounds unlikely – but remember, this was a different world. So – as this story goes – a "court of honour" was held in (or near) St Petersburg, with a committee of old boys of the school sitting in judgement on Tchaikovsky. They discussed the matter for hours; then Tchaikovsky rushed out, distraught. A decision had been reached: the only way to save the honour of the school was for Tchaikovsky to kill himself.

A strange and horrible story – but can it be true? Why did nobody on the "jury" ever write about it? And why did the story only get told in the 1960s? Also, the whole poison theory is a bit unconvincing, because there's no poison that would have produced the same symptoms as cholera. Unless, of course, everybody who was present at his deathbed and wrote about it afterwards was lying; but that's a lot of people to share the same lies.

The glass of water story is a bit strange, as well. The evidence for him having drunk it at the restaurant is pretty unconvincing; and according to Modest, Tchaikovsky only drank it the next day at home, well after he'd become ill. It's true that he had been a little careless in the past about drinking unboiled water in other places; but surely he would have been careful in notorious St Petersburg, where cholera was fairly rampant – unless he'd really wanted to kill himself. But even if he *had* wanted to, why choose such an unreliable and painful way to do it? We'll probably never know the full truth. There is still talk today of exhuming the body, and testing it; that might give us some more definite answers about how he died (though probably not *why*). But for the present, all we can do is to make informed guesses. My guess – and it is just a guess – is that Tchaikovsky didn't take poison; and he didn't drink a "fatal" glass of water. I think that what *may* have happened is that he caught cholera from someone with whom he'd had a brief love affair, who was perhaps living in unclean conditions. St Petersburg's outbreaks of cholera spread mostly through the unhygienic slums of the city; it was rare that people living or staying in the cleaner areas contracted the disease. If that's how Tchaikovsky had become infected (and it is possible to catch cholera from other people) the family would have wanted to keep it quiet, hiding the truth as they always did about Tchaikovsky's secret life; so perhaps that's why they would have invented the glass of water story. But maybe I've got it completely wrong.

Whatever – the point was (and is) that Tchaikovsky was dead, at the height of his powers (among his future plans had been a flute concerto and – gnash – a cello concerto). People throughout Russia were in shock; they had identified so deeply with his music that they felt now that something inside themselves had been torn away. And that, I'm afraid, is where we'll have to leave them, and him. The next chapter will be more cheerful – honestly . . .

Facts of Life

·1·

Pyotr Ilyich Tchaikovsky was born on April 25th, 1840 – or May 7th, 1840, depending on where you were at the time. According to our calendar, he was born on May 7th; but Russia's calendar was twelve days behind that of most of the rest of the world throughout the nineteenth century. (So the Russian people could enjoy twelve more days of passion and suffering than everybody else.)

Beloved parents . . .

Tchaikovsky's father Ilya was a warm, affectionate and trusting soul; sometimes that made life tricky for him. Not only was he cheated out of that job when Tchaikovsky was eight; later he lost all his savings, when a woman with whom he was besotted lured him into a bad investment. Still, he seems to have been a cheerful, lovable character. He was married three times: once before he married Tchaikovsky's mother, and again, after her death, to a woman known to her stepchildren as "the Bun". "The Bun" was lovely, even though Tchaikovsky complained about her being a bit too fat and lazy.

Tchaikovsky's mother, Alexandra Andreievna (i.e. "daughter of Andrei"), was apparently cooler than her husband; but Tchaikovsky, in his later recollections, transformed her into a saint. He remembered her as amazingly beautiful, with wonderful eyes and the most perfect hands; probably because of this, in later life he became strangely obsessed with people's hands. If he was in love with someone who got an infected finger, and Tchaikovsky happened to see it, he would fall out of love immediately. Yet another peculiar quirk.

· 2 ·

Tchaikovsky wasn't great, but nor was he hopeless, at his school-work; and the same could be said of his efforts at the Ministry of Justice. He received some commendations from his boss there; but in the summer of 1862, he failed to get the promotion for which he'd been hoping. This disappointment probably set him even more firmly onto his new path as a musician. Anyway, he'd never have been much of a success in the Ministry; he was too dreamy. There was a story told in his family that once Tchaikovsky was carrying an official document, which he was supposed to deliver; on the way, he stopped to talk to somebody. Distracted by the conversation, he kept tearing off little pieces of paper while he was talking, putting them in his mouth, and chewing them; suddenly he noticed that he'd eaten most of the document! No, Tchaikovsky wasn't cut out to be a civil servant.

A changed man . . .

It's really difficult to recognise the Tchaikovsky we know in 1890 from his early photos; he looks completely different. But perhaps that's not surprising; he was *completely different. The only threads that seem to have run consistently throughout his whole life were his deep sensitivity, and his love of the arts – books, theatre and dance, as well as music. (He was less enthusiastic about the visual arts – painting, sculpture, and suchlike.) During his time in the Ministry, Tchaikovsky doesn't seem to have been very shy at all – what a contrast with his later self! One of the few friends who knew him during both the early 1860s and the 1890s remembered walking with him along St Petersburg's most famous street in the 1860s and making rather slow progress, because Tchaikovsky was endlessly raising his hat to all his elegant acquaintances. Thirty years later the two men took the same walk together; this time Tchaikovsky, now one of the most famous men in Russia, knew no one.*

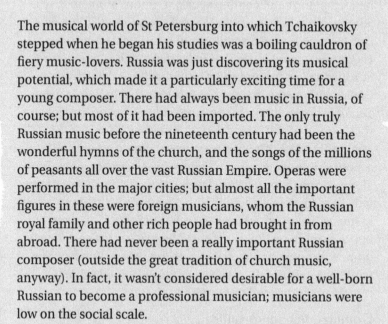

·3·

The musical world of St Petersburg into which Tchaikovsky stepped when he began his studies was a boiling cauldron of fiery music-lovers. Russia was just discovering its musical potential, which made it a particularly exciting time for a young composer. There had always been music in Russia, of course; but most of it had been imported. The only truly Russian music before the nineteenth century had been the wonderful hymns of the church, and the songs of the millions of peasants all over the vast Russian Empire. Operas were performed in the major cities; but almost all the important figures in these were foreign musicians, whom the Russian royal family and other rich people had brought in from abroad. There had never been a really important Russian composer (outside the great tradition of church music, anyway). In fact, it wasn't considered desirable for a well-born Russian to become a professional musician; musicians were low on the social scale.

But now all that was changing. In the mid-1830s, a man called Glinka wrote an opera in Russian, called 'A Life for the Tsar'. The story was Russian, and the music sounded Russian, its melodies based on folksongs and church hymns. It took time for the work to catch on. At first, people ignored it: "Your opera's a clinker, Glinka," they said. (No, actually they didn't say that – I just made it up; but I'm sure they used words to that effect.) Gradually, though, the opera, and the ideas it represented, became more and more popular, and led to a whole flowering of Russian music; by the time Tchaikovsky was ready to start taking music seriously, the situation for Russian musicians had changed completely. But, this being Russia, the opening up of this new artistic world aroused deep passions; and these passions led to violent quarrels.

Basically, there were two musical camps: on one side was a famous pianist and composer called Anton Rubinstein, who felt that what Russia needed to make it into a great musical centre was classical discipline and traditional education. He wanted young musicians to learn from the great Central European masters; and so he founded the St Petersburg Conservatoire, the first proper music school in Russia, where Tchaikovsky studied. On the other side of the musical fence was a group of composers known as either "The Five" or "The Mighty Handful". Their mission was to found an entirely new school of Russian music, initially using classical models but also drawing on purely Russian sources, as Glinka had done; only then, they felt, could their beloved country express itself in music. They started up a "Free Music School", in direct opposition to the Conservatoire. The two camps hated each other with truly Russian fervour; in later years, Tchaikovsky, with his gentle charm, was one of the few people able to remain on fairly good terms with both sides.

Domineering personalities . . .

Both camps were composed of amazing, unforgettable characters. Anton Rubinstein, only ten years older than Tchaikovsky, was a major celebrity, and a human whirlwind. He composed mountains of music, and was a fine conductor and, above all, a thrilling pianist, whose performances roused his audiences to fever-pitch. His energy was astonishing; he would tour all around Europe (and later America) giving solo recitals that lasted at least three hours – and the next morning he would repeat the whole programme free of charge so that poor music students would be able to hear it. The Conservatoire was a project very close to his heart; whenever he was in St Petersburg, he would spend countless hours at the school, teaching and administrating.

Tchaikovsky worshipped him (in a complicated sort of way,

of course); for many years Rubinstein's portrait was almost the only decoration on his wall. In later years, Tchaikovsky described Rubinstein (in public, at least) as "the greatest of artists and the noblest of men". Unfortunately, although he was very good to Tchaikovsky, Rubinstein never quite returned the compliment. He liked Tchaikovsky and respected him, but he never treated him as an equal. Strange, since Tchaikovsky was so obviously the greater composer; perhaps that was the problem.

"The Five" were a completely different bunch of people. They all had professions other than music; some of them did really well in their other lives, as well as being marvellous composers. (One of them, for instance, Alexander Borodin, was perhaps more highly thought of as a chemist than as a musician during his lifetime – at least in some circles. When Borodin was a young man, his chemistry professor was dismayed by his favourite student's interest in music, and advised him to give it up: "You can't hunt two hares at the same time", he warned.) The least talented of the five composers, César Cui, was a music critic; he wrote a series of nasty reviews of Tchaikovsky's music over the years – but would then write him very friendly private letters. Most odd. The leader of "The Five", Mily (not "Milly", but "Mily", meaning "dear" or "sweet" – rather inappropriate in this case) Balakirev, was the strangest character of all. He was a fanatical bully, who in later years became a religious bigot. Tchaikovsky was quite scared of him, and felt that Balakirev's company weighed him down "like a stone". Still, in his insufferable way Balakirev did Tchaikovsky some good; in fact, it was he who suggested that Tchaikovsky write 'Romeo and Juliet', his first great success. Then he tried to tell Tchaikovsky exactly how to compose it; luckily, Tchaikovsky ignored him, and managed to keep Balakirev quiet by dedicating the work to him – a good move.

· 4 ·

Having established himself in Moscow as a professor, but still relatively unknown as a composer, in 1866 Tchaikovsky began working on his most ambitious task yet – writing a symphony. Composing a huge piece like that for the first time is rarely easy for any composer; and for Mr Neurotic Tchaikovsky, it was pure hell. First, he worried that he was going to die soon and leave it unfinished; then he decided that he hated the whole human race, so there was no point in writing music for it; then he couldn't sleep, had hallucinations, went numb in all his extremities – and so on. Nice relaxing time all round, in fact. At one point, a doctor was brought in to examine him and announced that the patient was "one step short of madness". (Sounds like quite a short step!)

Eventually, though, he finished the piece. His First Symphony, 'Winter Daydreams', isn't a great work, perhaps, but it has many beauties; and when it was finally performed in 1868, it got people talking. Some of the talk wasn't nice, especially from the critics – usually the case when a new voice makes itself heard. (In fact, there are still quite a few people today who don't appreciate Tchaikovsky's music – well, it's their loss.) But it was generally accepted that, like him or not, here was a composer with something important to say. And Tchaikovsky kept improving; always deeply self-critical, he actually burnt his first two operas, despite the months and months of work they'd taken. He certainly didn't do things by halves!

Humiliation from a friend ...

The Moscow Conservatoire, where Tchaikovsky started to teach as soon as he'd finished his studies in St Petersburg, was found-ed and run by Anton Rubinstein's younger brother, Nikolai Rubinstein. He was another larger-than-life character. Also a

*famous pianist – though never as celebrated as his brother –
he used to pound his poor pianos so hard that they'd collapse
under his hands into stacks of wood and sawdust; a spare
instrument had to be kept on hand for all his concerts! He had
a violent temper, too; once, when he felt that a clarinet student
at the Conservatoire had played badly in a concert, he went up
to him and kept slapping the poor clarinettist around the face
until the boy, not surprisingly, burst into tears. Still, Nikolai
had a kind heart underneath all the bluster, and he was very
good to Tchaikovsky; he insisted that Tchaikovsky live in his
house for five years, so that he wouldn't need to pay any rent.
Nikolai also conducted the first performances of many of
Tchaikovsky's new works.*

*He was really a bit much at times, though, even to those
closest to him. Soon after Tchaikovsky had moved to Moscow,
Nikolai discovered that his young friend was easily frightened;
so he had lots of fun jumping out at the poor neurotic
composer and startling him, reducing Tchaikovsky to a state of
near-constant twittering. The most famous story about the two
men doesn't show Nikolai in a good light at all – which is a bit
unfair, considering how much he did for Tchaikovsky. It was all
rather unfortunate, really. Tchaikovsky had written a piano
concerto, his first, and wanted to dedicate it to Nikolai; so he
played proudly through the first movement for his friend.
Silence. Tchaikovsky, increasingly nervous, played the other two
movements. "Well?" he asked. At this point (according to
Tchaikovsky, at least), a torrent of abuse poured out of Nikolai:
the concerto was useless, worthless, horrible. Humiliated,
Tchaikovsky left the room; but Nikolai followed him, and went
on and on, insisting that Tchaikovsky should rewrite the whole
piece. Tchaikovsky put his foot down; no, he announced – he
would publish the concerto just as it was. And that was what
he did, dedicating it – not surprisingly – to someone else. What
is surprising is that Nikolai later decided that he really liked*

the concerto, and performed it with great success. Funnily enough, Tchaikovsky's Violin Concerto was to suffer a similar fate, with its original dedicatee refusing to play it. Oh well – today both concertos are among the most popular ever written.

· 5 ·

While teaching at the Conservatoire (a job that he found increasingly oppressive), Tchaikovsky used to dream of escaping to the country – preferably to Kamenka, the estate of his sister, Sasha, and her family. He could only manage it during the holidays, but at least it was something he could look forward to throughout term-time. He loved Kamenka – not so much for the place as for the family life he found there. Tchaikovsky adored babies and young children, so he was thrilled when Sasha kept producing more offspring; there were seven of them in the end. But sadly, his love for several of the children (apart from Bob, of course) was to turn sour. Worst was his eldest niece, Tatiana: having been a beautiful, lovable child, she turned into a walking disaster, with a serious drug problem, bringing unhappiness to all around her. In love with a young musician who showed no interest in marrying her, she got pregnant by him, which in those days was a terrible thing to happen to a young girl. At least these difficult circumstances brought the best out in Tchaikovsky, allowing him to show what a good uncle he could be. He took Tatiana to Paris, stayed there with her for several months, and took care of the baby boy, making sure he was looked after by trustworthy people. Eventually the baby was adopted by Tchaikovsky's older brother Nikolai and his wife. (Tatiana's parents never even knew that the boy existed!) Poor Tatiana – she had a sad life, and a short one. Still in her early twenties, she collapsed and died at a ball in St Petersburg, the very same night that Tchaikovsky made his first successful appearance as a conductor.

"Uncle Petya" had a major effect on the life of another of his nieces as well. In a truly extraordinary arrangement, Tchaikovsky and Nadezhda managed to marry Tatiana's younger sister Anna off to one of Nadezhda's sons, Nikolai – really just in order to strengthen the bond between themselves! A curious thing to do, even by their standards; but luckily, and surprisingly, the marriage turned out OK.

Strange and wonderful friendships ...

When reading about Tchaikovsky's relationships, one has to remember that he lived in a different world from ours, as well as being a unique character; perhaps that explains why some of his friendships seem so strange to us. During his first years in Moscow, for example, one of his friends was an older man, who would invite Tchaikovsky for dinner; then, in a strange ritual, he would cut up an apple, peel it, and feed it bit by bit to Tchaikovsky, groaning, sighing deeply and intoning: "Oh my little father! Oh my dear friend!" Tchaikovsky wouldn't be allowed to go home until he'd finished the last piece; that was the old man's way of being affectionate.

Tchaikovsky's sense of humour can seem very odd, too. Once, he wrote a series of anonymous letters to a friend; the letters contained lots of untrue bad news, ending up with the tidings that Tchaikovsky had been shot. That doesn't sound too funny to us, perhaps, but Tchaikovsky thought it was hilarious. And then he had a hearty laugh when his servant Alexei had an illness that puffed out his cheeks and made him look like a hamster. Hmm ... perhaps Tchaikovsky's best jokes were reserved for his music, which is often delightfully witty.

Some of Tchaikovsky's relationships were lovely, though, and very productive; for instance, he never seems to have had any major quarrels with his publisher, Jurgenson, who supported him through thick and thin. (It's true that Tchaikovsky was one of the few composers – along with Schubert – who

wasn't greedy in money matters; that must have helped.)
Another fine friendship was with his most talented student
from the Moscow Conservatoire, a marvellous character
called Sergei Taneyev. Taneyev started out as Tchaikovsky's
pupil, but ended up almost as a musical father-figure to his
old teacher. He would give Tchaikovsky a no-holds-barred,
blow-by-blow opinion of each new work as it came out. Some-
times his opinions seem to us plain wrong – he was very hard
on Tchaikovsky's monumental Fourth Symphony, for instance
– but Tchaikovsky took his scoldings without complaint. He
knew that Taneyev's judgements were completely honest and
totally unmalicious, and was thrilled on the rare occasions
that Taneyev was actually satisfied with something. (Taneyev
was strict in other ways too; if Tchaikovsky visited him and
wanted to smoke, he was sternly banished to the kitchen and
told to puff up the chimney – quite right!)

Anyway, Taneyev was even more critical of his own works;
for many years, Tchaikovsky was almost the only person to
know that his former pupil had composed anything at all,
because Taneyev kept his music hidden. But he was actually a
unique and wonderful composer; he wrote huge, serious,
impassioned works that are perhaps too complex ever to
become really popular, but are glorious in their own way. As a
teacher, he was greatly loved by his students; these included
Rachmaninov (one of the most popular composers of all time;
you'd probably recognise his beautiful Second Piano Concerto if
you heard it – it gets everywhere, especially into film scores);
Scriabin (another famous composer, a thoroughly peculiar
character who ended up as a mystic preaching a sermon to the
waters of Lake Geneva – I wonder if they listened?); and my
grandfather Julius Isserlis. So Taneyev was a very important
figure in the history of music!

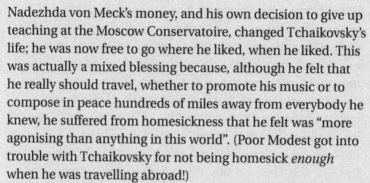

· 6 ·

Nadezhda von Meck's money, and his own decision to give up teaching at the Moscow Conservatoire, changed Tchaikovsky's life; he was now free to go where he liked, when he liked. This was actually a mixed blessing because, although he felt that he really should travel, whether to promote his music or to compose in peace hundreds of miles away from everybody he knew, he suffered from homesickness that he felt was "more agonising than anything in this world". (Poor Modest got into trouble with Tchaikovsky for not being homesick *enough* when he was travelling abroad!)

From his letters, one gets the impression that unless he were travelling with his brothers, Tchaikovsky spent a large proportion of his time abroad crying his eyes out. But when he wasn't weeping or in a depression, he was capable of having a good time on his travels. Paris, for instance, was one of his favourite haunts; he loved the city, and spent long periods there. Another beautiful city where he lived for several months was Florence; here, though, Tchaikovsky's reaction was typically twisted. In 1890, having been there several times before (including the trip with Nadezhda) he decided to spend two and a half months there, working on an opera for which Modest had written the libretto. While he was there, he did nothing but complain about how miserable he was, how he hated the place, etc.; but when he returned to Russia, he wrote a string sextet called 'Souvenir de Florence', one of his happiest and most warmly nostalgic pieces, with an obvious love of the city flowing out of every note. (His attitude to that sextet was typical, too: as he was finishing it, he wrote to Modest, telling him how wonderfully charming his new piece was; then, in one of his very next letters, he says that it's probably time for him to give up composing, because the sextet proves that he's lost all his talent. Pyotr Neurotich Tchaikovsky.)

167

Sometimes quite funny things happened to him on his travels. For instance, there was the time he was travelling incognito on a ship; somehow, however, it became known that this distinguished-looking gentleman could play the piano. So he was bullied into accompanying a lady singer who was on board, and who wished to give the assembled company the inestimable pleasure of hearing her sing. It turned out that the song she chose was by Tchaikovsky! So she started to sing it – badly. Her accompanist ventured to make some simple suggestions; but she stopped him with a condescending smile. Excuse me, she said, but actually her teacher had studied the song with the great Tchaikovsky himself – so perhaps her accompanist would just shut up and allow her to sing it in the right way?

Patriotic fervour ...

Tchaikovsky's fanatical love for Russia was by no means unique; almost all Russians seemed to worship their "motherland". These were turbulent times in Russia's history, though; there was a lot of political unrest, both among Russians and among some of the many nations who were dominated by the Russian Empire, including Poland. Once, there was an assassination attempt on the Tsar of the time, Alexander II, by a young man who was rumoured to be a Pole. The next night, Tchaikovsky happened to be going to the main opera house in Moscow to see Glinka's opera, 'A Life for the Tsar'. There's a scene in the opera in which a group of Polish soldiers kill the Russian hero; that night, however, things turned out a little differently. Rather unexpectedly, the hero, instead of allowing himself to be killed, suddenly lashed out and knocked down several of the "Poles" (who were actually Russian singers, of course). The public broke out into wild applause and cheering. At that point, all the other "Polish soldiers" threw themselves onto the ground; the audience loved it – but Tchaikovsky, patriotic though he was, thought that that was going a bit too far. Glinka's music was sacred!

*Later, Alexander was assassinated. Tchaikovsky was
horrified, as were most Russians, who practically worshipped
their royal family – in a complex sort of way, of course. (Was
anything ever simple in Russia?) Tchaikovsky knew an old lady
whose husband had been part of a failed revolution against
Alexander's father, Nicholas I, and as punishment had been
exiled to freezing Siberia; the old lady would have had good
reason to hate the royal family. But no – instead, when she later
in life she developed cataracts in her eyes, she was convinced
that they were caused by her frenzied weeping after the deaths
of Nicholas and Alexander.*

· 7 ·

Once Tchaikovsky's conducting career was launched, engagements to take part in concerts of his music started to pour in.
He was in demand in many countries, conducting in Poland,
Germany, France, England (where he was awarded an honorary
doctorate by Cambridge University), and so on. The furthest he
went was to America, in 1891, for the grand opening of
Carnegie Hall – still the most famous hall in New York. (It's nice
to think, as one goes to Carnegie Hall today, that Tchaikovsky
was there all those years ago.)

The beginning of the journey was awful, because Tchaikovsky
had just learned of the death of his sister Sasha, who had died
after a long and painful illness. Tchaikovsky was in France at
the time, as was Modest; Modest knew what had happened, but
tried to keep it from his brother until Tchaikovsky was safely
and busily in America. Unfortunately, just before he left,
Tchaikovsky happened to pick up a Russian newspaper in
Paris, and read about it there – *not* a good way to find out
about the death of a sister. To add to that disaster, there was
an upsetting incident shortly after Tchaikovsky's ship set sail,
when one of the passengers threw himself overboard and

drowned. Furthermore, Tchaikovsky was an extremely nervous traveller, very upset by any turbulence. So all in all, rather a rocky start to his first (and, as it turned out, last) transatlantic trip.

But when he got to America, Tchaikovsky enjoyed many things – especially the realisation that he was a genuine celebrity there. He was written about in all the newspapers, in a very enthusiastic and friendly fashion. (A little *too* friendly sometimes: one of them referred to Tchaikovsky as "Pete" and to his teacher Anton Rubinstein as "Tony" – it doesn't sound right, somehow.) There are lots of vivid descriptions of Tchaikovsky from this trip, most of them complimentary about his appearance and manners – although he was very offended when, on the day before his fifty-first birthday, one newspaper wrote that he was sixty! On the whole, though, he was impressed by all the attention, and by the luxurious American hospitality he experienced: at one dinner he ate oysters with turtle sauce – expensive, even if it sounds rather revolting. He was also impressed by the tall and majestic buildings in New York. He got upset, however, when he went onto the roof of a building with thirteen floors; too high for Tchaikovsky – he felt dizzy. (A good thing he's not there now!)

His concerts in America were a wild success; but perhaps the wildest successes Tchaikovsky ever experienced were his performances in his last years in some of the towns spread throughout the Russian Empire – places such as Tiflis in Georgia, where Anatoly was living by then, or Odessa in Ukraine (a very beautiful city, where, incidentally and irrelevantly but interestingly – to me, anyway – my father was born). The people in those far-off places went completely crazy! Groups of students would push Tchaikovsky into a chair and carry him in triumph from the concert hall back to his hotel – a touching gesture, even if it was probably more torture than pleasure to a nervous traveller like Tchaikovsky.

Distinguished colleagues ...

*For us, perhaps the most interesting encounters that
Tchaikovsky had on his travels were with other famous composers. He was very fond of French music in general, and was
on friendly terms with several of the leading French composers.
One of his friends was the fascinating composer Camille Saint-
Saëns (pronounced "San-sonce"). Once Saint-Saëns visited
Moscow to give some concerts there, and he and Tchaikovsky
spent an evening together. The two men discovered that they
were both ballet freaks; so they improvised a ballet, with
Nikolai Rubinstein providing the music at the piano. It
must have looked hilarious! (Tchaikovsky had always loved
imitating famous ballerinas; once, on a train, he suddenly
launched into a passionate Polish dance – rather to the surprise
of the passengers who didn't know him.)*

*The major German composers were more of a problem for
Tchaikovsky. The two most famous ones at that time were the
opera composer Richard Wagner and the composer of virtually
everything except opera, Johannes Brahms. Tchaikovsky never
met Wagner, but he did attend the festival in Bayreuth (in
southern Germany) that Wagner had set up to glorify his own
works. Tchaikovsky recognised that Wagner was a genius in
some ways; but he found his operas a bit much. "Earlier," he
wrote, "music was supposed to delight people – now it torments
and exhausts them."*

*He met Brahms a few times, but they never became friends;
the main problem was that Tchaikovsky really didn't like
Brahms's music. Curiously, they got on better once he'd told
Brahms that! (Brahms was so self-critical that he probably
agreed with him.) They did spend one enjoyable evening
together, along with another wonderful composer, the Norwe-
gian Edvard Grieg. All three were invited to dinner at a house in
Leipzig. At first Tchaikovsky and Brahms were separated at the*

table only by Mrs Grieg; suddenly, though, she got up. "I can't sit between these two! It makes me too nervous," she exclaimed. So Grieg himself took her place, and with his relaxed charm, made the evening go with a swing. One highlight was when Brahms seized a pot of strawberry jam, flourished it in the air, and announced that he was going to have it all, and wouldn't leave any for anyone else. Good to know that these great men communicated on such a profound level . . .

· 8 ·

Tchaikovsky had mixed feelings about his increasing fame. To Nadezhda, he wrote proudly: "I spit, spit, spit upon it all!" (He was always spitting, actually; every time he said something and then worried that he was tempting fate – and that was quite often, because like most Russians, he was highly superstitious – he'd spit hastily, three times over. He loved sneezing, too – yet another oddity.) Despite his constantly growing reputation, he still suffered from a genuine lack of self-confidence. In 1891, after the first performance of a large-scale orchestral tone-poem which had been criticised by his friends, he went straight back to his dressing room and, to everyone's horror, tore up the score. (Luckily the orchestral parts survived, so the work could be performed again after his death; this time some of the same friends who hadn't liked it at first hearing decided that it was a beautiful piece after all – a bit late!) The next year, Tchaikovsky destroyed a symphony on which he'd been working for several months; this time, though, his nephew Bob was so upset at his uncle's rash action that Tchaikovsky, who could never deny his nephew anything, recycled a lot of the material, and used it instead in a new piano concerto.

So nothing was getting any easier as Tchaikovsky grew older; he kept wondering whether he'd lost his gift and should give up composing. He asked himself (and others, of course!)

whether perhaps he should devote himself full-time to his new hobby, gardening, rather than relying on old triumphs to carry along his new creations? And – a major worry – was he standing in the way of young composers?

In fact, he was helping them. He supported the careers of all sorts of young artists, from Russia and abroad, both by using his influence to help them, and by assisting them financially. One young composer to whom he was wonderfully helpful in his last years was Sergei Rachmaninov (the one who wrote that famous piano concerto). Rachmaninov was Tchaikovsky's grand-pupil, as it were, through Taneyev. In 1891, Tchaikovsky had written a one-act opera (with a libretto by Modest), called 'Iolanta'; by chance, the nineteen-year-old Rachmaninov had also written a one-act opera, 'Aleko', as an examination piece for the Moscow Conservatoire, where it won the Great Gold Medal. One day Tchaikovsky approached his young colleague and asked whether Rachmaninov would mind if he arranged for the two operas to be performed together on the same evening. Rachmaninov couldn't believe it. Would he mind? It would be a dream come true.

Tchaikovsky was like a father to many young musicians; a strict one, it's true – if a young composer sent him a score, Tchaikovsky would tell him *exactly* what he thought of it, with no mincing of words. But he was a loving father, and that's what mattered. Strangely enough, one young composer whose talent Tchaikovsky does not seem to have appreciated was a Frenchman who was a protégé of Nadezhda's; this young man lived in Nadezhda's house for two summers, teaching her children the piano, and playing for his patron so that she could listen to music without having to go out. His name was Claude Debussy, and he was to become one of the greatest and most influential composers of the twentieth century.

An apparition from the past . . .

Tchaikovsky may have been the grand old – or at least middle-aged – man of Russian music; but one meeting less than a year before his death brought his early childhood vividly back to life. On New Year's Day, 1893, he went to see his old governess Fanny in Switzerland; the two had not met since Tchaikovsky was a little boy. Before the meeting, Tchaikovsky was terrified; in a characteristically cheerful letter to Modest, written on New Year's Eve, 1892, after mentioning that he was so miserable that it was amazing that he had not gone mad (that sounds familiar!), he told his brother that he felt that by meeting Fanny, a figure from so far in the past, he would be stepping "into the realms of death". In the end, his panicking proved to be quite groundless. Fanny received him with simple pleasure, as if she'd seen him only a year before. She talked about Tchaikovsky's childhood, and showed him the letters and school exercises of his that she'd kept. Tchaikovsky was thrilled. At one point, Fanny asked him which of his brothers he loved the best; all of them, Tchaikovsky replied vaguely. Fanny – who had never met the twins, and remembered only how close Tchaikovsky had been to his older brother, Nikolai, when she'd been governess – scolded him: surely Nikolai must be his favourite, she said. Suddenly, Tchaikovsky decided that she was right, in a way; and immediately wrote letters saying so, not just to Nikolai, but also to Modest. Typical – poor Modest. Still, it was quite a magical way for Tchaikovsky to enter the last year of his life.

· 9 ·

After Tchaikovsky's death, his body was laid out in Modest's apartment; hundreds of people waited for hours for the chance to view the body as it lay dressed in black and covered

up to the neck in a transparent shroud, the room dimly lit with flickering candles. The question has often been asked why, if Tchaikovsky had really died of cholera, his coffin was left open; wouldn't the people who came to see the body have been in danger of catching the disease? Others, though, insist that by then there was no danger, that the body would no longer have been contagious. Anyway, the apartment was sterilised and someone stood at the head of the bed, continually touching the lips and nostrils with disinfectant solution. (A famous cellist insisted on kissing the face and head of the corpse; that seemed a bit risky – but he was probably so drunk that he didn't know what he was doing. Cellists . . .) Fervent Russian Orthodox Requiems were sung over the body, as friends said their farewells. At nine p.m. on the day he'd died, Tchaikovsky's body, wrapped in a disinfectant sheet, was placed in a metal coffin; the coffin was soldered and placed inside an oak coffin that was then screwed shut. So maybe there *was* still a danger of infection? It's so hard to know where the truth is hiding in this story.

The next morning, the coffin was carried through the streets in a procession that stretched for over a mile, while vast crowds of people lined the streets, watching and weeping. The Tsar himself had agreed to pay for the funeral, which meant that it was a grand state occasion. There was a long service at the main cathedral in St Petersburg, before the body was taken to a beautiful cemetery at a monastery in the city. Last speeches were made at the grave; then everyone made the sign of the cross over themselves, and damp earth started to cover the coffin. Tchaikovsky was gone.

A final deception . . .

There were still quarrels to be fought, though. Even the funeral itself caused problems. Several friends thought that he should be buried in the grounds of his house in Klin; others felt equally strongly that his body should be laid to rest in his favourite city, Moscow. But by the time these grumbles were heard, Tchaikovsky was safely underground in St Petersburg, so there was no point in arguing, really. (Not that that stopped the grumblers.) Then something worse happened: in his will, Tchaikovsky had left his money to his niece's illegitimate son (with an annual provision for Antonina, which was decent of him), most of his royalties to his beloved nephew Bob (though with some left over for Modest, whom Tchaikovsky had always supported financially), and most of his possessions to his servant, Alexei. So far, so good. But Modest, wanting to preserve the memory of his adored brother as perfectly as possible, decided to purchase the last house in which Tchaikovsky had lived in Klin – he'd only ever rented property, never bought it – and to turn it into a museum. To keep the house as it had been in Tchaikovsky's lifetime, Modest would need to buy Tchaikovsky's furnishings; so the roguish Alexei, knowing that Modest would have to have them at any cost, charged him a ridiculous amount for them. Then Modest set about buying the house itself; and was flabbergasted to discover that the house had been sold already – to Alexei! That rat had managed to raise enough money to nip in before Modest could; and, of course, he charged Modest a fortune for it. Shocking. Well – Tchaikovsky loved him, anyway.

Poor Modest – he could never escape from his brother's shadow; perhaps he didn't really want to. Until Tchaikovsky's death, Modest's plays and other writings had been largely ignored, except for his libretti for two of his brother's operas; and even those had been heavily criticised. Now he produced his only really famous work: a biography of Tchaikovsky, a slim little book (!) in twenty-five parts, quoting from about three thousand of his brother's letters. After that, he settled down to running the museum, to writing, and to helping gifted young artists – poets, musicians etc. – until his death in 1916. Anatoly had died a year earlier; and sadly, Bob had come to a tragic end ten years earlier, developing a drug problem (as his older sister had done), and finally killing himself at the age of thirty-four.

As for Antonina – Mrs Tchaikovsky, in fact, since she refused ever to divorce Tchaikovsky – her fate was awful too. She got together with a poor lawyer and had three children by him; but she didn't keep them, sending them off to a home for orphans, where they died. She ended her days in a "Home for the Emotionally Disturbed", supported by the money Tchaikovsky had left to her. To do him justice, Tchaikovsky had always made sure that she was supported financially after the marriage fiasco; but he never showed much sympathy for her, usually referring to her in his letters as "the reptile" (or occasionally, for variety, as "that spawn of hell"). She seems to have been far kinder about him. After his death, she wrote a brief memoir of their relationship, painting an almost entirely positive picture of him, and saying that "he never spoke ill of anyone" – a good thing she didn't read his letters about her! It's true that she had occasionally made veiled threats to expose his homosexuality to the world; but basically, she hadn't troubled him nearly as much as she might have. She even sent him shirts she'd made herself as a thank you for his financial help; and at his funeral, the most ornate bouquet of flowers was hers.

Right; that's quite enough sad stories for one chapter. Let's move on . . .

The Music

Well, his story may be awful – but Tchaikovsky's music is anything but! In fact, it's gorgeous. Nobody wrote more soaring, impassioned melodies than he did; and few composers have written such elegant music, either. In one piece, he'll take us down to the depths of his own suffering; in another, he'll sweep us into a nineteenth-century ballroom, complete with bright candles, swirling dresses and fabulous dancers. His music is wonderfully exciting, too; he can build up vast climaxes of brass instruments, percussion, woodwind and strings – the whole orchestra, in fact – playing with all the strength they can muster. It can be almost deafening – but it's thrilling! Tchaikovsky is a many-sided composer, and all his sides are larger than life. Every note he writes communicates something from the depths of his heart; it's as if he's revealing his soul to us.

The 'Pathétique' Symphony is a good example of his many aspects. The first movement opens mysteriously, but blossoms into unforgettably beautiful tunes and boiling passion; the second is one of his dance movements, all elegance and luscious textures; the third is a thrilling march, which takes your breath away; and then, suddenly and powerfully, he plunges us into the weeping tragedy of the last movement. The despair of the ending wouldn't be nearly as overwhelming if it hadn't been preceded by all the contrasting elements of the other movements.

The 'Pathétique' is obviously an autobiographical work; but not *all* of his works so clearly describe his own inner life. The charming ballets, for instance, are just that – charming ballets. (But they're so lovely! He lifted the art of ballet music to a completely new level.) Everything Tchaikovsky wrote is warm, full of feeling – and ultimately uplifting, no matter how sad. Tchaikovsky had no desire to inflict his own sufferings on his listeners; he just wanted to speak to people, to share everything he thought and felt with anyone who would respond to his music. And in that, he succeeded marvellously; he is one of the most popular and beloved of all composers.

What to listen to

Well, I suppose that the most essential Tchaikovsky pieces of all must be the Fourth, Fifth and Sixth Symphonies; they really sum up his life's work. Listen to 'Romeo and Juliet', too, following the story in the music. Then, all three ballets – 'Swan Lake', 'Sleeping Beauty' and especially 'Nutcracker' – are gems. (If you like ballet, it's worth going to see them being danced, or getting a video; if not, the music works perfectly by itself.) If you're in the mood for lots of noise, the '1812 Overture' is fun – battle music, with cannon-fire at the end.

The best of the operas are stunning; try 'Eugene Onegin', for a start. Among the chamber music, 'Souvenir de Florence' for string sextet (or string orchestra) is a winner – teeming with energy and excitement. There are many beautiful songs, almost all of them in Russian – a perfect language for music. He wrote some lovely piano music, too, including a special 'Children's Album', Op. 39. (Great to listen to – and to play, if you're learning the piano.)

So – that's a beginning; and I'll bet that, once you get started, you'll want to hear more and more. That's the effect Tchaikovsky has on people ...

Antonín Dvořák

1841~1904

O ur next composer isn't as shy as Tchaikovsky was, but on the other hand, he's not exactly one of the world's great talkers, either. So it might be a bit tricky to strike up a conversation with him; but it's worth a try. We have to make sure that we start on the right tack, though. Were we to go and ask him, in no matter how polite a voice: "Excuse us, Mr Antonin Dvorak, could you please tell us what you're composing at the moment?", he'd be likely just to look at us suspiciously – his deep-set brown eyes glowing, his beard and moustache bristling, the furrow in the middle of his forehead crinkling sternly. This might be for one of two reasons. If he wasn't composing anything, and was having difficulty deciding what to write, he'd probably be in a foul mood "this composing is a terrible business, before you get down to it", he grumbled to a friend) and wouldn't want to be disturbed. If he *were* composing something, on the other

 *Antonín Dvořák*

hand, he'd be in a much better mood ("happy and contented in my work as I have always been and, God grant, may always be"); but he'd probably be quite secretive about the work in progress, and wouldn't want to talk about it to strangers like us – and he still wouldn't want to be disturbed.

So that question wouldn't be a good way to start the conversation. In fact, we'd have already put our foot in it in a big way, because his name isn't Antonin Dvorak at all – it's Antonín Dvořák. That little slant and curl on the top of his surname – making it look, as one American composer said, like a "name with foreign hair" – mean that it's pronounced, not Dvorak, but Dvor-jahk (with the emphasis on the "Dvor", and then a slight lingering on the "jahk", if you want to be *really* authentic-sounding). The reason why the signs matter so much is because they're part of the Czech language – and definitely *not* part of the German language; and Dvořák was a proud, passionate, bouncing Czech, who, like all Czechs, resented the fact that his nation was governed by the German-speaking rulers of the enormous Austro-Hungarian Empire. He adored his country – or rather, he adored his nation, because in Dvořák's time, the Czechs didn't really *have* a country. Dvořák was from Bohemia, which is part of what we now call the Czech Republic; and he, along with his fellow Czechs in Bohemia, neighbouring Moravia and other places, dreamed of the day when they would be free to rule themselves.

So he'd prefer us to ask him a question in Czech rather than German, if we can manage it – even though he certainly can speak German fluently, and spends a lot of his life doing so. In fact, his written German is more formally correct than his written Czech since, like most of his compatriots at that time, he's been educated mostly in German; but he speaks Czech better. If we can't manage Czech, though, English would be fine. His English is quite good, because he has visited England nine times, and lived in America for three years; and he likes to show off his

181

English in front of his Czech friends. It would probably be a good move at this point to buy him a glass of beer – or two . . . or perhaps, to be on the safe side, three. He does love beer – although if there were another alcoholic drink around, he'd be broad-minded enough to try that instead. After he's quaffed the beers, he might possibly be prepared to discuss music with us, so long as we asked him first about recent performances of his works. I think he'd be happy to tell us about those; he certainly wrote endless letters describing his triumphs, so presumably he'd enjoy boasting about them in person, as well. It's not *really* boasting, though – at least, not to him – because he's convinced that the only reason he writes such wonderful music is that God has given him a priceless gift; and by acknowledging the value of his own music, he is only showing his gratitude. (Dvořák is deeply religious, a committed Catholic, putting a little thank-you to God at the end of all his manuscripts – like Haydn.) Besides, every time his pieces are successful, Dvořák feels that it is a triumph, not just for him, but for the entire Czech nation. Other Czechs agree with him on this, too; he is the pride and joy of his poor mistreated country.

There's still a chance that music could be a bit of a tricky topic, though; he's quite touchy on the subject – for instance, he thinks that all bad composers should be sent to prison. So perhaps it's safer to stick to other subjects: his six children, perhaps – or, probably better still, pigeons. Yes, pigeons. Dvořák kept lots of them (of various different breeds) at his country house in a place called Vysoká; and he *adored* them! (In fact, if we *were* to ask him about his recent work, he'd be quite likely to tell us about the pigeon-house he's just built – not exactly the sort of work we'd have had in mind.) He would sit for hours at a time watching his multicoloured birds – not everybody's idea of a thrilling afternoon, perhaps; but for him, pigeons were the bees' knees. Because he was fascinated by them, he presumed that everybody else must be too; and he

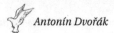

could – and would – talk about them endlessly. Perhaps at times he slightly overestimated their attractions; when the little daughter of his caretaker at Vysoká died tragically, Dvořák sent a letter of condolence. "I am pleased that our pigeons can cheer you up," he wrote. Hmmm . . . I doubt it, somehow.

Pigeons aside, Dvořák's deep love of the countryside, and of all that lives and grows in it, was one of his strongest and most attractive characteristics; and one can hear that in his music. As a great Czech conductor put it, "Dvořák knew how to listen to nature." All his pieces – his works inspired by Czech folk dances, his big symphonies, operas, religious music and so on – sing with the natural voice of the Czech people and their world. His music is organic, additive-free – and simple, in the best sense. Perhaps that's why it is so easy for people of all ages and tastes to love it.

But it wasn't *just* nature that fascinated Dvořák; he loved some man-made things as well – trains, for a start. When he wasn't in Vysoká, he lived in an apartment in the main city of Bohemia, Prague (a gorgeous city – now the capital of the Czech Republic). While there, he would make his way almost every day to the main station, where he would board the trains, inspect the engines, talk to the drivers, take notes, and generally

gather stacks of totally useless information. If he were too busy to go himself, he'd send one of his children to find out the vital facts for that morning; one of their main tasks was to remember the numbers of the locomotives (so important for the future of mankind). Once he asked his favourite pupil and prospective son-in-law, a wonderful composer called Josef Suk, to fulfil this urgent mission; unfortunately Suk got muddled up and wrote down the number of the coal-car instead of the engine. Dvořák was not impressed – this was the man his daughter wanted to marry? But he forgave him; at least it wasn't a sin on the scale of a dreadful crime committed by another of his favourite pupils. This unfortunate young man visited the master at Vysoká, and unwittingly managed to frighten the pigeons. The other people who witnessed this disaster were aghast – and amazed: where on earth had Dvořák managed to learn all those swear-words?

It wasn't just other people who suffered for Dvořák's hobbies: sometimes he himself got into trouble, as well. There was the time a letter from his publisher, Mr Simrock, urgently needed an answer; Dvořák's wife Anna kept nagging at him to reply to it, and eventually Dvořák got fed up. He informed her that he'd written the letter, and just needed to address the envelope. Then Dvořák went out; while he was out, Anna found the envelope, addressed it and sent it. When Dvořák got home and discovered what she'd done, he was embarrassed; he hadn't written to his publisher at all – the letter had been to one of his train-driver friends, all about engines! Mr Simrock must have been a touch perplexed . . .

During his stay in America, Dvořák lived mostly in New York, where – disaster! – only passengers were allowed onto the station platforms. So Dvořák had to travel for an hour by tram in order to get to a high bank from which he could see the trains going by; that took up a lot of time – and besides, it wasn't the same as actually getting on board and studying the trains. Luckily, rescue was at hand: ships. The harbour was quite near Dvořák's house, and he soon discovered that he was allowed to board the vessels before they sailed for Europe; from then on, he was down there constantly, talking to the captain or his assistants, and inspecting every inch of every deck. Then he would spend ages talking about the ships once they'd left, wondering at how many knots they would be travelling, where they'd got to, and so on. Each morning, the first thing he'd do would be to read the shipping news in the paper – and then he would probably announce the glad tidings to the assembled company. His breakfast companions must have been thrilled, I'm sure.

Hmm . . . on second thoughts, perhaps when we try to talk to him we shouldn't mention pigeons, trains *or* boats – the conversation might become just a tad boring (for us, anyway). Actually, Dvořák might decide not to talk at all, about anything, no matter how hard we struggle to say the right things. Once, a singer called Marák was performing in an opera; he was told that Dvořák was looking for him. He could hear the great man's voice in the passage: "Marák, Marák, where is Marák?" The composer sounded agitated, so Marák ran out and confronted him: "Here I am, Master." Dvořák was all red in the face from excitement – but he didn't say anything. "Is there anything you wish, Master?" asked Marák hopefully. Silence. Then, "No, nothing," said Dvořák – and off he stomped, leaving Marák totally discombobulated.

Perhaps Dvořák's silences came about because he needed time to think about things at his own pace; he wasn't always the quickest of conversationalists. Shortly before his sixtieth birthday, Dvořák, along with a famous Czech poet, was awarded a great honour by the Emperor in Vienna: life membership of the "Herrenhaus", the Austrian equivalent of the House of Lords. Actually, Dvořák only ever attended one assembly; what impressed him most were the wonderful pencils that the noble lords were given for their note-taking, so he pocketed some of them. (The pencils, not the lords.) But it was an important recognition, and Dvořák and the poet took a special trip to Vienna to thank the Emperor for the honour he had bestowed on them. On the way, Dvořák looked out of the window of the train and remarked how beautiful the Bohemian countryside was. The poet replied (rather too prosaically for a poet, really) that he wouldn't want to spend the summer there, because of the mosquitoes. Silence from Dvořák. The men arrived in Vienna, stayed there, and had their audience with the Emperor. After this memorable occasion, Dvořák decided that he had an important pronouncement to make to the poet: "Actually, I wouldn't like to be beside those lakes, either."

Not always the fastest or easiest of men, then, or the most brilliant of conversationalists. Nor always the most generous in money matters, either; having been really poor in his youth, Dvořák stayed poor inside, even when in later life he became rich. For that reason, it wasn't at all easy to make him part with his hard-earned cash. On one occasion, a poor friend of his, who'd been doing some work for Dvořák but hadn't yet been paid, turned up in a restaurant where Dvořák was eating, and joined the master for lunch. At the end of the meal, Dvořák apologised – he had only a couple of pennies with him, so could the friend please pay for both of them? The friend panicked; he hadn't any money on him either. Dvořák's face fell. "I was so happy to see you here, because I thought you could help me," he complained – so gracious. The situation looked dicey – until the friend saw a way out of it: "We could wash the dishes, so they'd let us off paying," he suggested. Suddenly, Dvořák found that he had enough money for both meals after all. Ahem . . . And while we're on his faults, or at least eccentricities: heaven help us if he forces us to play his favourite card-game, a Czech game called "darda". Although he's far too careful with his money to play for anything more than buttons, he'll get *furious* if he loses, and probably won't forgive us in a hurry – and yet he'll insist on playing at every opportunity.

Ah – but despite all these quirks, Dvořák was a wonderful man; one can feel it in the music, and one can see it in the accounts written by so many people who knew him. He was warm, he was honest, and he was totally without affectation (and actually, he *could* be very generous with his money – depending on his mood that day). Furthermore, his achievements in life were particularly amazing, because he started out with no obvious advantages: he was the eldest son of a local butcher and innkeeper in a tiny village. His family was very poor, and always had been; even the name "Dvořák" means "a servant in the manor house". Through his passion for music, and through unending hard work, Dvořák managed – eventually – to become a celebrated and beloved composer; but it was never a smooth ride.

At least he was lucky enough – unlike so many of the great composers – to enjoy a happy family life. In his youth, he'd fallen in love with a beautiful young actress called Josefina; but she turned down his offer of marriage, probably because he didn't earn enough money at that point. Eventually, Dvořák compromised, and married her sister instead. (Funny how many composers have done that – Haydn and Mozart being the two most famous examples.) Anna wasn't as beautiful as Josefina, but she was probably more sensible and supportive, and not quite as obsessed with money. (Josefina married a rich count instead, and the two families remained close; Dvořák built his country house on some land he had bought from the count, who owned the Vysoká estate.) Dvořák and Anna were married for more than thirty years. Sadly, their first three children all died very young; but then there were six more, who all gave their parents lots of joy – and lots of worries, as children do . . .

Dvořák was an affectionate father – if at times a severe one, who expected a lot from his children; if they got bad reports, Anna wouldn't dare show them to him. He could lose his temper at a moment's notice: Dvořák's youngest son Otakar remembered several canings – including one dreadful time when the boy broke some pigeon eggs, and another occasion when Otakar locked his mother's mother in the loo. Well, perhaps Dvořák had a point that time – grandmothers really shouldn't be locked in loos, as a rule.

Generally, though, Dvořák was lovely to the children – and they adored him. Otakar used to take great pride in cleaning his father's pipe (for a small fee – he was his father's son, after all), and in accompanying Dvořák on walks, as well as to evenings at the local inn in Vysoká. Dvořák was at his happiest and most relaxed there; he would spend hours talking with his friends (mostly local miners and farmers) about their work, his pigeons, and all his travels. Sometimes he would get a bit carried away with stories about his foreign adventures (Czech beer tends to be quite strong) and, lighting up his pipe, would launch into tall tales. But nobody – not even Otakar, who knew the truth behind the stories, but was frequently asked to back up his father – really minded; at some point towards the end of the evening, Dvořák might confess that *some* of what he'd been saying had been pure fantasy – but he would go on talking and puffing anyway, until his pipe burned out. (He had to make the most of his pipe in the inn; Anna wouldn't let him smoke it at home, although she let him smoke cigarettes there – a far worse smell, surely? Well, obviously not to Anna's nose.)

In his public life, Dvořák was a rather different man – at least on the surface. He would generally feel very awkward in grand society, and would turn down most social invitations; he didn't even attend many concerts or operas, preferring to get to bed early after a few games of darda. At the few parties he enjoyed, he would be apt to insist on hearing his favourite jokes, no matter how many times he'd heard them; they were usually about such deeply sophisticated matters as a boy with a stammer needing to go to the toilet. So he wasn't a natural society man; but great artists can get away with being different – and besides, he had his own unique charm.

As a teacher, he was different again; he could be *terrifying*. Fairly late in life, he accepted the post of professor at the Prague Conservatoire, and taught composition there for several years; he also taught during his time in New York. His pupils loved him, of course – everyone did; but sometimes (as Suk put it) he made them "howl". If he didn't like a piece they'd written, he was liable to hurl it to the floor and stamp on it, grunting like a wild boar – not exactly encouraging. To make things even more unnerving, he might praise something one day, and then decide the next day that he hated it. If he got angry with a student, he would often pull him around the room by the nose – making it a little hard for the pupil to maintain his dignity. And one had to say just the right thing at the right time, or else . . . Once, he was talking about Mozart: "Who knows what Mozart is?" he asked. The students were baffled; it was such a strange question. They stammered out whatever answers they could think of, but Dvořák was not impressed. "That just shows how little sense and feeling you have for music," he snorted. Getting more and more furious, he grabbed the nearest student by the shoulder (at least it was just the shoulder this time) and dragged him over to the window. "Now do you know? Do you see it?" thundered Dvořák. The unfortunate student saw nothing. "What?" Dvořák spluttered in disgust. "You don't see the sun?" The pupil admitted that he did. "Why then don't you say what Mozart is? Remember – Mozart is *sunshine*." I'm sure the pupil never forgot! At other times, Dvořák would sit at the piano and play through complicated orchestral scores for his students, very brilliantly; but even then he was liable to get into a bad mood, because his pince-nez (the half-moon spectacles that he wore in later life) had a bad habit of falling down his nose at the most exciting moments, causing him to curse alarmingly.

So Dvořák wasn't always a total joy to be with, it must be admitted, and it might be a tad nerve-racking to try to talk to him – but I'm sure it would be worth taking the risk. He was basically a very kind and good-hearted man. Anyone who had dealings with him seems to have realised that he never meant any real harm, despite all the huffings and puffings. Furthermore, Dvořák always felt guilty if he'd been angry, and tried to make up for it by being especially nice afterwards. It's clear that all the people who wrote reminiscences of him after his death had been terribly fond of him, and had found his tantrums funny – in retrospect, at least.

I suppose that in many ways Dvořák was like a child – a child who looked rather like a dog (even though the dogs I've met don't tend to have bristly beards). His character seems to have been open and direct in a childlike way – both the shining qualities and the faults; and the music he wrote reflected that openness. So maybe that's how we should sum him up: a musical genius with the heart and mind of a child, and the face of a dog. Come to think of it – what could be better?

Facts of Life

•1•

Dvořák was born on September 8th, 1841 in the little village of Nelahozeves (pronounced "Ne . . ." – no, on second thoughts, don't bother). He was the oldest of nine children – a large tribe for his poor father to support with his butchering and innkeeping. Not surprisingly, Dvořák senior was always in money difficulties. The Dvořáks had to share the houses in which Antonín grew up with lots of other families, which must have been noisy and probably quite tough. I doubt whether anyone in the village ever dreamed that a great composer might emerge from their midst; but there was some music around. Dvořák's father played the zither (a folk instrument) – at first to entertain his guests at the inn and later, when his main businesses failed completely, for a living. Bohemia was actually a famously musical area, with lots of travelling per-formers going from town to town, and masses of amateur music-making everywhere, music being played to celebrate every possible occasion. So young Antonín (or "little toothy", as his grandmother called him) got the chance to study violin and singing at the village school from the age of six; soon after that, he played his first violin solo in the local church. No doubt all the praise, and especially the coin he received after-wards from a neighbour, helped convince him that music was the life for him.

First attempts …

It didn't take too long for Dvořák to start to compose. The first piece of his to get played was a polka (a folk-dance, originally from Bohemia), which he wrote for a local fair in his home-town. The little orchestra started to play – but the music sounded awful! The trumpets seemed to be the culprits; the problem turned out to be that Dvořák hadn't realised that (for some reason) the notes that are written in trumpet parts are not the actual notes that sound. Once that was sorted out, the polka sounded – well, like a polka. And so, in a slightly unpromising way, a great career was born.

·2·

Dvořák's father might have expected his oldest boy to carry on his own profession; but young Antonín – despite having been given a tiny butcher's apron almost as soon as he could walk – was obviously drawn more to music than to butchery. Having spent six years as a pupil in his local school, at the age of twelve he was sent away for two years to a little town called Zlonice ("Zlon-it-se"), to study German and music. The music teacher there was good, if a little fierce: if his pupils couldn't play a passage properly, he would box them on the ears. (Perhaps that's why in later life Dvořák used to attack his own pupils on such a regular basis.) It was this ear-boxing teacher, however, who managed to persuade Dvořák senior that his oldest son was destined to create symphonies rather than sausages – so we should be grateful to him for that. After Zlonice, Antonín, now fifteen, went to a German school in another town for a year; and finally, in 1857, he travelled on the back of a peasant's cart (probably with vegetables for company) to Prague, where he lived in his uncle's house, attended a Catholic school called "The-Holy-Virgin-in-the-Snow" for a year, and began his studies at the Prague Organ School. He hated this first real taste of the musical world, partly because the school smelt of mould and partly because he felt that the other, more sophisticated, students were laughing at him. He must have done quite well, though, because when he left in 1859, he was judged to be the second best student in his year. It wasn't exactly the hugest success in the world, but it was something.

A troublesome lodger . . .

Even while studying at the Organ School, Dvořák had to get a job playing the viola in a local orchestra in order to earn some money. He was terribly poor – and also terribly bad-tempered, always furious about something or somebody. Sometimes he'd stop playing in the middle of an orchestral rehearsal and start humming to himself – which can't have gone down very well with the rest of the group. He wasn't exactly the perfect lodger or guest, either. From the time he arrived in Prague until his marriage in 1873, Dvořák lived mostly with his uncle, aunt and cousins. At first he couldn't afford a piano, which he needed for his composing, so he would go over to a friend's place to use his instrument – until the friend's wife objected to Dvořák leaving dirty footprints all over her nice clean carpet. So then Dvořák had to hire a piano (from his tailor) and put it in the room that he shared with two other lodgers at his uncle's. I pity those lodgers!

Sometimes, he would move out from his uncle's and take lodgings elsewhere; but he was a disastrous housemate wherever he was – especially if there were a piano in the house. Dvořák was apt to try out ideas for his new compositions at any hour of the day or night, quite forgetting that other people might just possibly prefer to sleep at times. Strangely enough, he was asked to leave his dwellings on a fairly regular basis. Best were the times when he was writing down a new piece, because then he'd sit at his table and, when he wasn't actually writing, put his pen between his teeth and try things out with his fingers on his jacket or his legs. The times when he'd just woken up weren't so bad, either: he might lie in bed and play passages on his eiderdown – at least that was quiet, if a little disturbing. But Dvořák couldn't act normally – he was obsessed! Well, at this stage, there probably wasn't much else in his life other than music (apart from food, that is: he famously ate thirty of his aunt's plum dumplings at one sitting). The sad thing was that many of these very early compositions, although they had inspired passages, really weren't that good; but he ploughed on, composing endlessly, even though he received little encouragement. Nothing was going to stop him.

· *3* ·

Having finished his official studies, and with no money coming from his father – who was in worse financial difficulties than ever – Dvořák needed a regular job. He tried to get a post as a church organist, but failed, so instead he joined a small professional orchestra as first violist. (Not a huge honour – there were only two of them!) This group played mostly dance music in restaurants; but in 1862, they were hired as the permanent orchestra for Prague's first-ever Czech-language theatre. This was definitely a step up, especially as the theatre, offered as a concession to the Czechs by their Austro-Hungarian rulers, was important politically as well as artistically. Dvořák was still earning very little, however, and had to give music lessons tool; this did not leave him enough time for composition. It did mean, however, that he got to teach, and fall in love with, Josefina – and so to be introduced to his future wife Anna.

The orchestra gave some exciting concerts – including some with Dvořák's hero, Richard Wagner. The starry-eyed Dvořák stalked the great composer through the streets of Prague; Wagner probably had no idea that he was being followed by the silent young violist with the glowing eyes. But despite these high points, the job was too time-consuming for Dvořák; in 1871, he gave it up and tried to support himself through teaching alone, which would leave him more time for composing. That was incredibly bold, because at this point he'd had nothing performed or printed. He had written stacks of music, including an opera which didn't receive its first performance until 1938 – just a tad late for Dvořák – and two symphonies, one of which he sent off to a competition in Germany, and never saw again. (It turned up again many years after his death, and is now known as his Symphony No. 1, 'The Bells of Zlonice'; it's not nearly as good as his later music, but it certainly has its moments.) There was also chamber music, vocal music, and so on – but virtually nobody knew about it, not even those who knew Dvořák. It can't have been at all easy for the fanatical young composer. Actually, he wasn't even *that* young – he was entering his thirties. No wonder he was silent and gloomy; he must have felt like a failure, writing all those unnoticed works – and then frequently burning the manuscripts. Still, there was a bright side to that: at least, as he said later, "I always had paper on me to light a fire!" Funny how many similarities there are between his story and Tchaikovsky's – but Dvořák was an even later bloomer, and he'd been trying for longer.

The father of Czech music ...

A few years after Dvořák joined the theatre orchestra, a man seventeen years his senior, Bedřich Smetana, was appointed principal conductor. He deserves a paragraph to himself here: not just because he was one of the first people to encourage Dvořák as a composer, and to perform some of his works; and not just because his surname means "cream" in Czech, and "sour cream" in Russian; but mostly because he was the real father of Czech music. He wrote the first great Czech opera, 'The Bartered Bride' (Dvořák played in the first performance); and lots of gorgeous works, including an orchestral piece called 'Má vlast' ('My Country'). You might recognise the principal melody of 'Má vlast' – it's a very famous tune. Smetana had a tragic life, though. In 1874, he quite suddenly went deaf, and had to give up his job with the orchestra; a couple of years later he had to move out of Prague to live with his daughter and her husband, who as a forester was much better off than the man who merely happened to be one of the greatest composers in the world. The good thing was that a lot of his greatest music – including 'Má vlast' – was written after he'd gone deaf, so we know that he wasn't crushed by that misfortune; but the bad – very bad – thing was that he eventually went mad, and died in a mental asylum. Hmm . . . another terrible story; sorry I brought it up. But Smetana was wonderful – he deserves our thanks.

· 4 ·

At long last, things started to look up for Dvořák. At the end of 1871, a song of his was performed in Prague: the next year, some more songs and an early piano quintet were played, and Smetana conducted the overture to Dvořák's second opera, 'The King and the Charcoal Burner'. It was the next year, though, that brought Dvořák his real breakthrough: in March 1873, his patriotic Czech cantata, entitled 'Heirs of the White Mountain', was performed by a huge choir in Prague – and triumphed. It was a major event in Dvořák's life; and in November came another one, when he and Anna were married. In order to support his wife and the family that they expected, Dvořák now needed some extra income to supplement his earnings as a teacher and an odd-job violist; so he took on a new post, as organist at the church of St Adalbert. It was very badly paid, but at least it was a steady job. He had to improvise before and after services (which he did adequately, though not especially well); and to accompany the congregation and the rather fine choir during services. Sometimes organists become very friendly with members of their choirs – but not Dvořák; every week, he would march in and place himself at the organ without a smile or word of greeting to anybody. I suppose he had other things on his mind.

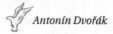

Operatic tribulations . . .

Dvořák's fortunes may have been improving gradually, but his humiliations weren't over yet. After the success of his cantata and other pieces, the management of the theatre where Dvořák had earlier played the viola became interested in his opera, 'The King and the Charcoal Burner'. Rehearsals started – and then stopped. The word was that the piece was unplayable and unsingable, and the score was sent back to the composer. Poor Dvořák! He must have been so thrilled – and then so devastated. His reaction, however, was amazingly positive; he took the same libretto and set it again, with completely different music – not a bar the same! Considering what effort and time it takes to compose an opera – some composers take years over it – that was really brave: suppose the second version had been as much of a failure as the first? Luckily, it wasn't; the second 'King and the Charcoal Burner' was produced the next year in Prague, and enjoyed a modest success.

· 5 ·

So now Dvořák was pretty famous in Prague, and probably throughout Bohemia; but Bohemia is a small place, and Dvořák, having worked so hard for so long, and knowing that his music was now at a stage where he could present it to the world, wanted more than that.

He was still desperately poor, so in 1874, he applied for a state grant for artists, awarded by a committee of bigwigs in Vienna. His application was successful; in fact, he received the grant for five years running. Finally, Dvořák was on his way to the financial independence he longed for, although it was not until 1877 that he dared give up his job as an organist. More important still, however – the real turning point for Dvořák, in fact – was that from the second year in which the committee

Antonín Dvořák

awarded him the grant, the bigwigs were joined by a bigbeard, the famous (and hairy-faced) composer Johannes Brahms, who lived in Vienna. Brahms recognised Dvořák's amazing talent, and took steps to help him; as well as awarding him the grant, he also wrote to his own publisher in Berlin, Fritz Simrock, recommending Dvořák's music to him. Simrock accepted some songs by Dvořák for publication – without giving Dvořák a penny, however. A bit rotten, especially since Brahms had told him how poor Dvořák was; but Dvořák was in no position to dictate terms. The songs were a success and were shortly followed by a series of 'Slavonic Dances' – Czechs being a Slav race, like Russians, Poles, etc. – for piano duet (to be played at home by musical amateurs) or orchestra (to be performed at concerts). These were a mega-hit and made Dvořák's name famous wherever classical music was played. Simrock's firm continued to publish almost all of Dvořák's new works for the rest of his life.

A helpful friend, an infuriating publisher ...

Brahms, often a grumpy character who could be fairly awful to young composers if he didn't think much of them, took a real shine to Dvořák. Brahms, for whom composing was never easy, was amazed by how many beautiful melodies arrived in Dvořák's head; he loved the freshness and cheerfulness of so much of Dvořák's music. At first, Dvořák was quite overawed by the fame and power of the older man (only eight years older, in fact – but the difference of their positions in life made it seem more); he wrote rather fawning letters to Brahms, referring to him as "Your Nobleness". In time, though, their relationship became a real friendship. Brahms, normally very secretive about his works in progress, would talk about them quite freely with Dvořák; the two composers would meet and spend time together whenever Dvořák could get to Vienna or Brahms to Prague (the two cities are quite close). Dvořák, as a devout

Catholic, was shocked by Brahms's lack of religion; but he was still very fond of his benefactor, and deeply grateful to him.

Their relationship was probably never quite equal. Brahms once wrote to a friend asking if he could bring Dvořák with him to a dinner, assuring the friend that Dvořák wouldn't be any trouble: "I will give [the meal] to him from my little plate and my little mug," he wrote – I can't imagine Dvořák writing about Brahms in that tone! But on the whole, Brahms was really wonderful to his younger colleague; later, while Dvořák was away in New York and it took ages to send music between Europe and America, Brahms proofread Dvořák's new works for Simrock, so that their publication wouldn't be delayed – an impressive compliment from such a busy man. And towards the end of his life Brahms, who was by then very rich but had no family of his own, offered to pay whatever it would take to get Dvořák to move with his family to Vienna. (Dvořák refused, but gratefully.) It is a lovely story of friendship between two great artists.

Simrock, however, was a different matter; he and Dvořák had a real love-hate relationship. Dvořák's letters to to his publisher might begin "Dear Friend"; but they were just as likely to start, with very un-Dvořák-like coldness: "Dear Simrock", or "Dear Mr Simrock". The two men drove each other crazy! Simrock drove Dvořák crazy (a) by being condescending about Czechs in general, and translating both the titles of Dvořák's pieces and his name into German ("Antonín Dvořák" became "Anton Dvorak", which did NOT go down well with the composer, who was quite likely, if he saw his name spelt like that in a shop window, to go striding into the shop and correct it); (b) by completely renumbering all Dvořák's works in the order that his firm happened to have published them – so that, for instance, Dvořák's Fifth Symphony, which was the first that Simrock had published, became 'Symphony No. 1' (actually, Dvořák also complicated things by referring to it as his Fourth, *since he thought that the first one was lost for ever – but that's no excuse for Simrock); (c) by constantly asking Dvořák to compose little pieces that would sell easily, whereas Dvořák was quite rightly more interested in writing big symphonies, operas, etc.; and (d) by offering Dvořák too little money. Dvořák drove Simrock crazy by (a), (b), (c) and (d) – demanding too much money! Dvořák often got his way: for instance, having been paid 300 marks for his first series of 'Slavonic Dances', he managed to get 3,000 marks for the next series, eight years later – not bad as wage increases go. Only once can Simrock have been pleasantly surprised, when he received a letter from Dvořák offering him a few works for the eminently reasonable sum of 1,000 marks; unfortunately, this was swiftly followed by another letter, saying that Dvořák had actually meant 10,000! Their relationship was full of bickering: Simrock asked whether Dvořák really wanted to send him mad, while Dvořák wondered whether Simrock really wanted Dvořák's family to starve. And so the two men went on squabbling, until Simrock's death in 1901.*

· 6 ·

From the time that his first set of 'Slavonic Dances' appeared, Dvořák became a famous figure throughout the musical world. Everyone knew about this rather strange-looking Czech, whose pieces, full of folk-inspired dances and songs, sounded so different from most modern music. His melodies sounded so simple and straightforward; but out of these materials, Dvořák could conjure wonderful large-scale works, equal to anything being composed by the most famous Germans and Austrians. A lot of important conductors and powerful music journalists championed his music – but it wasn't all sweetness and light, especially when it came to Dvořák's operas. There was a particularly virulent critic in

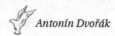

Vienna called Hugo Wolf ("Volf"), who was himself a famous composer of songs; he was also a manic Brahms-hater, which probably influenced his attitude to Dvořák. After an opera of Dvořák's had been performed in Vienna, Wolf wrote: "It is bad enough to meet Dvořák in the concert hall. That this embarrassment should insinuate itself into the opera house is truly deplorable." Gulp. (Oh well – Hugo Wolf was prone to violent outbursts; in fact, he ended up going mad, his life ending tragically, like Smetana's, in a mental asylum.) Mostly, though, Dvořák enjoyed a series of huge successes. His new symphonies were swiftly grabbed by orchestras in London, Berlin and Vienna; and the first all-Dvořák concert was given in Prague in 1878. Dvořák loved to read good reviews of his own works, chuckling delightedly if he saw himself praised to the skies. He also made friends with several other great composers of the day, including Tchaikovsky; the two of them got on very well, although their correspondence was rather slow> Dvořák would write to Tchaikovsky in Czech, and Tchaikovsky would reply in Russian – which meant that there were huge delays while the letters were being translated. Still, they were friends, and admired each other's music; Tchaikovsky even arranged for Dvořák to visit Russia in 1890.

A delicious reception . . .

England was the European country that took Dvořák most closely to its heart; several of his major works received their first performance there. Dvořák's first visit, in 1884, was a stunning success: he conducted his religious choral work, 'Stabat Mater', at the Royal Albert Hall in London, with a huge choir and orchestra; Dvořák was ecstatic! (In a letter to a friend back home, he claimed that the choir was a thousand strong, the orchestra had 160 members, and that there was an audience of ten thousand. Funny – these days the Albert Hall can only hold around five thousand people. It must have shrunk – or perhaps,

just possibly, Dvořák might have been exaggerating a bit . . .)
He enjoyed everything on this trip, his first outside Central
Europe: the parties (he stayed up till 2.30 a.m. at a reception
given for him – unheard of for early-to-bed Mr Dvořák); the
women (he tactfully wrote to his wife about how many
beautiful ladies he'd met at a breakfast party); and above all,
the attention he received from everyone around him.

Perhaps the most striking evidence of England's love for
Dvořák came when he was doctored – so to speak – by
Cambridge University in 1891, two years before Tchaikovsky
received the same honour. Actually, Dvořák was a little
dismayed at the ceremony by the fact that everybody made
their speeches in Latin, a language he couldn't understand; he
consoled himself by thinking that it was more important to be
able to compose great music than to speak Latin. There's a
rather funny photo of him taken that day, dressed in the cap
and gown that he wore for the ceremony; to his delight, he was
allowed to keep them. Probably his favourite part of that trip,
though, was the reception after the concert he'd
conducted the night
before the ceremony;
having already
impressed the other
guests with his music, he
now impressed them
further with the number
of sandwiches he was able
to consume. After devour-
ing a vast plateful, he
made an important
announcement to the
assembled company, in his rather
individual English: "Now my stowmack is betterer."

·7·

At this point in his life, Dvořák was so celebrated a man –
perhaps the most famous living Czech – that everybody
wanted to celebrate him! Honours were heaped upon his
balding head; more and more concert organisations asked
him to write pieces for them; and he was offered the job of
Professor of Composition at the Prague Conservatoire. At first
he refused this appointment, saying that he wouldn't have
the time; but eventually he was persuaded, and started
mistreating (well, teaching) his new students in 1891.
However, something rather more unexpected was afoot: that
same year, Dvořák received an offer from a rich lady in New
York called Mrs Thurber. She wanted him to become Director
of the new National Conservatory of Music that she had just
opened there. Dvořák thought about it. There were snags: he
didn't really want to leave his beloved Bohemia; his children's
education couldn't easily be disrupted; he'd just started
teaching at the Prague Conservatoire; and so on. On the other
hand, the financial offer from New York was pretty amazing –
he'd earn almost his monthly salary from Prague in just one
day; and Dvořák wasn't the sort of man to ignore such things.
So he hummed and he ha-ed, and he argued about the
contract, and he talked endlessly to this and that person
about it, and he fussed and worried and panicked. Eventually,
he just couldn't make up his mind, and might have decided to
stay where he was; but the practical Anna, who knew what
was what, realised that if he took the job, just for a couple of
years, he'd never have to worry about money again (even
though I'm sure she realised that, Dvořák being Dvořák, he
would worry about it!) So one day at lunch, Anna organised a
vote among the eight family members – was Dvořák going to
go to New York or not? It was a split decision, but there were
more for than against, so Anna took Dvořák (probably

grumbling about his unfinished lunch) by the hand, propelled him into the study, handed him a pen – and the contract was signed. He came back to the table, still grumbling, pointing out that signing a contract didn't mean anything, that he hadn't sent it yet, etc.; but Anna took the contract, hid it, and, when Dvořák was out of the way, mailed it herself. So that was that.

Around this time, Dvořák met a young Czech-American – born and raised in America, but in a community of Czech émigrés – called Josef Jan Kovarik, who had just finished studying the violin at the Prague Conservatoire. Dvořák (who didn't know much about America at that point) decided that since he came from America, Kovarik must somehow be American-Indian; so he used to call him "Little Indian" (when Dvořák was in a good mood) or plain "Indian" (when he wasn't). Actually, poor Kovarik had started out with an even worse nickname than "Indian". The first time the two men had met, Kovarik had been sitting in a music shop, reading a newspaper and minding his own business, when Dvořák walked in. Someone pointed at Kovarik and informed Dvořák that behind that newspaper was a "real American". Dvořák, never one for the niceties of social etiquette, went running over, snatched the newspaper away, and growled: "OK, Red Face – can you speak English?" "Red Face", indeed. Kovarik must have been a bit nonplussed by this charming introduction (so perhaps he did go red!); but he admitted that yes, he spoke English – and that was it. Dvořák needed someone to help him with the trip to America – and obviously that was going to be Kovarik's job. From that point, and for the next three years, the poor man was practically kidnapped. He'd been planning to go home to his Czech community in America, in a little place called Spillville in Iowa; but Dvořák wouldn't let him go, dragging him off instead to the family residence in Vysoká until the Dvořáks were ready to go to New

York. Once there, Kovarik might have thought he was going to go home, having not been there for five years – but he wasn't. Dvořák wouldn't let him out of New York: Kovarik had to live with the family, and act as secretary and frequent companion to the great man – not always the most relaxing of jobs . . .

On September 10th, 1892, after giving a huge series of farewell concerts throughout Bohemia, Dvořák set sail, accompanied by Anna, Kovarik, and the two eldest children (the others were left behind in the care of Anna's mother, who'd been let out of the loo by this time). Dvořák enjoyed the sea trip immensely. He seems to have been quite a star on board (except for a regrettable habit of stealing the long-suffering Kovarik's cigars). He was the only one of the two hundred or so passengers not to get seasick, and sometimes the ship's captain and Dvořák were the only two to be found eating in the dining room. On September 26th, the ship docked in New York. Because of quarantine restrictions, the Dvořáks had to wait for a day (during which poor Toník, the eldest son, dropped his hat into the ocean); but when they finally arrived in New York City, they received a royal welcome. The large Czech community in America was especially thrilled by Dvořák's arrival; to have such a celebrity from their country being given a hero's reception made them all feel proud – especially since so many of them, having escaped poverty back home in the hope of better things in America, were actually having a very hard time there.

In the end, Dvořák spent three years in America – with a few months' break in 1894, when he went home for the summer vacation. After the first year, to their great joy, the Dvořáks were joined by the four missing children; but for practical reasons, they had to leave five of them behind again when they returned to America after their summer at home. This time, only Otakar came with them. That was a hard year; they spent most of the time worrying about the children they'd left

behind, and Anna would spend many a long hour crying her
eyes out. Nevertheless, Dvořák's time in America was on the
whole happy and productive – and of course lucrative.
Needless to say, he drove the unfortunate Mrs Thurber up the
wall with his constant panics about money (especially after he
discovered that her husband was having financial problems).
If she'd agreed to pay him his fee on the 20th of the month,
he'd be sure to write by the 15th, wondering why he hadn't
received it yet. She adored him anyway, though, like just about
everyone else.

Dvořák enjoyed life in New York, especially since everybody
made such a fuss of him, and kept giving him things; bakers
would send him their tastiest little morsels, and the leading
piano firm in New York lent him a grand piano (which meant,
Dvořák wrote, that "we have one good piece of furniture in the
parlour" – not *quite* the point, I'd have thought). Furthermore,
he discovered that he could eat a HUGE meal every night,
with wine, beer and coffee included, for $1.70, which pleased
him mightily. But he was always homesick. Letters sailed
between his house and Bohemia, and Dvořák took pride in
knowing exactly which ship would be carrying those he'd sent.
The children wrote to him, and he to them; in his first letter he
begins talking about his teaching, but then continues, rather
typically: "I suppose this is not very interesting to you, so I'm
going to write about myself." Hmm . . . it was actually quite
rare for him to write about anything else! Except for his
pigeons, of course: he wrote detailed and anxious letters
about them to the caretaker at Vysoká, having apparently
given him ninety-nine instructions for their care before he
left. One of his regular correspondents was his old love, and
now sister-in-law, Josefina. She reported on the health of the
children left behind in Prague (sometimes a real worry), and
also about her favourite topic: money. A typical letter from
her, written late in 1892, ends: "Let our Lord present you with

plenty of money . . . I wish for Otila [i.e. Otylie, the Dvořáks'
eldest daughter], as I already wrote, a millionaire; to Tonik – a
very nice and expensive surprise for Christmas and also to
Mr Kovarik that he . . . would find some good and very rich
American girl." She was dotty about the stuff! And perhaps
Dvořák remained somewhat dotty about her, too – so the
rumour goes, at least. There's nothing too romantic in her
surviving letters to him (his to her are all lost) – in fact, her last
one tells him off for writing too much about the weather – but
then, she knew that anything she wrote would be read by the
family. And Dvořák, who knew that her health was failing, was
certainly thinking of her when he wrote the last major piece
that he composed in America, his wonderful Cello Concerto:
in the slow movement, he quotes from a romantic song he'd
written many years earlier, a song that Josefina particularly
loved. Sadly, she died a month after the Dvořáks returned
home for good; Dvořák said farewell to her in his own
personal way by adding a long extra passage to the end of the
concerto, again quoting from her favourite song. Was it a
lover's parting? It's certainly a deeply poignant, incredibly
beautiful passage – but we'll probably never know for sure
what his real feelings were. Perhaps it's right that we shouldn't.

An unexpected legacy . . .

*Dvořák wrote what would become his most famous and
popular work, his Symphony No. 9, 'From the New World',
while he was in New York. At the time he arrived in the United
States, there had been no great American composers. This was
really why Mrs Thurber was so anxious to have Dvořák
teaching at her school: she hoped that, through his pupils, he
would help create a distinctive style of American music.
Having been so deeply influenced by the folk music of his own
country, Dvořák felt very strongly that if an American school
of composition were to be successful, it would have to be*

rooted in the music of the native people; for Dvořák, that meant the melodies of the black and American-Indian communities. This was a fairly shocking idea for a lot of white Americans, and caused a lot of arguments. The enormous success of the first performance of the 'New World' Symphony shut up many of the doubters: the work was so obviously influenced by the native music Dvořák had heard – and yet it was a classical symphony. People still quarrelled about it, though, with some critics accusing Dvořák of stealing melodies and adapting them. This was rubbish, as Dvořák was quick to point out. It was quite true that he couldn't have written a work like the symphony (or some of the other pieces he wrote during his time there) had he not lived in America; but he didn't need to use other people's themes – he had more than enough of his own inside his head! The fact that his head was in America, listening to so much homegrown music, meant that some of the melodies he wrote there came out with an American accent, as it were. But they were still pure Dvořák – and Dvořák was pure Czech. It sounds a bit contradictory – but the music itself makes perfect sense. The title of the symphony says it all, really: 'From the New World'. A message from the New World, indeed – but to where? To Bohemia, of course, which was where Dvořák's heart firmly belonged.

He was right, by the way, about a great school of American music springing out from native folk songs; but I think that he'd have been rather surprised to see how it turned out. An American school of classical composition certainly did develop; but the music that really fulfilled Dvořák's predictions of a national, folk-based style would be jazz, blues and – eventually – rock. Funny to think of Dvořák as the father of rock 'n' roll!

Not surprisingly, Dvořák sought out the company of Czechs in New York wherever he could find them. His most constant companion, though – apart from Anna and the children – was Kovarik. In later years, Kovarik wrote a lot about his time with Dvořák. He was hugely grateful to have spent three years with the great man, and also for Dvořák's help with his career as a violinist; but it wasn't the most peaceful of existences. The worst days would be concert days. (Dvořák conducted several concerts of his own music in New York, as well as conducting the student orchestra at the Conservatory.) On these days, Dvořák would be nervous – and when he was nervous, he was unbearable. He would be horribly restless, and would drag Kovarik out for walks; but almost as soon as they were outside, he'd be in a hurry to get back to the house. Kovarik would try to distract Dvořák by talking about something other than the coming concert. Dvořák's usual reaction would be to chase him out of the room, shouting insults after him; but then he'd get lonely, and Kovarik would have to rejoin him, pretending that nothing had happened. What fun those days must have been!

Another "fun" activity – ahem – in which Kovarik was forced to participate was Dvořák's beloved card game, "darda". At first, Dvořák had Anna to play with; but once they had moved into a New York apartment (having spent their first few weeks in a hotel, which was *far* too expensive for Dvořák), Kovarik made the mistake of unpacking his large collection of books – a disaster! Anna started reading them endlessly; and Dvořák, who as a rule never worked in the evenings, was now left to entertain himself. He was desperate. One night, the fateful call came for Kovarik: "Little Indian – come here, I am going to teach you darda." Poor Kovarik had no choice. Dvořák was a conscientious teacher; but he was so passionate about the game that he would lose his temper when he felt that Kovarik was being slow. Later, of course, when Kovarik had learnt *too* well, Dvořák would lose his temper when Kovarik won. Another easy situation . . .

Kovarik's most colourful account of his life with Dvořák, though, concerns the summer of 1893. The original plan for Dvořák's first trip to New York was for him to go home after the first year's teaching; but as the summer approached, he was heavily involved in composing the new symphony, and realised that to go home in the middle of writing it would be extremely disruptive. So gradually, he and Anna came to the decision that instead of rejoining the four missing children in Bohemia, they would have to bring the children out to them in New York. In fact, the 'New World' Symphony was completed on the very day that Dvořák received a telegram telling him that the four children were safely on their way to America – a happy day on all fronts!

But the Dvořáks didn't want to spend the summer months in New York; they wanted to go into the country. One day, Dvořák – apparently innocently – asked Kovarik to tell him about his hometown in Spillville, Iowa. Kovarik described it, mentioning that the principal language there was Czech – quite a few of the inhabitants didn't even speak English. The next day, Dvořák asked for some more information; a plan was obviously forming in his head. He made Kovarik draw a plan of the village, and needed to know the name of the owner of every house, and also about the woods, the birds, and so on, in the surrounding countryside. Dvořák was not one to plan a holiday lightly! Soon he knew more than Kovarik did about Spillville and its fifty-nine Czech families. Finally, he came to a decision: "All of us are going to Spillville," he told Kovarik graciously, "but I warn you – if I don't like it there, you'll be in trouble!" Such gratitude. And so the party of eleven – the eight Dvořáks, Kovarik, and two helpers – prepared for the great trip.

Given this amount of pressure, Kovarik was understandably nervous. When they finally arrived at the local station after the thirty-six-hour train trip (which had fascinated Dvořák, of course), Kovarik had to look after all the luggage, which meant that he had to stay on at the station while the Dvořáks went ahead to the village. (No matter that Kovarik hadn't been home for six years now – his job was to administer to Dvořák's comfort.) As he eventually made his way to the village, on a farm wagon loaded with trunks, Kovarik was suffering from anxiety attacks; but the sight that met his eyes when he arrived reassured him instantly. Dvořák, obviously enjoying the after-effects of a good meal, was standing in front of Kovarik's family home, smoking a pipe and smiling. "Welcome to Spillville!" the great man shouted benignly.

In fact, the Dvořáks had a wonderful summer in Spillville. Dvořák would get up at four every morning (yuk) and go for a walk. (He managed to make Kovarik feel guilty for sleeping until the lazy hour of six.) After breakfast, he would go to the church and play the organ, accompanied by the singing of his family and the Kovariks. At first, the old ladies in the congregation were shocked by all this noise in their usually silent services; but they got used to it. After chatting with people outside the church – Dvořák was fascinated by the life-stories of the Czech emigrants – Dvořák would go home to work; he was to compose two of his happiest pieces, his 'American' string quartet and string quintet, in Spillville. Later, he might take another walk. Striding along, he would write down new musical ideas on his shirt-cuffs (much to the disgust of the lady who did his laundry there), and would go home only when he'd run out of space to write – an unusual way to compose! At other times, he would visit some of the oldest Czech settlers, with whom he became particularly friendly; or he would surprise the local saddler, who happened to own an old harmonium (a strange-sounding keyboard instrument, rather like a small organ), by charging into his shop, trying out a few chords, and charging out again. When his new pieces were finished, Dvořák and the Kovariks would spend their afternoons playing them through.

In the evenings, it was back to darda – but at least there were now several people around who could play it. Still, Kovarik and Dvořák managed to quarrel again. Kovarik's holiday task was to make a neat copy of Dvořák's new symphony; one evening, after Kovarik had won too many times at darda, Dvořák, obviously looking for trouble, asked him how the copying was going. Fine, replied Kovarik; he was getting through four pages a day. Dvořák exploded: "Look, Indian – you're lazy!" Kovarik was offended – how could Dvořák call him lazy? So next day, he copied sixteen pages, and proudly reported the fact that night. Dvořák exploded again: "Sixteen? Are you trying to commit suicide? You're supposed to be on holiday!"

Luckily, at one point during the summer there was a two-week distraction from darda: a group of American Indians came to Spillville to sell their "magic medicines". Every evening they put on a show, playing drums, singing and dancing. Dvořák was intrigued, attending their presentations every night and making friends with the chief, Big Moon, and his wife 'Large Had' (apparently a misspelling of "Head"); they presented Dvořák with their photos, which he kept in Vysoká for the rest of his life. One can really hear the influence of their music in the 'American' quartet and quintet; and one can also detect hints there of the bird songs that so delighted Dvořák on his tramps through the local woods. Dvořák used everything!

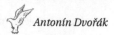

Later in the summer, Dvořák had to leave for a bit, to attend a "World Exposition" in Chicago, where on "Bohemian Day" he conducted his compositions for a crowd of six thousand cheering Czechs. But after that, he was thrilled to get back to Spillville – to his new/old friends, to the woods, to darda; and to the pitchers of beer that the local children brought to him on a regular basis. What more could he want from life? All in all, it was a wonderful summer – and one he would remember, and talk about, for the rest of his life.

The master gets his come-uppance ...

Kovarik, the "Little Indian", may have had a tough time – but of course he loved Dvořák; and besides, he occasionally got his revenge for all the insults heaped upon his innocent head. One memorable chance occurred during the journey to Spillville that summer. Dvořák was very upset that he couldn't buy any beer on the train: "The land of freedom! Free country! And one can't get a glass of beer here!" he grumbled. So when the train stopped in Pittsburgh station for twenty minutes, Kovarik kindly offered to go and find some. He managed to do so in an inn near the station, and walked back carrying three large bottles. When he got back to the station, he found that the train had been moved to another platform; no problem – he waited on the new platform, stretching his legs, and boarded the train just before it left. He went to the Dvořáks' carriage, anticipating the master's joyous gratitude when he saw the beer – but not a bit of it! Dvořák was in a foul mood. "Go away, you! I don't want to see you, Indian!" he roared. Kovarik showed him the beer. Dvořák swore at him: "I told you already – go away! And throw your beer out, I don't want it!" Perplexed, Kovarik stole away, and hid the beer bottles in an ice-box. He found Anna, who explained what had happened: when Kovarik hadn't reappeared in their carriage before the train left, Dvořák had got into a complete panic, convinced that Kovarik had missed the train, and had been left behind in Pittsburgh – and Kovarik had the train tickets! Understandable, in a way – but Dvořák's behaviour was still appalling. So Anna and Kovarik waited till the beer was nice and cold, and then took a bottle into the next compartment to the one in which Dvořák was sitting and sulking; they drank the beer noisily, praising its excellent taste. Eventually Dvořák couldn't resist; he came in – and saw that the bottle was empty! And he obviously hadn't noticed that Kovarik had brought more than one bottle. More temper tantrums: "You lousy Indian. You had a beer, but not for me. And you knew how thirsty I am." Kovarik pointed out that Dvořák had told him to throw the beer out – "but why should I? We were thirsty, too." Now Dvořák went all pathetic: "You drank it, good – but you could have offered a little to me, too. You knew full well that I didn't mean to do you any harm," he whined. Finally Kovarik took pity on him, and produced the other two bottles. Dvořák swore at him some more – but somehow his tone of voice was a little friendlier this time . . .

· 9 ·

Back in Bohemia, rumours abounded that Dvořák had emigrated to America for good, and would never come back. As so often, rumours were wrong. On his first visit home, in the summer of 1894, with all the children in tow, he went to Vysoká. It was so thrilling to be back there that, in a fit of generosity, he donated a new organ to the local church and had a skittles alley built – skittles being his favourite game (after darda, of course). It must have been hard for him and Anna to tear themselves away to go back to New York at the end of the summer; but it wasn't for long. In May 1895, Dvořák, Anna and Otakar (without Kovarik, who stayed behind to make a life for himself) left America for the last time, sailing home on a new, especially fast ship – very

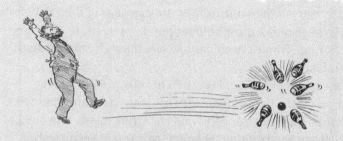

exciting. Dvořák hadn't ruled out the possibility of returning to New York, and allowed Mrs Thurber to advertise him as Director of the Conservatory as late as the 1897–98 academic year; but in the end he didn't go. It was time to settle down again in the place where he belonged.

He was by now a seriously grand public figure; but he hadn't really changed much. He stayed in his old, rather shabby apartment in Prague; at Vysoká, he and Anna still had to sleep downstairs in the dining room, because there wasn't a bedroom for them; he still tried (unsuccessfully) to get free season tickets to the National Theatre; he gave his son Toník a bicycle, as a reward for doing well in his studies – and then went into a state of panic when Toník actually started riding it. And he would still visit people, start talking, stop in mid-sentence to hum some new musical idea that had just occurred to him, and then march off suddenly, perhaps returning a few days later "to finish what we were talking about". He had a lovely reunion with Brahms, and visited his old patron four times in Vienna – and then, sadly, had to make a fifth visit for Brahms's funeral in April 1897. Appointed director of the Prague Conservatoire, he resumed his teaching there; and carried on his quarrels with Simrock. He also continued to write boastful letters to his friends – ending one catalogue of his many triumphs with the modest words: "So you see how fond people are of me everywhere." But it was true – they were!

Dvořák and Anna celebrated their silver wedding

anniversary at the same time as the marriage of their daughter Otylie to Dvořák's most brilliant pupil, Josef Suk, in 1898; and in 1901, the whole Czech nation celebrated Dvořák's sixtieth birthday.

One major change did occur in his musical life: having completed his last symphony ('From the New World') in 1893, and then his Cello Concerto and last string quartets in 1895, Dvořák stopped writing "abstract" music (i.e. music without any specific story attached to it), and after that wrote only music with a definite tale to tell. First, he wrote some "symphonic poems" for orchestra, retelling some old Czech legends in music; and then, for his last few years, he wrote only operas. Strange – in 1893, he'd lamented having spent so much time on operas in the past; but just a few years later, he decided that he didn't want to write anything else. In an interview very late in his life, he declared that he wanted to devote all his powers "to the creation of opera . . . I consider opera the most suitable form for the nation. This music is listened to by the broad masses, whereas when I compose a symphony I might have to wait years for it to be performed." That last sentence is actually very misleading; perhaps the interviewer misquoted him (as interviewers so often do), or perhaps Dvořák had been enjoying a bit too much beer before the interview – because it's just not true. If Dvořák had written a new symphony, it would have been seized upon by orchestras around the world; whereas opera, which is so complicated and expensive to put on, always caused him no end of difficulties.

Perhaps he felt that the glory of a successful opera made all the problems seem trivial by comparison. It is true that one of his late works, 'Rusalka', first performed in 1901, gave Dvořák his greatest success in the opera house. He didn't always have good librettos (or even libretti), but this one was excellent – although his librettist, Mr Kvapil, had to get used to Dvořák dropping in on him at 7 a.m. on his way back from inspecting the engines at Prague station, and then talking about anything except the work they were preparing, before abruptly striding off. Anyway, the results of their collaboration were spectacular; and 'Rusalka' is still very often performed today.

But with Dvořák's last opera, 'Armida', the problems were horrendous: the first director pulled out; the second quarrelled with Dvořák; one of the most important singers got ill just before the first performance, and had to be replaced at short notice; and so on. The whole thing was a nightmare, and had a bad effect on Dvořák's health: many years later, the original director felt so guilty about his behaviour that on his deathbed, he asked to see Anna Dvořák, and begged her forgiveness for having caused her husband's death. 'Armida' was actually pretty well received at its premiere (although Dvořák had to leave before the end because of a pain in his side, which may have been an early sign of his last illness); but it has never become popular. Nevertheless, at the time of his death, Dvořák was already working on a new opera story – one that would feature miners. With great pride, he told his miner friends at his favourite restaurant near Vysoká that there would be a mineshaft represented on the stage, and promised to take them all to Prague to see the production. Sadly, it was never to be.

A sudden end ...

Dvořák's health had always been remarkably good; he took lots of exercise, and even lifted weights in the mornings. Occasionally, he had had nervous attacks, causing him to cancel public appearances; but physically he'd been as strong as an extra-thick beer glass. So it was doubly worrying when he had to leave the premiere of 'Armida', and was then (apart from one brief trainspotting mission) unable to go out of the house for several weeks. Dvořák didn't seem to be too worried, though; he insisted that he was getting better. On May 1st, 1904, a Sunday, he got up very late – not a good sign; but at least he was in time for lunch. And a real Dvořák lunch it was: he ate a bowl of soup with great zest, and then complained that he was still hungry, so Anna made him his favourite meal, grilled steak with potatoes. After lunch Dvořák, still very weak, sat down in an armchair to rest. Then all of a sudden, he cried out: "Oh, my head is swimming," he exclaimed. A few moments later, he was dead. There's a photo of him lying in his coffin; that sounds ghoulish, but in fact it isn't. He looks quite beautiful; totally at peace, even his frown vanished – a child of nature returned to his roots.

It was sad that he'd died so young – at the age of sixty-two – but at least he had had, on the whole, a really happy, rewarding life: a wonderful marriage, a lovely family, lots of devoted friends, several extremely absorbing hobbies and, from his thirties onwards, a brilliantly successful musical career. As he put it himself: "I feel happy and contented while I am composing. God bless my good fortune . . . This is and always will be my motto: 'God – love – Homeland!'" And on that positive note, we can say goodbye to Mr Dvořák.

The Music

A lot of the magic of Dvořák's music lies in his rhythms. There are endless magnificent melodies and exciting textures, of course; but underlying everything he writes are the wonderfully natural rhythms that make his works so irresistibly alive. Dvořák's music is always either singing or dancing – or doing both at the same time.

At a time when most of his contemporaries were writing thoroughly "grown-up" music, finding increasingly complicated ways to express themselves, Dvořák remained childlike in his directness. A lot of his music is merry, sounding as though he has a lot to celebrate in life; then there is the other side of him, melancholy and inward-looking – but still never far from the spirit of folk music. There's a simplicity to his work that speaks to us with the voice of a friend.

Of course, there's lots of variety in his music too; some of it is quite complex – but his spirit is always clear-eyed and pure. And above all, whether he's writing an intricate string quartet, a grand opera or a simple little piece that skips around happily, his music is always lovable. It makes one feel good, because his love of life comes through loud and clear – and infects his listeners. A healthy infection!

What to listen to

Dvořák's symphonies are very good examples of his music; try numbers 6, 7, 8 and the last, No. 9 ('From the New World'). And every bit as important – ha! – is his Cello Concerto, Op. 104. That has everything: a glorious, heroic first movement; a peaceful, nostalgic slow movement; and then a joyous last movement that suddenly changes character at the end, as Dvořák bids Josefina a tender farewell.

Among his many beautiful operas, 'Rusalka' is a long but truly inspired work, with some gorgeous tunes, especially the 'Song to the Moon'; his religious music – the 'Te Deum', for instance – is very impressive, as well. But perhaps the best way of all to approach Dvořák is through his chamber music: try two wonderful quintets, the string quintet with double bass, Op. 77, and the piano quintet, Op. 81. (The piano quartet in E flat, Op. 87, is also a masterpiece.) Then, if you want to hear music from his American period, try the fizzing 'American' quartet, Op. 96; or another quintet, his string quintet, Op. 97. To hear the other, sadder side of Dvořák, listen to the 'Four Romantic Pieces' for violin and piano, Op. 75; the last of them is a magical, heartbroken lament. And so on ... Dvořák is a wonderful companion – enjoy his company!

Gabriel Fauré

1845–1924

there are probably quite a few people who, when they see the title of this chapter, will dispatch their eyebrows on a quick trip to the north. "Gabriel Fauré?"they'll exclaim (probably pronouncing the name wrongly, since they're so foolish in other ways – it should be Gabriel with an A as in "apple", "Faw-ray"). "He wasn't an important composer – he just wrote some pretty little pieces, and that's that." Well: if they do say that, look at them as witheringly as you possibly can, and tell them to put their eyebrows right back where they belong, on either side of the frown-marks at the tops of their noses; and then, for good measure, tell them that if they can't say anything more intelligent than that, they might as well keep their silly mouths shut for the foreseeable future – because what they say about Fauré is complete balderdash. Fauré was, in his quiet and gentle way, a genius; but he just wasn't the type to draw attention to himself. He didn't go around smashing musical windows, saying that everybody before him had got it wrong, and writing in a shockingly new-sounding style, as some famous composers did. It's true that a lot (though not all) of his pieces are on quite an intimate scale, almost as if they had been written for close friends; but that's one of his most wonderful qualities, not a fault. Fauré is a major musical figure, simply because he wrote some of the most angelically beautiful, pure, touching, and ecstatic music that has ever been written. And besides, he had a wonderful walrus moustache.

Well, I suppose he wasn't born with that last feature; but he does seem to have been born with an innate sense of beauty. Gabriel Urbain Fauré, to give him his full title, entered this world in a little village in the south of France at around 4 a.m. on May 12th, 1845. I'm sure that both he and his mother must have been exhausted for the rest of the day; and it seems as if Fauré never got over it, because he hated mornings for the rest of his life. He was the youngest of six children, and his mother didn't really want this new arrival; so poor Baby Gabriel was packed off to foster parents for his first four years. He must have felt a bit sad about that when he thought about it in later years; but he wasn't the type to feel bitter or angry, and it didn't stop him loving his family when he finally got to know them. By the time he came to live at home, though, the Fauré household was a pretty lonely place to be: his four brothers and one sister were away most of the time studying; his father, a headmaster at a boys' school, was busy with his job; and Mrs Fauré was fully occupied in the house. So little Gabriel, a quiet, well-behaved child, was left mostly to his own devices. He spent much of his time in a beautiful garden that was attached to the grounds of his father's school, and much of it in the school chapel, where there was a harmonium. Fauré would spend many happy hours playing this curious, wheezing instrument, badly (or so he claimed in later years) but enthusiastically; he even had some lessons on it from an old blind lady.

In time, it became clear that he had musical talent; strange, that, because nobody else in the family was at all interested in music. Fauré's gift was obviously so special, however, that a friend advised his parents to send the boy to a school of classical and religious music in Paris, the exciting capital city of France; the school was called the Niedermeyer School, after its founder and headmaster. Fauré's father was a bit worried – was it wise for his son to become a musician? (That's nothing new – the fathers of *every* composer in this book seem to have panicked, to some degree at least, when their sons decided to be professional musicians!) The friend was persuasive, though; and when Fauré senior discovered that, because of his small income, he'd only have to pay a quarter of the normal school fees, the matter was settled. Gabriel, now nine years old, set off with his father on the three-day coach trip to Paris.

Once at the school, the quiet, well-behaved little boy had to become even quieter and better behaved; it was a strict establishment, with not much time allowed for fun and games. At least the pupils received a good education, particularly in musical matters. They were introduced to lots of beautiful and ancient church music, as well as more modern music written for the concert hall; they were also taught to play various instruments, and to compose. Fauré seems to have been quite a favourite with both staff and students at the school, appreciated for his charm as well as his talent; Mr Niedermeyer himself was very fond of him, and became something of a father-figure to the quiet young boy. Fauré thrived, falling in love with the pure beauty of the historic music he sang in the choir; even in old age, he would enjoy getting together with surviving schoolfriends and singing the songs they'd learnt all those years earlier.

It was cramped at the school, though; the music room contained fifteen pianos, on which the boys had to practise – all at the same time. What a racket that must have made! But it certainly taught Fauré how to withdraw into himself, into his own world; no wonder that he became more and more of a dreamer. Maybe he was *too* much of a dreamer for some people's liking; when he went home for the school holidays, his brothers, far more down to earth, would tease him, sometimes cruelly. Once they woke him from his reverie by shoving a plate of spinach into his face; rather an extreme way to get his attention, but presumably it did the trick. Another time, some schoolmates sat on his face so hard that they broke his nose. But Fauré took it peaceably; he was too good-natured to make much of a fuss – and perhaps too dozy. On another occasion, as punishment for some small naughtiness, he was locked into a room; Fauré just went to sleep!

Meanwhile, his inner world developed and became stronger – maybe it was more vivid for him than everyday life? One can already hear his distinctive musical voice, with its mixture of church-like purity and garden-like beauty, emerging in his earliest compositions, written at the school. His very first song, he remembered later, was written in the dining room, with the smells of school dinner all around him. (Doesn't sound *very* inspiring – but he managed.) Fauré's composing was encouraged by a new arrival at the Niedermeyer establishment: a twenty-five-year-old man with an enormous nose, a flourishing beard and moustache, a loud, lisping voice and a winning smile. This was a piano teacher called Camille Saint-Saëns (pronounced "San-sonce"). (Actually, we already met him briefly two chapters ago, improvising a ballet with Tchaikovsky.) Saint-Saëns came to the school when Fauré was fifteen, and was to be extremely important in Fauré's life for the next sixty years or so. He's going to be very important to us too for the next three hundred seconds or so (depending on how fast you read), because he was such a fascinating, amazing character that he's going to have a whole paragraph to himself. And here it is:

Saint-Saëns was a child prodigy – and an adult prodigy. He started studying music at the age of two, wrote his first piano piece at the age of three, used to read scores of Mozart's operas for pleasure at the age of five, and at ten gave his first piano recital in Paris, offering at the end to play any of the thirty-two Beethoven sonatas from memory, in case the audience hadn't had enough yet. Sickening, really. And it wasn't just music that interested him, either. It's true that for his whole life he composed music "as an apple-tree grows apples", as he put it – and that he was also a brilliant pianist, a phenomenal organist, an expert on forgotten old music, an energetic organiser of concerts, a successful conductor, and a prolific writer about music. But other things were almost equally important to him: he wrote plays, books of poetry, books of philosophy, and travel books; he gave lectures on logic to learned societies; he was an expert on the science of acoustics and on ancient instruments; he was a distinguished astronomer, who designed his own telescope; and he was an energetic campaigner for animal rights. (He also composed Uruguay's national anthem, wrote a cantata to celebrate the glory of electricity, and was the first important composer to write film-music – in case you were wondering what he did with his spare time.) In short, Saint-Saëns was a phenomenon. He also had a phenomenally short temper, and during his long life managed to quarrel with an impressive number of people: at his own eighty-third birthday party, half the guests refused to speak to him! But he and Fauré remained the very best of friends for their whole lives. Furthermore, Saint-Saëns never stopped trying to help Fauré's career; in fact, he was far more ambitious for Fauré than Fauré was for himself.

It was Saint-Saëns who arranged for Fauré to get his first job when he graduated from the school: Fauré became the organist at a church in Rennes, a smallish town some distance from Paris. It really wasn't his scene, though; Fauré, despite his quiet,

Gabriel Fauré

thoughtful nature, loved parties and fun – and the people at his new church just weren't party animals. Far from it: when he arrived in Rennes, he had to live for a time with a strictly religious family who expected him to go to bed every night at eight o'clock! That wasn't the sort of life Fauré had in mind at all; somehow one has the feeling that he can't have been heartbroken when, after four boring years, he got the sack for turning up to play at a morning service dressed in full evening dress, having come straight from an all-night party.

So in March 1870, it was farewell to Rennes, and back to Paris. Paris was the place for Fauré; there he could find almost everything he really cared about – fine musicians, true music lovers, elegant surroundings, distinguished society and beautiful women. But Fauré, now twenty-four years old, also needed to make a living. Once again Saint-Saëns – "Grandfather", as Fauré called him – came to the rescue; he found his former pupil – "my large cat", as he called Fauré – a job as a church organist in the great city. The "large cat" was thrilled; at last he could start to live life as it was supposed to be lived!

Not for long, though. Later that year, war broke out between France and Germany; the dreamy, pleasure-loving Fauré was suddenly transformed into a soldier, fighting to defend his beloved home town. He took part in three battles, served as a messenger when Paris was under siege, and was given an award for bravery. Life in the city must have been awful: people were reduced to eating dogs, cats and rats. (Bad for the people; even worse for the dogs, cats and rats.) Not surprisingly, Fauré was relieved when it was over; when France surrendered in 1871, he found his way back home and slept solidly for twenty-four hours! Even after the war was over, though, Paris remained unsafe, and Fauré had to escape, using a fake passport. These were the first really dramatic series of events in his dreamy life (well, unless you count the plate of spinach).

Having supported himself during his exile by teaching at his old school, which had been evacuated to Switzerland during the fighting, Fauré finally returned to Paris in the autumn of 1871. Settling down in the capital for good now, he was appointed (with Saint-Saëns' help, as usual) to a couple of different jobs as organist, as well as boosting his income by giving music lessons. By this point, however, it was high time for Fauré to start thinking beyond his life as a jobbing musician. He'd composed some wonderful short pieces (one choral work he'd written while still a schoolboy, the 'Cantique de Jean Racine', is still one of his most famous works, and rightly so – it's gorgeous); but he was just too unambitious, and too busy earning his living, to write a really major work. Thank goodness for Saint-Saëns, that hive of nervous energy, constantly urging him on, as well as introducing Fauré to other strong, energetic people who kept trying to bully him into doing more with his talent. Fauré was charming and lovable; but he was also frustrating.

Let's take a brief look at him at this point in his life. If we look at him by himself and catch him at the wrong moment, we may be a bit disturbed; he suffers from occasional deep depressions, and from migraines so violent that he sometimes has to prop himself up against a wall to stop himself from keeling over. So there's a dark side to his life, which probably contributes to his lack of drive; but there's an extremely well-lit side to it, too. In the evening, we're likely to find him in a luxurious drawing room, or salon, to which he's been invited by music-loving hosts. Fauré is dressed up to the nines, in a smart dark suit with tails and a white bow-tie. He's thoroughly good-looking, with lots of black hair, deep-set dark brown eyes flecked with gold, tanned-looking skin, a graceful figure, and (by now) a classy moustache. He's completely at home in this elegant setting, wandering around the crowd of distinguished-looking people with a blissful smile on his face, and a far-off expression. His manners are charming, his voice husky but gentle, with a slight southern French accent that means he rolls his "r"s adorably; no wonder he captivates all hearts – especially female ones! (Men were extremely fond of him as well, though; Tchaikovsky, for instance, who met him in 1886, thought he was "delightful".) Now the handsome young composer sits at the piano and accompanies an enthusiastic lady singer in one of his beautiful songs; the women around him practically swoon, the older ladies dreaming of mothering him, the younger ones dreaming of other things . . .

But alas – the younger ladies were to be disappointed, at least in the long run; the trouble was that Fauré's heart may have been readily available for hire, but it wasn't yet for sale. In both his musical and romantic life, he was a bit directionless. He was composing small pieces, he was flirting – but it seemed as if an eruption were needed to make him settle down and take life seriously. Eventually, as he entered his thirties, that eruption took place.

Musically, it came about in the form of a violin sonata, his first major work. His friends practically had to lock him into a room to force him to get down to work and finish it; when he *did* eventually complete it, though, it changed his life. An enthusiastic friend sent the sonata off to a famous German publisher. To Fauré's astonishment, the publishers agreed to print it – though not exactly on generous terms (in fact, they didn't pay him a penny for it). So he was now an internationally published composer; and the first performance of the work, in Paris in 1877, took everybody by surprise. So far, the general attitude had been "Fauré's a jolly good fellow" – but was he anything more? This sonata showed that he was: this composer of charming songs and piano-pieces, which were so popular in sophisticated Parisian salons, could write a large-scale masterpiece. People were astonished and impressed. From that point onwards, Fauré would no longer limit himself to small forms; moreover, in small forms or large, he started to challenge himself more and more, to extend his range, his music becoming deeper and more meaningful – and so he became a great composer.

The sonata was soaring, brilliant and ecstatic; perhaps the ecstasy was partly to do with the other, non-musical eruption in Fauré's life. The work was dedicated to the son of a lady called Pauline Viardot, one of the best-known society hostesses in Paris. Pauline had been a well-known singer herself in earlier days; she was an extremely strong character who lived with her children, her husband and her lover, the famous Russian writer, Turgenev (whom her children, and Fauré also, addressed as "Godfather"). Pauline was a supporter of Fauré's, and he was made very welcome in her house; the Viardots became, for a time, almost like a second family for him – although a far richer and grander family than his own. He loved going there for lots of reasons: for a start, anybody who was anybody in Paris was likely to be found in Pauline's salon; then, there tended to be lots of dancing, and Fauré loved dancing; there was the pleasure of having his ego boosted by the support and flattery he received from the people he met there; and finally – and most crucially – there was the little matter of one of Pauline's daughters, Marianne.

Marianne was a rather surprising choice for Fauré: she was quiet, timid and shy, and not particularly beautiful – but the composer was smitten. For four agonising years he wavered, longing to marry her, but not wanting to frighten her by asking too insistently. He kept trying to get up his courage to demand an answer – but as soon as he got too bold, she'd slap him, which wasn't exactly encouraging. At last, however, he couldn't stand it any longer, and told her that he needed a decision; and she didn't say no! Oh Joy. She didn't actually say yes either, though; she asked for three months to think it over. Oh Less Joy. Three months more agony for Fauré, in fact. But then, finally –

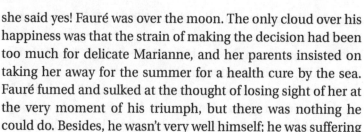

Gabriel Fauré

she said yes! Fauré was over the moon. The only cloud over his happiness was that the strain of making the decision had been too much for delicate Marianne, and her parents insisted on taking her away for the summer for a health cure by the sea. Fauré fumed and sulked at the thought of losing sight of her at the very moment of his triumph, but there was nothing he could do. Besides, he wasn't very well himself; he was suffering from a throat infection that was threatening to turn his already rather husky voice into a mere croak – and Marianne wouldn't have wanted to marry a man who sounded like a frog.

So Fauré took himself off to a different health spa, and from there wrote impassioned, imploring letters to Marianne. On the surface, he gave an impression of serenity; but underneath that tranquil exterior was a romantic tempest, which poured out in these letters. "I love you with all my heart, now and always," he exclaimed. "You are a pearl . . . and I am determined to worship you!" Strong stuff. His passion swept away some of his Parisian sophistication: he would sign his love-letters "Toto" – Marianne's pet name for him – and told her (rather embarrassingly) that he wanted to "kiss the little hairs on the side of your ear". He was, he told a friend, "living pure daydreams" – not that that was anything new for him.

So now, in the late summer of 1877, everything in his life looked rosy: his musical career was starting to look more promising; he was living in his favourite city, surrounded by devoted friends; he was going to marry the woman he adored. What could be better? Well – nothing, really; and in fact, things got considerably worse instead. Back in Paris, perhaps alarmed by the strength of his passion, Marianne asked to postpone the wedding. Fauré was upset, and showed it so violently that poor, timid Marianne was frightened; she broke off the engagement altogether, and returned all his love letters. Fauré was devastated. It was as if, with one sudden blow, his whole world had suddenly crumbled around him. He had lost not only Marianne, but also the golden family whose friendship had meant so much to him. Writing to Marianne's sister, he begged her not to abandon him completely; his "whole being", he said, was wrapped up in the Viardot family.

In later years, he acknowledged that it was all probably for the best. Not only was Marianne a bit of a weed (although Fauré was far too gallant ever to admit that), but her family had wanted to push him into writing grand, showy operas – and that wouldn't have been right for him at all. So in the end, perhaps he was grateful for Marianne's decision. For the moment, though, things were bad. He fell into what he described as an "appalling vacuum"; it was one of the lowest points in his life. As for Marianne, she ended up marrying a minor composer, and drooping off into, or out of, history. Or is that a bit unfair? Anyway, she vanishes from our story now.

Fauré recovered, of course – most people do; broken hearts tend to be more easily mended than broken necks, on the whole. By the next year, if not sooner, he was back to flirting madly – he couldn't help it! But he was still going through some tough times. "I am perturbed, disturbed, dismayed and overwhelmingly sad," he wrote to a motherly friend in 1879. "I am bleeding, and do not know where the wound is." That sounds worrying. Other letters written at around the same time show that he hadn't lost his capacity for having fun, though. Fauré's humour made him popular with children. In one letter, he complains that the children of friends of his are completely ransacking his room as he writes; one is between his legs, another on his back. "The situation is no longer tenable," he wails.

In another, he writes that he'd been a bit dismayed when he'd made a date with a pretty girl, and her brother had turned up instead. "He is very nice," he admits, "and has even more whiskers than his sister, but he is no substitute." Fair enough.

In general, however, he felt frustrated; he knew that his life was going to have to change if he were to achieve all the great things of which he was capable. He'd have to stop filling his schedule with unimportant jobs and frivolous amusements, and would somehow need to arrange things so that he'd get more serious work done.His friends were sure that he would never manage it on his own, and decided that the best plan for him would be to get married to someone who could offer him a steady home life. So at the age of thirty-seven, Fauré got engaged again; and this time it resulted in marriage. The story goes that one of his many middle-aged lady admirers put the names of three eligible young ladies into a hat, and made Fauré draw one out: that would be the name of his future wife. Hmm . . . sounds a bit unlikely to me. Anyway, the girl he chose – and who accepted him gladly – was called Marie Fremiet ("Fremi-eh"), the daughter of a distinguished artist and sculptor called Emmanuel Fremiet.

To outward appearances, Marie was as unexpected a choice for Fauré as Marianne had been. She was shy and silent, far from beautiful, and unhappy by nature; perhaps she even reminded Fauré of Marianne? Poor Marie was all too aware of her limits: "I am the dunce, the lame dog, the non-entity of the family", she wrote to Saint-Saëns – not exactly a fountain of self-confidence there. Her main trouble was that with a famous father and now a famous husband, she felt that there was no way that she could use her own talents, and fulfil her dreams of becoming an artist in her own right. (She did make lovely hand-painted fans for the first few years of the marriage, and boosted the family income considerably with them, but that wasn't enough to satisfy her; and her later attempts to become a sculptress ended in failure.) Even if they'd agreed that he needed a wife, several members of Fauré's smart set were bitchy about his choice. They mistook Marie's shyness for unfriendliness; she was "narrow and cold", wrote one particularly disapproving friend – and besides, he added sniffily, "she has no taste in clothes." Parisian wives in Fauré's circle were supposed to be socially accomplished, witty and elegant – but that just wasn't the way Marie was. In fact, she hated going out into society, and hated the fact that her husband wanted to do so almost every night. She took to "forgetting" to do the laundry, so that Fauré wouldn't have any clean shirts, and would be forced to stay in. It didn't work, though – Fauré would just go out and buy new shirts instead. Later, she would suffer deeply when Fauré fell in love with a succession of beautiful women, all more confident and outwardly successful than herself.

But Marie had her own very special qualities; and Fauré, despite his own completely different character, appreciated them. And although it's true that Marie and Fauré had a strange and rather unsatisfactory relationship, they stayed together – or at least semi-together – until his death. In his later years, he would confide all his musical plans and dreams to her, and she would understand and encourage him, kissing his manuscript paper to bring him good luck. In fact, in their rather curious way, they do seem to have loved one another. He adored Marie's parents, too, becoming particularly close to her father; as with Marianne and the Viardots, it almost seems as if he'd wanted to marry the whole family.

Anyway, as the day approached, Fauré was happy to be getting married at last. His descriptions of Marie before the wedding were far from the passionate outbursts in which he'd indulged during his engagement to Marianne; but he was, he told a friend, filled with a "deep, sweet delight" at the prospect of settling down with Marie. And so the wedding took place, in March 1883. The very best results of the union were the Faurés' two boys, Emmanuel and Philippe, born in late 1883 and 1889 respectively. Fauré adored both his sons, and they adored him. Writing to a friend when Emmanuel was three, Fauré complained about parents who were always going on about how wonderful their children were; but this was different, he continued – there really *was* "no sweeter, more intelligent, more sensitive, more perceptive" a creature than Emmanuel! Unfortunately both boys suffered from delicate health – which made their perpetually worried, obsessively hygienic mother more neurotic than ever. Poor Philippe couldn't even stand up until he was nearly six; but he, like Emmanuel, was extremely intelligent and lovable. Shortly before his sixth birthday, he wrote a letter to his daddy: "My darling Papa, I am almost walking, and we are very well. But I annoy Mummy a bit, and I have made a boat for Mummy, and I am very excited because I am going with Mummy. Darling Papa, I love you very much indeed." I'm sure that Fauré's heart melted when he read that.

So as the boys grew up, Fauré's life was in many ways far better than it had been before. But then again, in other ways it still wasn't all that good. For a start, having a family to support meant that he had to take on lots of boring new teaching jobs, which involved him spending three hours a day rushing around on trains – probably not what he'd had in mind when he'd decided to settle down. His finances improved a bit when in 1892 he was appointed as inspector of music schools throughout France; but that post was still far from exciting, and involved even more travel. He dreamed of getting a proper, challenging job, such as a professorship at the Paris Conservatoire, France's leading school of music; but the head of that great institution would have none of it. Fauré hadn't even studied at the Conservatoire, after all. "Fauré? Never! If he's appointed, I resign," he spluttered. Distinctly unpromising. So Fauré struggled on with his thankless tasks. He tried desperately to find time to compose; but even when he did manage to produce something, it was genuinely appreciated only by a handful of intelligent people. Would he ever be truly successful?

It wasn't until 1896 that his professional life really started to take off – at last. The head of the Conservatoire – the one who had threatened to resign if Fauré was given a post there – finally did resign. In fact, he resigned on a permanent basis – he died. After that, it wasn't long before Fauré, to his delight, was appointed as a professor of composition, and he quickly became famous as a teacher. He wasn't exactly a model professor; he would regularly arrive forty-five minutes late for his classes, and some days he would seem to be in such a dream that the pupils wondered whether he was listening to their works at all. But he was: fifteen years later, he might surprise them by suddenly mentioning a detail from one of the pieces they'd shown him in the class. Besides, he had the aura of a great musical figure, and the students revered him; sometimes without knowing quite how or why, they would make progress.

Fauré's pupils included some of the most gifted composers of the early twentieth century – most famously a well-dressed, super-intelligent young man called Maurice Ravel. Perhaps Ravel's most familiar work nowadays, unfortunately, is an oddly hypnotic orchestral piece called "Boléro". It crops up all over the place – film soundtracks, mobile phone ring-tones, supermarket muzak, etc. Poor Ravel – if he were around today, I'm sure he'd be horrified! (But rich.) What was really important about him, though, was that, along with another French composer of genius, Claude Debussy, he created a really new style of French music, both composers discovering whole new sound-worlds. (We heard about Debussy very briefly, by the way, when as a young man, he was being supported by Tchaikovsky's patron Nadezhda von Meck. Remember? . . . just checking that you've been concentrating.)

Actually, an episode in Ravel's early career turned out to have a big effect on the career of his teacher. Ravel had been trying for years to win the Conservatoire's biggest composition prize, the Prix de Rome, and in 1905, he tried for the fifth time. In previous competitions, he had done well, without actually winning the first prize, but this time he didn't even reach the final. It turned out that all six of the young composers who *did* reach the finals were pupils of one of the fusty old professors who still ran the Conservatoire; furthermore, this professor, by an inexplicable coincidence, just happened to be on the jury! There was a scandal; newspaper articles were printed, referring to "the Ravel affair". (It sounds better in French: "L'affaire Ravel".) The upshot of the uproar was that the director of the Conservatoire resigned and, with the support of the unstoppable Saint-Saëns, our gentle friend Fauré, now sixty years old, was appointed in his place. He was now officially a big-shot.

And perhaps not that gentle after all; the appointment had an astonishing effect on him. Thirty-five years earlier, he'd suddenly shaken off his dreams in favour of action and become a soldier; now it happened again. Determined to transform the Conservatoire into a living, breathing entity, Fauré forced out the boring twits who'd had their way for far too long. They were outraged. Earlier, his predecessor had been very firm about the purpose of the institution: "Monsieur, the Conservatoire, as its name indicates, exists to *conserve* tradition." Fauré would have none of that. He agreed completely that knowing the music of the past was important – but music wasn't a dead art; the students needed to know what was happening in their own times as well. So he introduced them to all sorts of modern music, brought important new musical personalities to the Conservatoire, and swept away anyone who objected. And because he was Fauré, because he was so charming and everybody – well, *nearly* everybody – adored him, he managed to get away with it. He was in his element; his son Philippe remembered him coming home every night "with the air of a conqueror". It was a good time for Fauré. Two years earlier, after several failed attempts to get the job, he'd also been appointed music critic for one of France's major newspapers; although writing was something of a torture for him, he wrote more than three hundred articles, his views influencing the musical life of France.

So finally everything looked rosy for Fauré – on the surface. He still didn't have nearly enough time to compose, but at least he was enjoying his work at the Conservatoire, in a way he'd never enjoyed any of his previous jobs. Another aspect of his life that he was enjoying was the company of a young lady he'd met in 1900; she was a wonderful pianist called Marguerite Hassel-mans, who would be a faithful companion to Fauré until his death. She was certainly not the first girlfriend he'd had since his marriage, but she was the one who lasted. Marguerite was a striking contrast to Marie. Outgoing, fluent in many languages, beautiful – and easily young enough to be Fauré's daughter – she could probably have caused havoc in his life; but she seems to have accepted that Fauré was a married man, and that was that. Fauré would go on long summer holidays with her, and sometimes entertained at her place in Paris in the winter – even though he was still officially living with Marie and the boys. It was quite an arrangement! And with his new standing as one of the most important and popular men in the musical life of France, hardly anybody seems to have criticised him for it.

But alas – hanging over Fauré's handsome head, and descending slowly but horribly surely, was a threatening cloud. In 1903, two years before he became Director of the Conservatoire, Fauré wrote to Marie: "The problems with my hearing remain fearful and depressing as ever." Disaster had struck – Fauré, like Beethoven a hundred years earlier, was going deaf. It wasn't just that he couldn't hear: the sounds that he *could* hear were distorted, high notes sounding higher than they really were, low notes lower. Many of his greatest works were yet to be written; but he would never hear them himself, except in his head. It made his job as Director of the Conservatoire difficult, as well as his job as critic (although a lot of music critics seem to be deaf to start with!) Fauré, however, managed to carry on for many years in both capacities, trying desperately to hide his increasing deafness from everybody except those closest to him. It was a horrible curse; but life went on.

By this point, his schedule had settled into a routine. During the winter months, apart from the occasional foreign trip to take part in concerts of his works (including the longest journey of his life, to far-off Russia and Finland, in 1910), he would be in Paris, running the Conservatoire, living with his family, occasionally reviewing concerts or operas, and going out to as many social events as possible (frequently with Marguerite). In the summer, he would go on holiday, usually to the south of France, accompanied by the faithful Marguerite; it was only during these trips that he could really devote himself to composing. It's sad for us that he had so little time to write music; but he had to live, and his compositions didn't bring in enough to support him and his family. (There was an added expense these days, too: he'd acquired a flat in Paris for Marguerite. How he justified that to – or hid it from – Marie remains a mystery.)

Anyway, his work at the Conservatoire was important, to him and to all the young musicians whose life he changed, directly or indirectly. The students were under his spell. I used to know an old gentleman who had studied at the Conservatoire when Fauré was Director; although he didn't have any direct contact with the great man himself, he felt that "Fauré's influence was somehow everywhere." Of course, it was whispered that a deaf man shouldn't be running such an important school; but actually, Fauré's deafness wasn't that much of a problem in musical matters. He could read a piece of music like most people can read a book, so he could judge young composers' works as easily as when he'd had his hearing; and he could tell how an instrumentalist was playing, or a singer was singing, just by looking at them and observing their style.

He carried on as Director of the Conservatoire until 1920; but then he was asked to resign. That hurt, especially since the newspapers announced his resignation before he did. (Not long after that, the newspaper for which he wrote also replaced him as critic without telling him – charm personified.) When he'd got over his hurt feelings, though, Fauré started to feel the positive effects of retirement. For the first time in his life, he was free to compose whenever he liked, not just during the summers. He had only another four years left to him after leaving the Conservatoire; but he made the most of them. As his body grew older and more feeble, his spirit seemed to become younger and stronger – one can hear it in his music. (Saint-Saëns said that Fauré was "ageless".) One can feel increasingly in Fauré's last works that he was on a unique journey, his inner world becoming ever more removed from the life around him (maybe partly because of his deafness). As his son Philippe put it, "his solitary spirit discovered new secrets . . . he soared towards the infinite."

We had a glimpse of him in a fashionable salon when he was young; now let's go briefly into his study (we don't want to go in for too long, because we mustn't disturb his composing) and visit him in his old age. He receives us kindly. His door is never closed in these late years, because he feels that he's alone enough with his deafness, and his increasingly dim sight, and he doesn't want to be even more isolated. He sits at his desk, looking up at us with his wonderful, wise eyes; we can hear him wheezing, because he suffers from bronchitis, made worse by far too much smoking. His moustache is more resplendent than ever – although stained yellowish now by nicotine. Snowy-white hair crowns his noble head; although his forehead is very high these days, he's far from bald. He sits, head bowed forward, trying to hear what we're saying to him. We have to say it three or four times over – but finally he's got it. Then he smiles, and his whole face lights up; even his moustache seems to perk up. He replies in the old husky voice – weaker now, but as charming as ever. He thanks us for coming, and we leave; as we go out, he turns back to the manuscript paper he has in front of him, then looks out of the window. He is back in his dreams.

As Fauré neared his end, he often had to stay in bed for weeks at a stretch; but when his health permitted, he still loved to go out and have a good time. Philippe remembered him coming back from a dinner in 1923 "in a mood of bravura . . . A sparkling dining room, bright dresses, a breath of society atmosphere . . . had been enough to lift his spirits and he declared himself 'ready to go and paint the town red!'" There were some celebrations of his life's work, such as a huge "Fauré Festival", attended by a glittering crowd of the great and the good, including the President of France (who got far less applause when he appeared than Fauré did – ha). These events pleased and touched Fauré, and brought in some very welcome money; but he felt that success had come too late for him really to enjoy it. Furthermore, he'd be critical of the works of his that were played; he felt that he could do still better.

So he kept setting himself new challenges. In the summer of 1923, he started on the first string quartet he'd ever written; he was nervous about it, feeling that nothing could ever be as great as the wonderful quartets that Beethoven had composed. Writing a string quartet was enough, he said, "to give all those people who aren't Beethoven the jitters". Still, he was going to try; so he began, slowly and secretly, in July. He finished the first and second movements by the end of the year; but that winter and the spring of 1924 were difficult. He was mostly too ill to compose, and was worried that he wouldn't finish the quartet; he probably knew that it would be his last work. First quartet, last composition – that somehow sums up his wonderful combination of old age and eternal youth. Furthermore, he used in the quartet two themes that he'd originally composed for a violin concerto he'd started forty-five years earlier, but never finished. Fauré's life was coming full circle.

Fortunately, his health gradually improved; by June, he was well enough to take his annual holiday. And so he set off for the south of France, where he was to spend the summer accompanied by both his sons, as well as Marguerite. As the train pulled away from Paris, the frail invalid was suddenly transformed; he became like a young man again. Fauré went to the restaurant car and devoured an omelette – "Incomparable!" he exclaimed. Once at his destination, he rested for three days, and then set to work. All through the summer, he worked slowly but steadily on the last movement of the quartet. On September 12th, 1924, he wrote to Marie: "Yesterday evening, I finished the Finale." His life's work was finished.

The quartet had soaked up almost all of Fauré's last fraction of strength; he was exhausted. There was still one more important task ahead of him, though: he knew he owed Marie a last apology for all the misery she'd suffered on his account. Probably aware that he wouldn't be able to tell her when he saw her, because he always communicated with her so much better in writing than in person, he wrote her a last letter, dated October 14th. "I am very well at the moment," he tried to reassure her. "My appetite is excellent. I am happy with the fine weather we have been having, happy with everything, and I should like everyone to be happy around me, and everywhere else!" It was a lovely way to start; but then he went on to more serious matters. He talked about her father's impressive achievements, and then – with apologies – about his own; he asked whether the achievements of her father and her husband had not brought some happiness to her. "Your life has been a sad one," he admitted, acknowledging her frustration at not having had an artistic career of her own. But, he asked anxiously, didn't her part in his and her father's achievements, and the consciousness of having brought up two wonderful boys, bring some comfort to her? "I do hope you will understand what I am trying to say and that these lines will convey to you all the sincerity I have put into them!" The letter finishes: "I kiss you from the depths of my heart."

It is an extraordinary document. I wonder how Marie felt when she got it? I imagine that she must have wept – for grief that her life *had* been so sad, that their marriage had been so unsatisfactory; and for joy that her husband had showed at the last that, deep down, he did love her, even if it was with a compassionate, rather than passionate, love.

After that, weak and unshaven, a shadow of his former self, Fauré was taken by his sons back to Paris, where he gave Marie all his old sketches (and perhaps love letters?) to burn; he wanted to tidy up before he died. He instructed his family to keep his condition a secret, so that he could die in private, with dignity. And he did just that. On November 3rd, he called his two sons to him, and told them "how tenderly he had returned the feelings of those who had loved him". He told the "boys" (now forty and thirty-five) not to worry if his reputation suffered a little after his death; it happened with most composers. Then came his very final words: "I did what I could . . . now let God be my judge." Early the next morning, he drifted away.

I wish he were still alive today (he'd only be 160, as I write – a youngster); but his death seems to have been as peaceful, as beautiful as death can be. Of all his works, probably the most widely loved is his 'Requiem'. Many composers, when they write Requiem Masses, concentrate on the dark mystery of death, and on the "day of wrath" supposed to come at the final judgement. Not Fauré: his 'Requiem' is radiant and comforting. Fauré saw death "as a joyful deliverance, an aspiration towards a happiness beyond the grave".

Marie survived her husband by only eighteen months – perhaps, despite everything, she missed him too much to carry on without him. Emmanuel continued his distinguished career as a biologist, while Philippe became a writer, whose books included affectionate biographies of both his father and his (Fremiet) grandfather. Marguerite Hasselmans lived until 1947, delighting those lucky enough to hear her play Fauré's music. Through his students, too, Fauré's spirit lived on; some became major composers, others passed on his legacy to future generations. One of his favourite pupils, an extraordinary lady called Nadia Boulanger, would herself teach many of the most important musicians of the later twentieth century; several of them are still performing or composing today.

Facts of Life

·1·

Fauré's parents had interesting names. His father was called Toussaint-Honoré Fauré, while his mother's maiden name was Marie-Antoinette-Hélène de Lalène-Laprade. They took names seriously in those days!

A protective father ...

Toussaint-Honoré was quite a distinguished schoolmaster, author of a little 'Treatise of Arithmetic' that was used in many schools. He was very much a self-made man, his father and grandfather having been butchers – shades of Dvořák there. Toussaint-Honoré was strict and severe – a real schoolmaster, in fact; but he was also kind. Perhaps he wasn't much fun, but he inspired respect and trust, and he really tried to do his best for his children. His letters to them were signed: "Your father and your friend". In his last letter to Fauré, he told him that he was "watching over" him – a comforting image for a father to leave his son.

·2·

Perhaps it was just as well that Toussaint-Honoré *was* strict, because otherwise the schedule at the Niedermeyer School in Paris might have been too much of a shock for little Gabriel. His weekdays there were busy: up at 5.30 to practise, and then almost constant work for the rest of the day. The nights weren't always that easy, either; one winter the roof leaked, and Fauré had to sleep in a soaking wet bed. The students were only allowed one walk a week – not very healthy; and they weren't allowed to leave the school by themselves except on Sundays, and then only to meet close relatives or appointed guardians. Until 1861, Fauré's guardian was the family friend who'd advised Toussaint-Honoré to send Gabriel to the school, and it is to him that Fauré's first surviving letter is addressed. "Sir," writes the nine-year-old boy politely, "I write these few lines to advise you not to bother to come and collect me in a fortnight's time as my aunt has promised to come and collect me." Then, just in case his guardian had missed the point the first time, he adds: "I am advising you in order that you shall not bother to come and collect me" – Fauré liked to be clear about these things. From 1861 onwards, though, Fauré had a new guardian: Saint-Saëns' mother . . .

Quite a lady . . .

Well, we gave Saint-Saëns a whole paragraph to himself earlier; so I think we'd better give his mother a paragraph to herself too, or she may get cross – and we definitely don't want to get on the wrong side of her. She was fierce! *Saint-Saëns, an only child, never knew his father, who died just a few months after his son was born, so he was brought up entirely by two formidable women: his mother and his great-aunt. Saint-Saëns was devoted to them both; but he can't have had an easy childhood – or adulthood, for that matter. If his mother decided that she didn't like a piece that Saint-Saëns had written, he'd have to start all over again; and, even when he was well into his twenties, she'd insist on reading, in front of him, all the letters he received. Her personality shines (?) through a letter she wrote to Saint-Saëns when, in his mid-thirties, he was going to perform at a huge music festival; he'd told her that he was worried he might not play as well as some of the other great pianists who were performing there. "Dear Friend," she replied graciously, "I found your letter upon my return from Mass. You make me ill with your fears. You are merely a coward. I treat you with contempt. I believed I had brought up a man. I have raised up only a girl of degenerative stock. Play as you ought to play – an artist of great talent. Either you will play well, or I will renounce you as my child." What a sweetie. Still, Fauré doesn't seem to have had any problem with her. He probably charmed her as he charmed everyone else; in fact, he is sure to have made an extra effort to keep on the right side of her, because he loved her cooking.*

· 3 ·

In his eleven years at the Niedermeyer School, Fauré did very well, winning several prizes. Some, not surprisingly, were for piano-playing and composition, but there were also two for literature and one for religious studies. In addition, he had a real talent for drawing cartoons; he did some particularly good caricatures of Saint-Saëns, having fun with his teacher's truly enormous nose. Still, it was his composition that was most outstanding, of course; and it's frustrating that after having produced some beautiful short piano pieces and songs, as well as the 'Cantique de Jean Racine', while still at the school, it was to take him until his thirties to produce his first large-scale masterpiece (the first violin sonata). So many years practically wasted! To be fair, it wasn't *just* because he spent most of his time either earning a living or going to parties; there was another major problem as well. If a French composer didn't want to write an opera – and Fauré didn't at that point – there was really almost no chance of getting his or her music performed outside the Parisian salons, which were of course strictly private. Life wasn't easy if you decided to be both French and a composer.

Saint-Saëns and some friends decided to do something about this state of affairs; trying to rebuild French morale in the aftermath of the disastrous war of 1870, they founded the "National Society of Music", putting on concerts consisting entirely of modern French music. Fauré became the Society's secretary in 1874 – although he soon got into trouble for his "deplorable unpunctuality". It was the National Society that presented the first public performance of his violin sonata, as well as many other works of his. Fauré admitted that without the Society, he wouldn't have written the sonata; French composers weren't *supposed* to write works like that. In fact, Fauré's is the first famous French sonata for violin and piano.

Problems with publishers ...

So perhaps it's not surprising that it was a German publisher, not a French one, who accepted the sonata; but that relationship didn't last. In fact, Fauré was to have a hard time with publishers for most of his life. His first major contract was with a French firm called "Hamelle". (As in many French words, the "h" isn't pronounced – I don't why it's there, really. The French do waste letters, don't they? At a time when the earth is running out of natural resources, it does seem a pity. Still, we English-speakers can't be too smug – think of "Wednesday", for instance. And what's the "h" doing in what? But sorry – I'm wandering off the point.) He signed up with them in 1879, and stayed with them until 1906. It's hard to know why; they couldn't have cared less about him – it was said that Mr Hamelle's wife

(Mrs Hamelle, in fact) used unsold copies of Fauré's works to cover her jam-jars! Also, Hamelle kept giving Fauré's pieces unsuitable titles. Once, for instance, Fauré wrote a children's piece named after a dog called Ketty; Hamelle didn't like that name, so he changed the title to "Kitty". (The dog must have been livid!) And Hamelle never listened to Fauré's protests.

No wonder Fauré snapped. In 1896, he wrote a letter to Hamelle: "I am simply unable to tolerate any longer your indifference to the fate of my compositions. I am fifty-one . . . but you treat me as though I was some student just out of school," he raged. "I've had enough." It's a good letter, but it didn't lead to much. Either Hamelle managed to calm him down with false promises, or Fauré's laid-back good nature got the better of him. Whichever it was, Fauré stayed on for another ten years before moving to another publisher for a few years, changing again in 1913. But he still wasn't free of ham-fisted Hamelle; towards the end of Fauré's life, Hamelle agreed to produce a good new edition of Fauré's complete piano music (from which he'd already made a fortune, incidentally). One of Fauré's favourite pupils spent months editing out all the mistakes in the original editions, and writing intelligent introductions; Fauré also took immense trouble over it, checking everything over and giving Hamelle explicit instructions. And what did Horrible Hamelle ('Orrible 'Amelle, rather) do? Waited until Fauré had died, then brought the pieces out as cheaply as possible, without introductions and ignoring Fauré's wishes. Gggrrrr . . .

·4·

After the premiere of Fauré's first violin sonata, his former teacher Saint-Saëns said that he felt the pain of a mother whose child finally grows up and doesn't need her any more; Fauré was now a musical adult. Practically, though, it didn't change much in his day-to-day existence. Three months later, Saint-Saëns arranged for Fauré to become choirmaster at the Madeleine, one of the most famous churches in Paris. It was certainly the best job Fauré had had so far, and he would continue to work at the Madeleine for about eighteen years; but he didn't enjoy it much – he referred to his choir, rather rudely, as "my gaggle of geese". His life was still basically that of a jobbing musician. It must have been really difficult for Fauré to watch mediocrities becoming famous, while he just about managed to survive. He was so little known outside Paris that people would often confuse his music with that of Jean-Baptiste Faure (with a silent "e"), a celebrated singer who composed a bit on the side; that would make Fauré's teeth gnash. (Funnily enough, there was also a writer called Gabriel Faure, who knew Fauré quite well, and many years later wrote a book about him: Gabriel Fauré by Gabriel Faure.)

For all his modesty, Fauré was longing for some recognition of his stature as a musician; one thing he needed to boost his standing (and his ego) was membership of the "Institute". The Institute was a society of the most successful people in the arts in France; if you were in, you were in for life – but if you were out, you were definitely out. Membership was by invitation only, after a vote held among existing members. Everybody in the artistic world of France was desperate to be elected to the Institute, but since the number of members was limited, the only chance for a new candidate to get in was when an existing member died. So every time there was a death in the Institute, artists throughout France would say how sad they were, shed a few tears, and then immediately start rushing around getting all their member friends to vote for them. Fauré was longing to become part of this magic circle. He first tried to get elected in 1894. Saint-Saëns and others plotted and planned on his behalf and mustered all the support they could for him; but in the end, all Fauré got was four measly votes, while his rival, a composer now totally forgotten, got in with twenty. Fauré kept trying over the years, but he was continually humiliated. It wasn't until 1909 that he finally, finally got in; even then, Saint-Saëns had to rush home from Algeria to whip up support for his old pupil, with help from Fauré's father-in-law. And even *then*, it took five ballots before Fauré was declared the winner. It was all politics, really; art and politics have always been practically the same thing in France.

Star of the salons . . .

Most decisions about artistic life in France weren't made in government buildings, though. They were really made in the elegant salons where Fauré would spend his evenings; these were the lifeblood of artistic life in Paris. Almost all of Fauré's influential friends attended the parties held in these salons, and it was there that he met people who commissioned his new works, recommended him to publishers, and so on. So these gatherings, as well as being fun, were really important to him; a famous violinist later remembered Fauré dragging him out of his sick-bed at eleven at night, just because some people had decided that they wanted to hear Fauré's violin sonata at a late-night supper party. Fauré wasn't by any means the only composer to have supporters among fashionable Parisians; many composers had their fans. The supporters, even more than the composers themselves, would squabble and intrigue, trying to prove that their hero was the best. It could turn quite nasty at times; rather like football – or politics, in fact.

The most lavish parties in the greatest salons must have been amazing: careers and friendships being made and broken; the richest, the most talented, the wittiest, the most affected people in Paris all gathering and eyeing each other, exchanging news about the ones who weren't there that night (or who were there, but out of earshot); romances beginning, flourishing, withering and ending, all under the gaze of fan-wielding old ladies whose most important task in life was to gossip. It really was an extraordinary world. Of course, there were lots of laughs as well. A highlight of one of Pauline Viardot's parties was the time that Saint-Saëns, with a long blonde wig which went nicely with his beard, sang an aria in the style of an eminent but ageing soprano of the day, singing painfully sharp throughout. Cruel, perhaps; but it was a major hit.

The most famous description of this world is in a book by a writer called Marcel Proust – 'Remembrance of Things Past'. If you've got a free afternoon sometime, you should read it: it's only about 3,000 pages long. Proust was a great admirer of Fauré's and wrote him a fan letter, telling him that he'd like to write a three-hundred-page book about his music. He never did; but a violin sonata that he describes in detail in 'Remembrance of Things Past' may perhaps be based in part on Fauré's first violin sonata. Proust writes that the fictional sonata contains an "ineffable joy which seemed to come from paradise".

·5·

In 1885, Fauré's father died; and his mother followed in 1887. Between these two dates, Fauré composed the bulk of his most famous work, the 'Requiem' (though being the perfectionist he was, he kept tinkering with it for years afterwards, as well as adding extra movements, so it's difficult to date it exactly). Although it must have been connected with his parents' deaths, Fauré claimed that he hadn't really written the 'Requiem' for any specific occasion, but rather "for fun" – what a strange thing to say about a Requiem! It's true that the first presentation of the Requiem in 1888 wasn't really a performance at all; it was sung by the choir at the Madeleine to accompany the funeral of a local architect, who had had nothing to do with Fauré. There were a few such "performances" of the Requiem within a service at the Madeleine; if Fauré wanted friends to hear it there, he'd ask them to come in a few at a time and sit separately, so that it wouldn't look like a concert. (A vicar at the Madeleine had ticked Fauré off after the architect's funeral: "Monsieur Fauré, we don't need all these novelties." Twit.) The first concert performance didn't take place until 1892, under the auspices of the National Society. After that, its fame spread – how could it not? It is such an incredibly beautiful piece – radiant, other-worldly and, as Fauré put it, "as gentle as I am myself".

Traveller's tales ...

Until he got his job as inspector of music schools in 1892, Fauré was very poor, despite constantly rubbing shoulders with extremely rich people; and he had to watch his finances, or Marie and her parents, who kept an iron set of eyes on his outgoings, would give him hell. Sometimes they'd even discourage him from travelling abroad to perform his music, because of the expense involved; that does seem a bit mean. Fauré's better-off friends knew about his financial problems, so in the summer of 1888, some of them held a lottery to raise funds for Fauré and a composer friend of his to go to the festival at Bayreuth devoted to Wagner's operas (the same festival that Tchaikovsky had attended a few years earlier). Thrilling though this was for Fauré, the trip didn't start promisingly. He wanted to see the grave of one of his favourite composers, Robert Schumann, who was buried in Bonn, several hours'

Gabriel Fauré

journey away from Bayreuth; so the day before they were to see their first opera, Fauré and his friend went off and inspected the grave. They then spent a sleepless night in Bonn, and set off at dawn on the journey back to Bayreuth. They just made it back in time for the beginning of the Wagner opera; settling into their seats, they waited for the great event to begin – but just before it did, both of them fell fast asleep and, to the great disgust of their neighbours, snored their way right through it! After that, however, Fauré had a wonderful time at the festival (although like most Frenchmen, he hated German food – he was very shocked when Wagner's widow, Cosima, served cold legs of mutton at a dinner party).

Fauré often had his best times travelling; the freedom from his "squirrel-cage", as he called his life in Paris, was intoxicating. Despite this, though, he usually found quite a lot to complain about – the boat-journey from France to England, for instance: "Oh, for a bridge, a tunnel, a balloon, anything at all to get rid of these absurd crossings!" he groaned in 1898. If only he'd been around a hundred years later! In Brussels, he moaned about having to play his music with a lady violinist who, he claimed, looked like a smoked fish; and he was always whingeing about being too tired. Furthermore, he was constantly having little disasters – losing things, breaking things, and so on. (It's surprising he managed to get anywhere safely, really – he was so dreamy. Once, he went into a post office to buy some stamps for a letter; he paid, collected his change, put the stamps on the letter, then put the letter into his pocket, and the change into the post-box.)

251

*Poor abandoned Marie appears to have been quite under-
standing about his need to be away from her in order to
compose, so long as the trip didn't cost too much. She doesn't
seem to have really wanted to go with him on concert trips,
anyway – she was probably too shy. Besides, she knew he'd
always come back before too long; in some strange way, he
needed to be in Paris, much though he detested some aspects of
his life there. He loved the city – and he hated it. He admitted as
much in a letter to Marie, written from Germany: grumbling
about everything there – the people, the food, the weather – he
concluded, "So I prefer Paris, and when in Paris I prefer everything else to Paris!" Rather awkward . . .*

· 6 ·

In 1900, Fauré conducted the first performance of his biggest
piece yet, 'Prométhée'. He was interested in historical Greece,
and had harmonised an ancient Greek hymn that had been discovered in the 1890s. So when he was asked to write a massive
piece on a massive subject for a massive concert, he chose the
(massive) ancient Greek story of Prométhée. The story of
Prométhée (whom we call "Prometheus" in English) is interesting: Prometheus is commissioned by the gods to create man; he
does this very well, and his employers are pleased. Then, however, he decides to give man a little extra coming-to-life present
– fire, which is really meant only for the gods. His employers are
rather annoyed by this, and he gets cast down in chains as a
result; that's what happened in those days if you didn't follow
orders. Also included in the piece (at no extra charge) is the
story of Pandora, who loves Prometheus, but thinks he's been a
twit about the fire business; she dies, but then comes back to
earth holding a box. This is no ordinary box; it has all sorts of
nasty things in it, which cause all sorts of trouble ever afterwards – but it also contains hope, which makes some of the

trouble worthwhile. The story might not be everybody's idea of a fun night out, but it does have a certain timeless power.

The reason Fauré had been asked to write such a huge work was that Saint-Saëns (him again! He does crop up a lot in this story; I think he really wants a chapter to himself. Well sorry, Camille – not this time . . .) had met a rich winemaker in the south of France, Mr Castelbon, who wanted to put on a vast open-air festival in his local town. Saint-Saëns, who was very interested in the open-air theatres of ancient Rome, liked the idea and wrote a large-scale choral work, also based on an ancient Greek story, for the festival. It was a big success, and Castelbon asked for another work; this time Saint-Saëns refused, but put him onto Fauré. So Fauré was commissioned to write his work in what was for him a very short time; a lot of it was written during a heatwave, and Fauré, shut into a boiling room, spent quite a lot of the time cursing, and vowing never again to compose to order. He managed to get it finished on schedule, though, and 'Prométhée' was performed out of doors, in front of an amazing setting of giant rocks and mountains, with narrators, solo singers, 450 instrumentalists (including thirteen harpists, placed in a row at the front of the stage, and three wind bands) and a vast chorus, many of them local wine-growers – all conducted by Fauré. The audience was enormous, too: seventeen thousand people over the two nights. (Actually, the premiere had to be postponed by twenty-four hours: Fauré was about to give the first beat, when suddenly a terrifying thunderstorm broke out and drenched everybody – as if the gods were still angry!) The work was a major success, and Fauré got his first taste of real celebrity: a local clothes shop advertised a new line of boots called "The Elegant Gabriel Fauré"! More lastingly, the spirit of Ancient Greece seem to have affected Fauré's music from then on; one can feel that he is no longer writing for the salons, but for a different world – a world of less elegance but more strength.

The straying husband . . .

*It was at these performances that Fauré met Marguerite Hassel-
mans. It's sad to think of Marie that hot summer, at home in
Paris, presumably trying – unsuccessfully – to work on her
sculptures, looking after the boys, and waiting for letters to
arrive from her absent husband. What must she have thought
of Marguerite? She* must *have known about her eventually;
Fauré spent so much time with Marguerite, both in private and
in public, and his sons knew (and liked) her. So how did Marie
cope? Not very well, probably – but who can blame her? Not the
easiest of situations, to put it mildly. And when Fauré was at
home, he often wouldn't communicate with Marie; his silence,
she claimed, "crucified" her. Only in his letters would he really
open up to her – curious.*

*It's a pity that most of Marie's letters to Fauré are missing. His
later letters to her (apart from the very last ones) make it seem
that their relationship had become rather like that of two very
serious pen-pals; he tells her all about his music and very little
about himself. I wonder whether her letters to him were
warmer? Perhaps not – perhaps they were just angry, at least
when she talked about anything other than his music. But the
few that survive, dating from much earlier, when the children
were young and she was protecting them like a tigress with a
nervous breakdown, are lovely, if a bit mournful. His to her are
far more affectionate at that stage, too. "You are everything I
could wish for," he had told her – which was a good thing
because, as she wrote to him, "one word of disapproval from
you is enough to put me into a panic." While he was in London,
probably misbehaving, she wrote to him: "I am happy to know
that you are happy over there . . . Now make sure you don't
come back until you want to." She promised to increase her
health twofold – and her sweetness. All in all, she comes across
as a truly good person, who suffered deeply from her lack of*

self-confidence. Fauré's love affairs can't have helped; and she couldn't do much to stop them, seeing as little of him as she did. Even in Paris, in later years, he'd sometimes stay at an apartment near the Conservatoire rather than go home to her at the family house, which was a train ride away – his rather feeble excuse being that by avoiding the journey, he'd escape catching flu from the other passengers.

Marguerite was the most significant and presumably the last in a long line of relationships in which Fauré got involved after his marriage. The first major heart-flutter (as far as we know) was in 1891, when a rich princess invited him to join a group of friends in Venice for a summer holiday. Fauré went, leaving the family in Paris; over the course of the summer, he fell madly in love with the princess (who was also married, incidentally). And yet all the while he was writing daily to Marie saying how much he missed her – hmm . . . Then there was a singer called Emma Bardac, who was later to marry Debussy. For Emma, Fauré produced probably his most famous song-cycle, 'La Bonne Chanson' ('The Good Song' – somehow that doesn't sound quite right, though. Again, it sounds better in French, as so many things do – such a lovely language, for all its wasted letters.) There were rumours that Emma had produced something very beautiful for Fauré, too – a daughter, Dolly. Hmm again . . . After that, there was the wife of a publisher in England. This publisher took a great interest in Fauré's music, and printed several of his works. That professional relationship somewhat withered, though, after the publisher's wife abandoned him and their two children in order to go and live near Fauré in Paris. Hmm for a third time. (At this rate, my lips are going to stick together!) And so on – there were probably endless women in Fauré's life; it was as if his love life was out of control.

Poor Marie – what a situation. Strangely, though, when it came to Marguerite, she may possibly have been less jealous

than another Marguerite, a pianist called Marguerite Long.
Marguerite Long's husband was an old friend of Fauré's; and
this Marguerite (unlike Marguerite Hasselmans) was deter-
mined to use Fauré's friendship to further her own career. At
first, Fauré was pleased by her apparent devotion to his music;
but later, when he saw her for what she was, he realised that
she was a "shameless woman". For his last twelve years, he
wouldn't speak to her. After his death, though, Marguerite Long
somehow managed to make out that she was the only one who
understood how to play his music, and that Fauré had appointed
her as his sole musical representative; she made sure that
Marguerite Hasselmans was pretty much ignored and forgotten.
Had it not been for Fauré's sons, who appreciated her devotion
to their father for his last quarter-century, nice Marguerite
would have been almost completely abandoned; while of
course nasty Marguerite's career flourished. Not fair! But things
have an unfortunate tendency to turn out that way . . .

· 7 ·

Fauré had been trying to find a suitable opera libretto for
years; in 1907, he finally found a librettist he liked, along with
a subject that appealed to him, and started to write 'Pénélope',
his only opera. It was to take him five years. (Not too bad,
considering that his first piano quintet took him sixteen years,
on and off; Fauré was *not* a fast worker.) Again, the story was a
legend from Ancient Greece; Fauré was really taken with the
ancient Greeks! Pénélope's husband, Ulysse (Ulysses to us),
has gone away, and may be dead; in his absence, various
suitors turn up and try to persuade the beautiful Pénélope to
marry them instead. She refuses them, however, convinced
that Ulysse will come back to her. Eventually, an old beggar
appears; in a test, it appears that he can draw a huge bow
that none of the suitors can move at all. He turns out to be –

surprise, surprise – Ulysse in disguise; the suitors are all slaughtered (seems a bit harsh – they only asked, after all) and they all live happily ever after. Well, Ulysse and Pénélope do, anyway.

The opera, dedicated to Saint-Saëns, was a huge success at first; but unfortunately, a combination of circumstances – its first producer going bankrupt, the First World War, and so on – conspired against it. Fauré worried about the fate of the opera for the rest of his life; and it's true that it's never become really popular. Still, the few people who know it well really love it. That's true of most of Fauré's later works: the better one knows them, the more devoted one becomes to them – but they're not as easy to understand as his earlier works. He was aware of this himself; in 1906, he told Marie "Deep down, I have a definite feeling that what I am doing is not within everybody's comprehension."

An even-tempered man – usually . . .

Fauré's lovable character put him in a unique position in French musical life. While Saint-Saëns and the others shook their fists at each other and formed warring camps, Fauré managed to get on with almost everybody (except, presumably, for the stuffy old Conservatoire professors whom he fired). In 1910 a new musical society, the Independent Musical Society, was formed in direct opposition to the old National Music Society, causing all sorts of cursing and swearing from both sides. Fauré was elected President of the new society, but somehow managed to remain on good terms with the members of the old one. The National Society was run by Fauré's contemporaries; to them, he was a beloved friend. The Independent Musical Society was run largely by Fauré's pupils; and to them Fauré was an adored father-figure. Fauré had an amazing effect on people; if the students at the Conservatoire were being unruly, for instance, Fauré just had to appear and they would all calm down.

On the rare occasions that he did get cross, there was always a very good reason for it. Nasty Marguerite Long was one of the people who incurred his fury; another was a famous pianist named Alfred Cortot (pronounced "Corto", with a long "o" and a silent "t"). Cortot was a truly great musician, but a rather unpleasantly ambitious man. He always sucked up to Fauré, writing him letters telling him how much he adored his music; and Fauré had done a lot to help his career. Cortot hardly ever performed any of Fauré's works for piano, however, even after Fauré dedicated his 'Fantasy' for piano and orchestra to him. Eventually, after receiving yet another toadying letter from Cortot, Fauré lost his temper; he wrote him an uncharacteristically fierce letter, in which he asked why Cortot kept playing the music of virtually all the other famous French contemporary composers, "for which it is clearly your opinion that mine are no match", but not his? Why, Fauré asked, was Cortot "more modest about me than I am about myself?" It's quite a letter; I bet Cortot's hands were shaking as he read it! Unfortunately, his reply – if there was one – is lost. It's somehow good to know that Fauré had those moments; he knew his worth.

· 8 ·

The First World War broke out in 1914, and Fauré, like so many people, was caught by surprise. He was actually on holiday in Germany – the enemy country – when it all started; not the best place to be! He tried to get back to France, but the border was closed. His only escape route was to Switzerland; the journey, partly on foot, took him "three appalling days with my blasted luggage" – an unpleasant experience for a man of almost seventy. It was weeks before he was able to get back to Paris. Once there, he continued with his duties at the Conservatoire, even though staff and students were being called up to the army almost daily. Fauré and his friends tried in various

ways to keep Parisian musical life alive; and Fauré was asked
to play the piano in some charity concerts. Sadly, his
performing days were really over; he just couldn't hear what
he was playing, or what other people were playing or singing.
Ploughing on regardless, he would leave his fellow musicians
floundering, trying desperately to follow him. Still, Fauré's
name was famous enough now to fill a hall, and that helped
the war effort.

Aside from composing his own music – some of it extremely
stark and tragic, not surprisingly – Fauré spent much of his
time during the war years editing other people's piece's. The
biggest project was beginning a new, thirty-seven-volume
edition of Schumann's piano works, since the usual German
editions were no longer available. That must have provided a
welcome distraction from worrying about Philippe, who
fought throughout the war; neither Fauré nor Marie could
relax until he returned home safely in 1918. As for so many
parents, their son's absence was a constant shadow over their
lives; at least it turned out that they were among the lucky
ones . . .

A fighter to the last . . .

*So Fauré survived the war pretty much intact. Still, it was
inevitable that, as Europe emerged blinking into peace in 1918,
the world that he knew had largely disappeared. Aside from the
casualties of war, many important figures in his life were
vanishing. His much younger colleague, Debussy (never a real
friend, but undeniably a major musical force, whom Fauré
respected highly) died in 1918, as Paris was being bombarded.
His death left Fauré's former lover, Emma Bardac, a widow;
Fauré wrote her a (lost) letter of condolence, which brought a
grateful, if miserable, reply. She didn't mention her history with
Fauré in the letter, and presumably he didn't in his letter to her;
but it can't have been far from their minds. Later the same year,*

Fauré's last surviving brother died, just as the war ended. Then, even closer to Fauré, Saint-Saëns died in 1921, at the age of eighty-six; always the restless traveller, he was in Algiers at the time. Mentally, Saint-Saëns was as young as ever – and rather proud of his age. Passing an old beggar, Saint-Saëns asked the man how old he was. "Seventy-five", croaked the beggar. "Ah – youth is a wonderful thing," sighed Saint-Saëns. Continuing to compose and to practise the piano till the end, he spent the last evening of his life playing dominoes – and won! A good way to go.

Maybe because he was still so young in spirit, Saint-Saëns remained as pugnacious as ever, too. He couldn't stand the discordant sounds of the music that was being composed in his last years: "It is as if we were taking pleasure in eating live crayfish or cacti bristling with spikes," he fumed. Even Fauré's post-1900 music baffled him, although for once he was too tactful to say so to the composer. Fauré's music wasn't really "modern", though; it was just from a different world. What was modern was the music of an egg-headed Russian composer called Igor Stravinsky. His savage, primitive ballet, 'The Rite of Spring', was first performed in Paris in 1913, within a few days of the Paris premiere of 'Pénélope'. 'The Rite' provoked a riot, which has gone down as one of the most famous events in musical history. Fauré studied a two-piano score of the piece; we don't know what he thought of it, but it's unlikely to have been polite. (Stravinsky wasn't particularly polite about Fauré, either; he said that everybody who loved Fauré's music had a "Fauré-shaped head". What a peculiar thing to say! But then, he was a peculiar man.) We know exactly what Saint-Saëns thought of 'The Rite'; he hated it. Sitting through the first performance in horror, he kept muttering, all too audibly: "He's mad, he's mad!" Still, he went back for the first concert performance (without the dancers) the next year. 'The Rite' begins with a very high solo on the bassoon, sounding nothing like a bassoon had ever sounded before. "What's that instrument?" demanded Saint-Saëns furiously. "A bassoon," someone replied. Saint-Saëns got up: "It's a lie!" he shouted, and stormed out, slamming the door as loudly as he could. And that's where we leave him – or rather, he leaves us.

·**9**·

So now Fauré was lonelier than ever; and by his last years he was almost totally deaf. His forced retirement from the Conservatoire in 1920, which he felt had been forced upon him, was made even more bitter by a horrible and unnecessary wrangle over his pension. He'd been working for the government since 1892, when he had started his job as inspector of music schools; so he'd been a state employee for twenty-eight years. Officially that wasn't enough, though. Some bureaucratic toad contacted him to say that employees had to have been working for the government for thirty years in order to qualify for a state pension; so – sorry, and enjoy your retirement. Fauré was furious, humiliated and panic-struck. In the end, some high-up people who appreciated his worth sorted it out; but Fauré could have done without that worry. Even with the pension, Fauré felt that, after all his hard work and achievements, he didn't have "a sou (a French penny) I can call my own". (Mind you, one could point out that he would have had rather more sous to his name if he hadn't been paying for

Marguerite's apartment as well as his own home; but perhaps that would be a touch tactless – and anyway, it can't have been a huge expense.) Luckily, several admirers of his, mostly from America, heard about his plight, and sent him gifts; Fauré was embarrassed , but touched.

His life wasn't easy, then; but he carried on, refusing to give in to his frail health. "Among so many faults," he wrote to Marie, "grant me at least one virtue, that I never complain about anything." (Again, not *strictly* accurate; he spent rather a lot of his time complaining, in fact – but at least he never lost his sense of humour. And he did have rather a lot to complain about.) The most impressive thing about these final years was that he was still developing musically. His second-from-last work was a piano trio; his friends listened in astonishment to this extraordinary piece, further along his own individual path than ever, and asked each other where Fauré would go in music if he lived to be 100.

After that, but before he'd finished the string quartet, there should have been a final song, to round off the glorious series that had started in the school dining room more than sixty years earlier; but bad luck intervened. 1924 was the four-hundredth anniversary of the birth of a marvellous sixteenth-century French poet called Ronsard; to celebrate the occasion, a special edition of France's most important musical journal was planned, and several leading composers were invited to set his poems to music. Fauré liked the idea, and started to work on a striking poem, in which the poet bids farewell to his soul – perfect for a last song. But then, alas, Fauré discovered that his old pupil Ravel had chosen exactly the same poem for his contribution. Ravel was horrified when he found out, and immediately offered to withdraw his song; but it was too late – Fauré had already destroyed his. What a pity. Perhaps, though, the last words of Fauré's final surviving song, written in 1921, are apt enough: "I have in me a hunger for great journeys yet

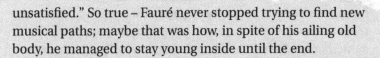

unsatisfied." So true – Fauré never stopped trying to find new musical paths; maybe that was how, in spite of his ailing old body, he managed to stay young inside until the end.

The last rites . . .

Fauré's funeral was a grand state affair, held at the Madeleine, where he had worked for so many years. It was almost a small private affair, though. In order for it to be an official state funeral, the Minister for Arts had to give his permission. The Minister, a certain (or in this case, a rather uncertain) Mr Albert, was asked for his signature. His response was far from impressive: "Fauré? Who's he?" he asked. Fortunately, he was soon persuaded that Fauré was important enough to merit all the pomp the government could offer; a few days later, in fact, he gave a speech at the funeral, getting highly over-emotional in the process! Strange, that . . . Rather more genuine was the speech given by Nadia Boulanger. She addressed the Master directly: "I want to thank you one last time," she said. "It is sweet for us to know that when all else is over your noble soul will still be here and the memory of your boundless goodness intact." Couldn't have put it better myself.

The Music

You may perhaps have noticed already that I adore Fauré's music. Actually, I adore the music of all the composers in this book – otherwise I wouldn't have written about them! But there's a difference: the others are generally acknowledged as great composers, whereas a question mark seems to hover around

Fauré. I warned you about the silly eyebrow-travel-operators who sneer at him; then there are also many people who really like his music, but wouldn't go overboard about it. Finally, though, there are those listeners who adore Fauré, and think that he was a major genius. I hope you'll join that last group!

It sounds rather as though I'm trying to initiate you into a strange cult; but I'm not – nothing could be healthier or more uplifting than Fauré's music. Fauré denied that his works were particularly French; for him, music was universal. But one can't help hearing the soft sounds of the French language in all his pieces – not just the vocal ones. His music is always refined, even when it's dramatic or angry; and it's always radiant, with an amazingly ecstatic feeling that means that it never seems to touch the ground. The purpose of music, Fauré felt, was to lift us "as far as possible above what is". And how he succeeded!

It is true that he doesn't immediately reveal his inner secrets to us – as Tchaikovsky, for instance, does. But you'll find that the more you listen to one of Fauré's masterpieces, the more you'll fall in love with it. Have you ever heard the expression: "Still waters run deep?" Well, whoever made it up could have been thinking about Fauré. The beauties of his music are endless – and timeless.

What to listen to

Much though I love the late music – and there are many Fauré fans who think it is far more important than his early music – I think that you should begin with some of the earlier works. They're so exquisite; and they're easier to understand on a first hearing. Start with the 'Requiem'; it is sublime – heavenly, in fact. Also, try to find the shorter choral works: the 'Cantique de Jean Racine', the 'Mater Maria Gratiae' (written in 1888) and the 'Tantum Ergo' (1894), for instance, are among my very favourite Fauré – pure beauty.

Moving into his chamber music, the first violin sonata sounds as

Gabriel Fauré

fresh today as it must have done at the first performance. The two piano quartets are magnificent, as well; in both, it's as if one can hear the sea surging, trees waving, church bells ringing – like great musical paintings. There are lots of wonderful short pieces, too; Fauré could produce magic in just a few bars. Try the 'Berceuse' (Lullaby) for violin, and the 'Sicilienne' or the 'Elegy' for cello.

The songs are important, too; songs suited Fauré. Try the 'Cinq Mélodies de Venise', Op. 58, or the song-cycle written for Emma Bardac, 'La Bonne Chanson', Op. 61. Help! I'm giving you too many suggestions, and you're going to become confused and not listen to anything; and it'll be my fault. So I'll skip over all the solo piano music, and 'Pénélope' and 'Prométhée' (there's no recording of the latter available as I write, anyway – shocking), and try to choose a couple of late works for you.

Well, I think I'd try the piano trio and the second cello sonata. They may take a few listenings, but (provided the performance is good, by players who understand the music – not always the case, by any means) I'm sure you'll get to feel at home with them, and will adore them, after a bit. Or maybe not even after a bit – perhaps I'm exaggerating the difficulties, and you'll understand them at first hearing. Finally, there's the string quartet. I must confess that I'm still working on that one. I keep listening to it, and each time I understand it a little more; but it's taking me time. I *know* it'll be worth it in the end, though; it's by Fauré!

Musical Words

Canon
Nothing to do with guns – that sort has two "n's" in the middle. A musical canon is a piece, or a passage in a piece, where two voices sing (or play, if it's an instrumental canon) the same music, but at different times; one starts, and the other imitates. A short sung canon is also known as a "round", because when one voice comes to the end, the other has already started again; so it can go on for ever – or at least until one of the singers collapses.

Chamber music
Pieces for two or more instruments with one player for each part. (Sonatas for two instruments count as chamber music.)

Choir
A group of singers singing together.

Choral music
Music for the group of singers to sing together.

Chords
Groups of notes played at the same time.

Chorister
One who sings in the group of singers who sing together.

Concerto
A piece, again usually in three or four movements, for orchestra with one or more solo instruments. The solo instrument has more to do than the orchestral instruments, and usually gets to show off!

Conductor

The man or woman who stands in front of the orchestra, beating time and somehow managing to convey to the orchestra how the piece should sound. It's funny, that: the conductor doesn't actually make any noise, but an orchestra will sound quite different with one conductor rather than with another – magic!

Elegy

A piece of music written in memory of someone who has died.

Flute, clarinet, oboe, bassoon

"Woodwind" instruments: instruments that are blown, and are – or used to be – made of wood. (The materials have changed a bit in recent times; for instance, modern flutes are usually made of metal.) All these instruments have distinctly separate personalities.

Harmonies

The sounds produced by notes played or sung at the same time.

Instrumental music

Music for any musical instrument except the voice.

Keys

As well as being the name for the things you press down on a piano to make sounds, the word "key" has a larger meaning (in music, that is; nothing to do with locks and doors). Musical notes go from A up to G, and then start again on A; there are also some notes in between the main ones, which are known as "sharp" or "flat" notes. Each note has its own "scale" (nothing to do with fish or weighing) – a series of notes beginning and ending on that note. There are two basic sorts

*of scales, the "major" and the "minor": the major tends to
sound cheerful, the minor sad. Between the early seventeenth
and early twentieth centuries, almost every piece had one of
these scales as its "home", with the main note known as the
"key" of the work; each movement of the piece would start with
notes taken from the home scale, go on a journey through lots
of "keys", and then come back to end on notes from the same
scale. Phew! Complicated for a three-letter word; but a key is a
good way of identifying a piece. For instance, if we talk about
Brahms's G major violin sonata, people will instantly know
which of his three violin sonatas we're talking about. Far more
important, though, is the satisfying feeling one gets (even if one
doesn't know why) from coming home at the end of a long
musical trip – as if the story has reached a proper ending.*

Libretto
The words to an opera – often rather silly – and
Librettist: *a person who writes librettos – often quite silly too.*

Lieder
*German for "songs", generally for voice accompanied by
piano.*

Movement
*A large section with its own beginning, middle and ending,
complete in itself, but part of an even larger work; usually
there are breaks between each movement of a piece – as there
are between "acts" in plays.*

Opera
*A play set to music, involving singers who also have to act,
accompanied by an orchestra. It often features people dying
tragically, but somehow managing to sing very loudly, and
for quite a long time, as they expire.*

Opus

Often shortened to "Op." Italian for "work". Most composers' music is catalogued in order of "opus". For instance, the first works that Beethoven had published in Vienna are his three piano trios, Op. 1, written when he was in his mid-twenties; the last works he wrote are his string quartets, Op. 130–135.

Orchestra

A large group of musicians – playing wind instruments, string instruments, percussion instruments and (sometimes) keyboard instruments – who all make music together; an impressive sight and sound!

Percussion instruments

There are too many of these to list – but basically they are instruments that are hit with a stick (like drums or triangles), bashed together (like cymbals) or mistreated in some other way; and quite a racket they make about it, too.

Piano, harpsichord, organ, clavichord, harmonium

Keyboard instruments, which can play more notes at the same time than other instruments; that's probably why virtually every composer's main instrument has been one of these. These instruments need dental help, though; they've all got lots of black teeth mixed up with the white ones. (Alright, they're called "keys" – goodness knows why – but they look like huge teeth.)

Posthumous

Often shortened to "post.", means "after death". Many composers' last works are described as "Op. post." This doesn't usually mean that they've written them after they've died,

which would be tricky – just that the works have been
published after their deaths.

Royalties
Share of profits earned by a composer for the performance or
sale of their music; never large enough, according to almost
every composer who has ever lived.

Serenade
A piece of music originally intended to be played out-of-
doors, preferably outside a lady's window.

Sextets
Not what you think – just music for six instruments.

Song-cycle
A series of songs that tell a whole story.

Sonata
A piece – again, often in three or four movements – usually
written for one or two instruments.

Symphony
A piece, generally in three or four movements, for orchestra –
occasionally with singers as well.

Trios
Pieces for three players; most piano trios are for violin, cello
and piano.

Violin, viola, cello, double-bass
"String" instruments – i.e. wooden instruments with four
strings (made of either steel, or gut – from animals' insides!)
played with a bow strung with horse-hair. Violins make the
highest sound, violas are in the middle, cellos make a
(lovely!) deep sound, and double-basses, lowest of all, are
the grand-daddies.

Virtuoso
Someone who is brilliant at playing his or her musical instrument.

Vocal music
Any music that is sung; therefore involves singers, which frequently leads to problems.

Thank Yous

One of the side benefits of writing this book is that I've come into contact with lots of people who know far more than I do about these composers. I have persecuted these unfortunate beings mercilessly, sending them endless emails about any point that might occur to me about anything that could possibly be slightly relevant. I am really grateful to everybody mentioned below for their patience and their willingness to help; and if there are any inaccuracies in this book, it's certainly not their fault. (It's not my fault either, of course; if you spot any mistakes, that's good – they were put there just to see whether you'd notice.) (Ahem.)

For the Handel chapter, I was helped greatly by two people the second of whom I've never actually met: Ruth Smith and Anthony Hicks, two of the most distinguished Handel experts around today. They both gave me wise advice, and also told me not to be *too* rude about various important people in the story. I was honoured that H. C. Robbins-Landon, the most famous Haydn scholar of all time, read through the Haydn chapter for me. Luckily, I was already friends with Brian Newbould, who has not only written two books about Schubert, but has actually completed ten of the works that Schubert left unfinished. For Tchaikovsky, I enlisted the services of David Brown, who very kindly took time off writing his own latest book on Tchaikovsky to go through mine; he doesn't actually have email, so we had some lengthy and enjoyable discussions (and occasionally arguments) on the phone. Then, I contacted Jan Smaczny, who has written lots about Dvořák and Czech music in general - including a whole book about Dvořák's cello concerto! (Very interesting it is, too.) And finally, when I came to Fauré, I dragged in Jessica Duchen, whom I've known since she was still at school; now, as well as having written lots about music, she's written her first novel, and is hard at work on her second. (Though, with the amount of questions I fired at her, she's probably missed her publishing deadline for those. Ah well.)

So, many thanks to all of those; and also to the innumerable people whom I bothered with single questions about all manner of things which cropped up as I went along. And many thanks to them for not getting cross if I don't mention them by name, otherwise this page would go on forever, and there would be no space for the index.

Of course, there are lots of other people who've been involved with this little volume. I wrote out the first version of every chapter in my appalling spider-who's-lost-his-glasses scrawl, so I needed someone kind-hearted and with good eyesight to type them out for me. Rosie Yeatman, who – when she isn't running the course in Cornwall at which I teach every year – helps me with all sorts of stuff, typed out the Handel and Schubert chapters. Then, however, in an appalling fit of laziness, she went off to indulge herself by having a baby! You just can't rely on some people. In her absence, our friendly neighbour (and hamster-sitter), Nicoline Sajjadi, typed out the Dvořák chapter; then Sarah Bruce, who had taken over for a bit from Rosie in Cornwall, came, sat elegantly at my computer and typed the Haydn and Tchaikovsky chapters. And finally, Rosie (having cleverly produced the adorable little Ben Greenberg) re-appeared just in time to process the Fauré chapter. (Actually, she did most of it, but not all. Unexpectedly, my son Gabriel, who's been interested in Fauré ever since he found out that he was partly named after him, volunteered to type out some of that chapter. I was touched – until certain sordid financial trans-actions, the details of which I won't reveal here, were forced upon me.)

When I felt that each chapter was somewhat ready, I would send it off to my lovely editors at Faber's, Belinda Matthews and Suzy Jenvey, and to my literary agent (writing that makes me feel so important!) Deborah Rogers, for approval. I would also give it to my considerably better other 45% (she's thinner than me) Pauline – without whom I wouldn't have time to play the cello, let alone write books. After that, there was more revision, and re-revision; and finally, finally, it was finished! So all that remained then was to write the little extra bits that make up the book, ending with – the thank-yous. So - thank you!

Index